"If the doctrine of the Trinity goes v
necessarily implode. The church fathers surely understood this. Yet within
evangelical circles, a departure from classical trinitarian thought is discernible
regarding the eternal generation of the Son. Kevin Giles has recognized this
drift, analyzes it well and calls us back to a better way."

Christopher A. Hall, Ph.D., chancellor, Eastern University, and dean,
Palmer Theological Seminary

"Rejecting the biblicism at the root of problematic presentations of trinitarian
doctrine among evangelical theologians, Kevin Giles mounts a vigorous defense of the Nicene teaching of the eternal generation of the Son. His book
exposits with uncommon depth and lucidity both the biblical background and
the traditional reception of the doctrine of the relation between the Father
and the Son."

Hans Boersma, Regent College, Vancouver, British Columbia

"Kevin Giles, who has established a reputation as an important voice in
support of the Nicene faith and of the traditional doctrine of the Trinity, en-
hances that reputation in this book by trenchantly illustrating why those who
today oppose the doctrine that the Son is eternally begotten of the Father end
up in opposition both to the biblical witness and to the Nicene faith. Giles
meticulously argues that those evangelicals today who reject this doctrine
have unwittingly embraced the very Arian views they themselves oppose.
This is a book that will challenge readers to understand Scripture and the
historical development of trinitarian doctrine once again before embracing
views that unwittingly undermine the Son's true deity. For anyone interested
in seeing the practical implications of sound trinitarian theology and Christology, this book is must reading."

Paul D. Molnar, professor of systematic theology, Department of Theology
and Religious Studies, St. John's University, Queens, New York

"Despite its prominent role in classic trinitarian orthodoxy, the eternal generation of the Son is routinely rejected by some evangelicals as unbiblical,
speculative and philosophically problematic. In conversation with the great
theologians of the church, Kevin Giles helps us understand the theological
importance of eternal generation for the doctrine of the Trinity and presents
a persuasive biblical and theological argument for why we, as evangelicals,
should embrace this doctrine."

Keith E. Johnson, author of *Rethinking the Trinity* and *Religious Pluralism:
An Augustinian Assessment*

"Kevin Giles has done the theological community a service with his detailed account of debates on the issue of the eternal generation of the Son by the Father. His work represents a fine example of a theological reading of Scripture drawing on the 'cloud of witnesses' throughout the ages to defend and explain this basic trinitarian doctrine."

Neil Ormerod, professor of theology, Australian Catholic University, Sydney, Australia

"In *The Eternal Generation of the Son*, Kevin Giles hits a home run in terms of defending the traditional, orthodox doctrine mentioned in its title. He does it in three ways: this doctrine is the only way reasonably to interpret Scripture; it is the consensual teaching of historic Christianity; it alone safeguards against the heresy of subordinationism of the Son. Game won; case closed. Let's move on."

Roger E. Olson, professor of theology, George W. Truett Theological Seminary

The Eternal
Generation
of the Son

Maintaining Orthodoxy in Trinitarian Theology

◆ ◆ ◆

KEVIN GILES

Foreword by ROBERT LETHAM

IVP Academic

An imprint of InterVarsity Press
Downers Grove, Illinois

InterVarsity Press
P.O. Box 1400, Downers Grove, IL 60515-1426
World Wide Web: www.ivpress.com
E-mail: email@ivpress.com

InterVarsity Press® is the book-publishing division of InterVarsity Christian Fellowship/USA®, a movement of
students and faculty active on campus at hundreds of universities, colleges and schools of nursing in the United States
of America, and a member movement of the International Fellowship of Evangelical Students. For information
about local and regional activities, write Public Relations Dept., InterVarsity Christian Fellowship/USA, 6400
Schroeder Rd., P.O. Box 7895, Madison, WI 53707-7895, or visit the IVCF website at <www.intervarsity.org>.

Scripture quotations, unless otherwise noted, are from the New Revised Standard Version of the Bible, copyright
1989 by the Division of Christian Education of the National Council of the Churches of Christ in the USA. Used by
permission. All rights reserved.

Cover design: Cindy Kiple
Images: Scenes from the life of Christ and the apostles at the British Library, London, Great Britain. The British
       Library/HIP/Art Resource, NY
Interior design: Beth Hagenberg

ISBN 978-0-8308-3965-0

Printed in the United States of America ∞

Library of Congress Cataloging-in-Publication Data

Giles, Kevin.
 The eternal generation of the Son: maintaining orthodoxy in
Trinitarian theology / Kevin N. Giles.
    p. cm.
 Includes bibliographical references and index.
 ISBN 978-0-8308-3965-0 (pbk.: alk. paper)
 1. Trinity—History of doctrines. 2. Jesus Christ—History of
doctrines. I. Title.
  BT109.G545 2012
  231'2.—dc23

                                                                2012005241

P	20	19	18	17	16	15	14	13	12	11	10	9	8	7	6	5	4	3	2	1
Y	29	28	27	26	25	24	23	22	21	20	19	18	17	16	15	14	13	12		

Contents

Foreword

◆ ◆ ◆

In various journals over the past few years, Kevin Giles and I have expressed our disagreements on certain aspects of trinitarian theology—and those differences remain—yet I am writing a foreword for this impressive exposition of the eternal generation of the Son. Giles rightly argues that this doctrine, which is at the heart of trinitarian doctrine, is not negotiable. For a number of reasons, this book is an important contribution to discussion.

First, Dr. Giles writes from the perspective of a confessional Anglican, committed to the teaching of the Thirty-Nine Articles. As a confessional Presbyterian, I have argued elsewhere that the Westminster Assembly was operating within the boundaries of confessional Augustinian Anglicanism. We therefore have much in common. Particularly, we both recognize that we cannot do theology in a vacuum. Systematic theology does not consist in simply collating a number of biblical passages and synthesizing them. The post-Reformation slogan *sola Scriptura* was never a claim that the Bible was the only source for theology. Instead, it asserts that Scripture is *the final and ultimate* authority. The Reformers and Puritans—including the Westminster divines—were students of the church's theology and built upon the teaching of the church's leaders. The great ecumenical creeds and the classic Reformed confessions represent the distillation of the best biblical exegesis of the past. God gave the gospel, and the Scriptures, to the church, not to freewheeling individuals.

Unfortunately, in contrast, large swaths of contemporary evangeli-

calism have a casual attitude to the heritage of the church. There is
much ignorance of the classic statements of the faith and the theology
that underlies them. Dr. Giles examines the causes of this malaise with
discernment and accuracy.

Second, Dr. Giles's book is an invaluable contribution in support of
the classic doctrine of the eternal generation of the Son. He understands this doctrine as the cement that holds together the larger doctrine of the trinity. Sadly, as a result of the widespread neglect of historical theology, many leading evangelical theologians have argued that
the doctrine of the eternal generation of the Son is unbiblical and
should therefore be abandoned. The consequences of this position are
far-reaching, and Dr. Giles explores them at length.

The root of this indifference to the classic trinitarian doctrine is in a
biblicism that requires express statements of Scripture to establish any
particular matter. This biblicism misses the point that, as the Westminster Confession of Faith puts it, the whole counsel of God is dis-
cernable not only in the express statements of Scripture but also in what
"by good and necessary consequence may be deduced from Scripture."
Many readers may be surprised to learn that, before the Enlightenment
of the eighteenth century, the main threats to the Christian gospel
came from the ranks of biblical fundamentalists. Basil the Great and
his friend Gregory of Nazianzus, key figures in the resolution of the
fourth-century trinitarian crisis, were confronted by such claims. Their
opponents demanded chapter and verse from the Bible to support the
doctrine of the trinity; the orthodox retorted that the doctrine de-
pended on "the sense of Scripture," on the interplay of the elements of
biblical truth, not on a simple list of "Bible verses."

The doctrine of the Trinity is a vast mystery, infinitely transcending
our intellectual capacities. Thank God that, even though we stand at
the periphery, he has revealed himself sufficiently to guide us in our
pilgrimage of discipleship. There are many ramifications that we can
and must explore, which can lead to differing questions and answers.
Giles, myself and others will no doubt continue to debate the *filioque*
clause, alleged differences between the Eastern and Western doctrines,
aspects of the relations between the trinitarian persons, and the con-

nection between the economic Trinity (the Trinity as revealed in the history of redemption) and the immanent trinity (the Trinity in itself). As we think hard and long about our great and ultimately incomprehensible God, we need to keep before us the central issues. In this, Dr. Giles places starkly before us the pressing need to give heed to the biblical exegesis of the whole church, not merely our own. He also correctly and forcibly directs us to the ways in which the Fathers held to the eternal generation of the Son—and in turn the eternal procession of the Holy Spirit—so as to maintain both the unity of being and nature of the persons and their self-differentiation. Dr. Giles's message is that if we abandon this doctrine, then we will be in grave peril. We thus need to hear and heed his claim.

Robert Letham
Wales Evangelical School of Theology

Preface

◆ ◆ ◆

This book began as a proposed journal article in reply to the growing number of contemporary conservative evangelicals who are either uncertain about or advocate abandoning the doctrine of the eternal generation of the Son. The more I researched this matter the more the work grew and the more I realized how important this doctrine is. It is hugely important because it was the focal issue in the fourth century conflict between the Arian theologians and the Nicene fathers, including Augustine; it is twice affirmed in both the Nicene and Athanasian Creeds; it is endorsed by the Reformation and Post-Reformation Protestant confessions, and it is foundational for the orthodox doctrine of the Trinity. This doctrine explains how the Father and the Son can both be God without any caveats, yet one is the Father and the other the Son. In this light it is surprising to find how little has been written recently on the doctrine of the eternal generation of the Son even though most modern theological textbooks have a short section on it, and some brief evangelical defenses of the doctrine exist in response to its critics.

Because so little has been published on the doctrine of the eternal generation of the Son in recent years, despite all that has been published on the Trinity, I found that I was largely exploring alone. Fortunately, I found on the Internet "a theological friend," an American evangelical scholar, Keith E. Johnson, who has published several articles on Augustine's treatment of this doctrine.[1] He is also the author of *Rethinking the*

---

[1] Keith E. Johnson, "Augustine's Trinitarian Reading of John 5: A Model for the Theological Interpretation of Scripture," *Journal of the Evangelical Theological Society* 52, no. 4 (2009): 799-811; Johnson, "Trinitarian Agency and the Eternal Subordination of the Son: An Augustinian

Trinity and Religious Pluralism: An Augustinian Assessment.[2] He agreed to read the original article, making many valuable comments, and he even suggested that it would make a good book. Subsequent to this he read a first and then the final draft of the book, again making many insightful criticisms, suggestions and comments. I thank him for his valuable counsel. He has helped me make the book what it is.

In recent years, I have had several debates about the doctrine of the Trinity in scholarly journals[3] and periodically in personal emails with Robert Letham, who has written the most informed book by an evangelical on the Trinity, *The Holy Trinity: In Scripture, History, Theology and Worship.*[4] The knowledge of the historical sources he exhibits in his book is excellent, and his survey of the thought of significant modern trinitarian theologians is equally impressive. I have learned much from him, and on most matters we are virtually of one mind. In what follows I frequently quote him in support. We have agreed to differ, however, on one important matter on the doctrine of the Trinity: whether the Son is *freely* and *eternally* "obedient" and in "submission" to the Father. What has delighted me in our private and published scholarly debates on this matter has been the generosity of spirit and courteousness that he has expressed. In chapter ten, where I argue against those who differentiate the Father and the Son, primarily if not exclusively on the differing authority they exercise in the immanent Trinity, I put forward the case yet again that neither the Bible nor the theological tradition teaches that the Son is eternally subordinate, submissive and obedient to the Father; indeed, I argue that these sources oppose this idea. As I

Perspective," *Themelios* 36, no. 1 (2011): 7-25; Johnson, "Augustine, Eternal Generation, and Evangelical Trinitarianism," *Trinity Journal* 32, no. 2 (2011): 141-63.

[2]Keith E. Johnson, *Rethinking the Trinity and Religious Pluralism: An Augustinian Assessment,* Strategic Initiatives in Evangelical Theology (Downers Grove, Ill.: IVP Academic, 2011).

[3]Kevin N. Giles, *"The Holy Trinity in Scripture, History, Theology and Worship,* An Extended Review," followed by "A Response by Robert Letham," *Evangelical Quarterly* 78 (2006): 85-94; Giles, "Is the Son Eternally Submissive to the Father?" (A four-part exchange with Professor Robert Letham), *Christian Research Journal* 31, no. 1 (2008): 11-21; Giles, "The Evangelical Theological Society and the Doctrine of the Trinity," with a response by Robert Letham and a rejoinder by me, *Evangelical Quarterly* 80, no. 4 (2008): 323-48. See also Letham, "Kevin Giles on Subordinationism," appendix 1 in *Holy Trinity,* pp. 489-96.

[4]Robert Letham, *The Holy Trinity: in Scripture, History, Theology and Worship* (Phillipsburg, N.J.: P & R, 2004).

neared the end of this book, I wrote to ask him if he would critically read the final draft and write a foreword to the book. I told him I knew of no other conservative evangelical and Reformed theologian better equipped to assess my work and offer criticism and suggestions. Much to my delight, despite our sharp difference on this one matter, he agreed. I warmly thank him for his work and support for this venture and yet once more for his largeness of heart and grace.

In my home country of Australia, I am pleased to know Neil Omerod, professor of systematic theology at the Australian Catholic University, Sydney, who is a very competent trinitarian theologian. He too agreed to read my work and, regarding Augustine and Aquinas in particular, made several important suggestions.

Professor I. Howard Marshall, whom I have known from my days as a postgraduate student in England in the early seventies and who has long been interested in the relationship between exegesis and systematic theology, agreed to read my chapter on "doing" evangelical theology. And Professor Paul Molnar, who generously helped me with my 2004 book, *Jesus and the Father*, agreed to read my chapter on the eternal generation of the Son in contemporary theology and the section on "Rahner's Rule" in chapter nine. His constructive comments on my first draft of this material helped me improve it significantly.

In writing books, libraries are essential and helpful librarians a godsend. In this regard I would like to thank Ruth Millard at Ridley Theological College, Melbourne, and Miranda Fyfield at St. Paschal Library, Order of Friars minor, Box Hill, near to where I live in the city of Melbourne, for all their assistance. One of Miranda's great virtues is fluency in Latin. More than once, she helped me work out the Latin of Tertullian and Augustine.

Finally, I would like to thank the staff of InterVarsity Press for seeing this book through publication. I was delighted to have again as my editor Gary Deddo, a competent and published trinitarian scholar. The book has been much improved by his insightful comments.

Kevin Giles
Melbourne, Australia

1

Introduction

◆ ◆ ◆

Thomas Torrance, whom Paul Molnar calls "one of the most significant English-speaking theologians of the twentieth century,"[1] emphatically asserts that the Father-Son relationship stands right at the heart of the Christian faith. It is the pivotal center of the Christian religion. "It is only in the Son . . . that God has revealed himself to us" for our salvation.[2] If we do not meet and know God in Christ, then we are without hope. "Everything," he says, "depends, then, on the relation and the nature of that relation that obtains between Jesus Christ, the incarnate Son and God the Father."[3] What explains and defines the relationship between the Father and the Son Torrance insists, is his eternal begetting or generation. Thus, he says, the bishops of Nicea concluded that

> to have faith in one Lord Jesus Christ is to have faith in one God the Father, and to acknowledge him as God equally with the Father. This unique relation of Christ to the Father within the oneness of God was spelled out by the phrase "the only begotten Son of God, begotten from his Father before all ages . . . begotten not made." . . .
>
> The import of these phrases was then gathered up in concentrated form by the emphatic, "of one being with the Father" [homoousios tō patri], to express oneness in being between the incarnate Son and God the Father.[4]

---

[1] Paul D. Molnar, *Thomas Torrance: Theologian of the Trinity* (Surrey, U.K.: Ashgate, 2009), p. 1.
[2] Thomas F. Torrance, *The Trinitarian Faith: The Evangelical Theology of the Ancient Church* (Edinburgh: T & T Clark, 1988), p. 110.
[3] Ibid., p. 117.
[4] Ibid.

Similarly Lewis Ayres, who has written possibly the best intro-duction to the emergence of the orthodox doctrine of the Trinity in the fourth century, is adamant that the doctrine of the eternal generation of the Son is foundational to the Christian faith. The prolonged and bitter fourth-century disputes over the Trinity, he says, focused "*first,* on de-bates about the generation of the Word or Son from the Father."[5] This was so because the Nicene fathers recognized that "these questions about the generation of the Son or Word—and consequently about the ontological status of the generated Son—then have immediate reper-cussions for how one understands incarnation and redemption."[6]

What both these highly respected theologians are arguing is that the doctrine of the eternal generation of the Son takes us to the heart of the gospel, the good news, that in Jesus Christ we meet with the God who saves.[7]

What is distinctive and unique about the Christian doctrine of God is that God is triune. The one God is Father, Son and Spirit. Thus the doctrine of the Trinity—which stands right at the heart of the Christian faith—is our most fundamental belief. If we get this doctrine wrong, then we are bound to get other doctrines wrong. Theologians across the ages have thought long and hard about how God can be one and yet three persons, reflecting continuously and debating with one another on what the Scriptures say about the Trinity. Possibly the most difficult specific question they have had to grapple with is, if God is one and yet three persons, *how* is he self-differentiated? The doctrines of the eternal generation, or begetting, of the Son and the eternal pro-cession of the Spirit are human attempts to answer this question in the

---

[5]*Nicaea and Its Legacy: An Approach to Fourth-Century Trinitarian Theology* (Oxford: Oxford University Press, 2004), p. 3. Italics added. Similarly P. Christou, "Uncreated and Created, Unbegotten and Begotten in the Theology of Athanasius of Alexandria," *Augustinianum* 13, no. 3 (1973): 399-409.

[6]Ayres, *Nicaea,* p. 3.

[7]For virtually the same conclusion see also Fred Sanders, *The Deep Things of God: How the Trinity Changes Everything* (Wheaton, Ill.: Crossway, 2010). The great strength of this book is that it connects belief in the Trinity with salvation in Christ. Sanders emphatically endorses the doctrine of the eternal generation of the Son and fully recognizes the importance of this doctrine. On my request he kindly sent me an unpublished essay on this topic he had read at the Far West Regional Conference of the Evangelical Theological Society in April 2010, "Relations of Origin in the Eternal Trinity: Biblical Warrant and Systematic Implications." It is an excellent piece of work.

light of Scripture. In this book I say very little about the doctrine of the eternal procession of the Spirit, not because I am uninterested in the Holy Spirit—far from it—but for two reasons. First, in the early church and today among evangelicals it is primarily the doctrine of the eternal generation of the Son, rather than the procession of the Spirit, that is questioned or rejected. And second, the church fathers rightly recognized that the question of the Father-Son relationship is the most difficult. If this can be settled, they reasoned, then the easier question of the Father-Spirit relationship is less of a challenge. I agree.

It is in defense of *the doctrine of the eternal begetting or generation of the Son*, so central to the doctrine of the Trinity, that I write; indeed, this is what the entire book is about. In it I seek to outline the biblical support for this doctrine, how this doctrine developed, what it teaches and why it is so important. The biblical language of "begetting" is integral to the doctrine of the eternal generation of the Son, but the doctrine and this one word should not be confused. The doctrine and the term certainly overlap, but one can imply or speak about the doctrine without using the word *begetting*. Invariably a specific doctrine involves far more than the usage of any one term in the Bible. The doctrine of salvation is analogous: it involves far more than the uses of the word *salvation* in Scripture. As we proceed, we need to keep in mind at all times our primary belief that the God revealed in Scripture is eternally triune and that this belief gives rise to the doctrine of the eternal generation of the Son. This doctrine sheds light on how the one God is self-differentiated for all eternity. Thus we are not asking whether God is eternally self-differentiated: this is agreed. What we are asking is, are theologians justified in transposing the biblical and earthbound metaphors of "begetting" and "generation" to the realm of eternity in seeking to understand and speak of the eternal self-differentiation of the Father and the Son? We cannot avoid this question. Theologians must grapple with it.

HOW THIS DOCTRINE EMERGED IN HISTORY

Almost invariably when human beings are confronted with difficult and complex questions, preliminary answers are in due course rejected, some because they come to be seen as wrong, others because they do not account for all the data. This is exactly how the doctrine of the Trinity in general and the doctrine of the eternal generation of the Son in particular developed historically. The church rejected inadequate or wrong answers, eventually developed an answer that seemed to account for all that the Bible said, and then refined this answer. In reply to the profound question, how can God be one yet self-differentiated as Father, Son and Spirit? Christians gave the following answers.

1. God is truly one but appears successively as Father, Son and Spirit (modalism). On this view, God appears in history to be self-differentiated. This divine self-differentiation, however, is not grounded in the eternal life of God. This solution honored the Bible's affirmation that God is one, but the church fathers rejected it because the New Testament clearly refers to three "persons" in historical revelation who have continuing existence in heaven. *Armufil* .

2. God is one, yet he has eternally within himself his Word and his Spirit, whom he brings forth in time for the works of creation and redemption (economic trinitarianism—held by, e.g., Justin Martyr, Irenaeus, Tertullian).[8] This view suggests that God in his ultimate inner and eternal life is a monad; he becomes triune in the economy (history). This answer did not win the day because in this construct God is yet again not eternally triune.

3. God is a monad who creates in time the Son and the Spirit, who are above all other creatures but less in being and power than the Father (Arianism in its various forms). This solution gained much support. Nevertheless, it was bitterly opposed by Athanasius, the Cappadocian fathers and Augustine, among others, and finally rejected because they recognized that it made the Son and the Spirit God in second and third degree. On this view, divine self-differentiation is again not eternal and within the life of God but rather results from the one true and almighty God contingently *creating* in time two lesser Gods. It thus excludes the belief that the three differentiated divine persons are all "true God," "coequal" in being and power, and thus it introduces the error of

---

[8]This is to be contrasted with Arian ontological subordinationism. Here we must remember that the orthodox doctrine of the Trinity developed in history a step at a time and initial answers to complex questions often gave way to better answers that came later.

"subordinationism"[9] (hierarchical ordering within the eternal life of God). And in addition, because it radically divides the divine three in being and power, it also undermines divine unity, introducing the error of tritheism.

4. God is triune for all eternity. In the inner life of God, outside of time, divine threefold self-differentiation takes place in a way that is beyond human understanding or description. Following biblical language, this eternal divine self-differentiation is best designated as the eternal begetting, or generation, of the Son and the procession of the Spirit. God's self-revelation in the economy (history) as Father, Son and Spirit reveals and confirms what is true apart from history— namely, that God is eternally triune. In other words, his triunity is not constituted by anything that takes place in this world; God himself constitutes his triunity by his own free and eternal decision. This is the view that triumphed and became orthodoxy. It triumphed because it made the most sense and integrated better than any of the other views the revelation in Scripture and that which is seen in the economy. The assembled bishops at the Council of Nicaea (325), who endorsed the conclusion that the Son is eternally begotten of the Father, and those at the Council of Constantinople (381), who also determined that the Spirit eternally proceeds from the Father, took a very important step forward in articulating the doctrine of the Trinity. All Christians from then on would explain divine self-differentiation in these terms. And they could then say how the one God could eternally be Father, Son and Spirit without undermining or denying divine unity or divine threefold self-differentiation. Believing that Scripture taught the eternal begetting or generation of the Son, the church could then agree to confess that Jesus Christ is "true God from true God, *one in being* with the Father."

---

[9]For long centuries all significant deviations from Nicene trinitarian orthodoxy were pejoratively called "Arian" or "Arianism." The English word *subordinationism* was first used in the mid-nineteenth century, and its equivalent, *subordinatianismus*, soon after appeared in German texts. See the *The Oxford English Dictionary*, 2nd ed. (Oxford: Clarendon, 1989), p. 1227. The term *subordinationism* is more specific than "Arianism." It refers to any teaching that ranks the Son and/or the Spirit under the Father in the immanent Trinity, thereby implying his/their subordination in divine being. Subordinationists seldom if ever say openly, "we are asserting the ontological subordination of the Son." This is the conclusion that orthodox theologians make about certain construals of the Trinity.

More than anyone else, Athanasius is to be thanked for developing and establishing this profound understanding of the God revealed in history and Scripture.[10] He saw clearly that speaking of the Son as "eternally begotten of the Father" unambiguously affirmed both the Father and Son's oneness of being and their eternal self-differentiation. Following from this affirmation, he drew the same conclusion regarding the Spirit. The Holy Spirit's eternal procession spoke of his *oneness in being* with the Father and of his self-differentiation within the life of God. Thus for Athanasius the linchpin holding together divine unity and divine threeness were the doctrines of the eternal generation of the Son and the procession of the Spirit. Athanasius's achievements in showing how the Father, Son and Holy Spirit can be the one God and yet eternally distinguished as three fully divine "persons," as a holistic reading of the Bible indicates, should never be underestimated. But, like all good answers to profound questions, subsequent theologians added their insights and refined his answer.

Athanasius held that the eternal begetting of the Son and its counterpart, the eternal procession of the Spirit, spoke of two necessary[11] acts of divine self-differentiation *ad intra* (within the life of God in eternity).[12] These acts produce nothing exterior to God. Augustine added to this insight by clearly distinguishing between what takes place in eternity and what takes place in history. He thus differentiated between the "mission" (sending) of the Son and the Spirit for the works of creation and redemption, divine acts *ad extra* (acts of God "outside" of the divine life, in space and time), and the eternal begetting of the Son and procession of the Spirit in eternity *ad intra* (within the life of God). Although not constituting the differentiation, what takes place in time and space (the missions) were for Augustine nevertheless indicative of differentiating acts (generation and procession) within the life of God apart from space and time in eternity. In other words, the revelation of God's triunity in the economy (history) reflects accurately what is true of God in eternity.

---

[10]Athanasius's teaching on the Trinity will be outlined and fully documented in chap. 4.

[11]That is, noncontingent willed acts.

[12]The terms *ad intra* and *ad extra* appear first in medieval theology and come into prominence with Aquinas. The Nicene fathers recognize the distinction these two terms represent, but they do not use the terms.

Given this brief account of the initial development and emergence of the doctrines of the eternal generation of the Son and eternal procession of the Spirit, we can see why they are foundational elements in the orthodox doctrine of the Trinity. Or to revisit the metaphor used above, why they are "the linchpin" that holds together divine unity and eternal threeness, the triunity of the God revealed in Scripture. Remove these two doctrines and the historic doctrine of the Trinity collapses. We are now in a place to see the necessity of a book in defense of the doctrine of the eternal generation of the Son. This book is a defense of the historic creedal faith of the church, which reflects the teaching of Scripture that the one God is Father, Son and Spirit. In other words, to deny that the Son is eternally generated by the Father is to undermine the very doctrine of the Trinity, which was developed to safeguard the full divinity of the Son. If the Son is not fully God for all eternity, then our salvation is in jeopardy. Only God can reveal God, only God can save, and only God should be worshiped.

HUMAN WORDS AND DIVINE REALITIES

In speaking of eternal divine self-differentiation, Eastern Orthodox and Western Protestant theologians speak of "the eternal begetting or generation of the Son" and "the eternal procession of the Spirit." However, most Roman Catholics, following Thomas Aquinas, speak of two eternal *processions* in God, one called "begetting" and one called "spiration." But whatever terminology is used we must recognize that this is human language reflecting creaturely reality with all its limitations. Its applicability to God, who is not a creature, is only safeguarded by the addition of the qualifying word *eternal*. The premise of orthodoxy is that God *is* eternally triune. He did not *become* triune at some point. The Son and the Spirit are not creatures contingently brought into existence temporally by God the Father. The Father, the Son and the Spirit are the one self-differentiated God for all eternity.

In speaking about God we must use human words—we have nothing else—and God must use human language to speak to us if we are to understand him, but human language is human language. Words that normally refer to things that are part of this world are inadequate when used of God, who is not a creature: he is uncreated and eternal. Thomas Aquinas put his able mind to work on this problem.[13] He argued that human speech used of God could be one of three things. (1) It could be *univocal*. Saying that God loves me means the same as saying that my wife or my parents love me. If our language of God were univocal, it would mean that God is just like human beings. (2) It could be *equivocal*. Saying that God loves me means something altogether different from saying that my parents or wife love me. If our language used of God were equivocal, we could not say anything factual about God. (3) It could be *analogical*. Saying that God loves me tells me something true about God but only captures part of the reality. If our language used of God is analogical, as Aquinas argued, it means we can speak of and understand God in the categories of human thought but never fully comprehend him. In his discussion of human language used of God, Aquinas says, "It seems that no word can be used literally of God. For as we have already said that every word used of God is taken from our speech about creatures, as already noted, but such words are used metaphorically of God."[14] By this he means that there can be an overlap of meaning between how we use a word in reference to creatures and how we use it in reference to God. Theology, then, is the discipline of finding where that overlap lies and also where the meanings diverge. But at every point we must make a distinction between a word's application to God and to creaturely realities. That is the very task of theology. Without this discipline we fall into idolatry and mythology, speaking of God as if God were a creature or projecting upon God creaturely understandings. The Fourth Lateran Council made this

---

[13]There is not one passage in Thomas Aquinas' writings where he discusses the limits of human language used of God and offers the three alternatives given above. I give the accepted summary of his conclusions. On this matter see the full discussion in Alan J. Torrance, *Persons in Communion: Trinitarian Description and Human Participation* (Edinburgh: T & T Clark, 1996), pp. 120-30. He also gives an alternative reading of Aquinas on this matter, pp. 130-212.

[14]Thomas Aquinas, *Summa Theologiae* 1, q.13, a.3.1 (p. 57). For a similar point see also pp. 67, 69. In this quote the term *metaphorical* is equivalent to *analogical*, and *literal* is equivalent to *univocal*. In modern discussions of religious language the meaning of the words *metaphorical* and *analogical* overlap, but generally the word *metaphorical* has a wider range of meanings and uses than the more technical and precise term *analogical*. For a good summary of this discussion see J. W. Cooper, *Our Father in Heaven* (Grand Rapids: Baker, 1998), pp. 167-80.

point forcefully when it ruled, "Between the Creator and the creature no similarity can be expressed without including greater dissimilarity."[15]

The limitation of human language used of God is an acute problem for theologians seeking to enunciate the doctrine of the Trinity. None of the key trinitarian terms—*Son, Father, person, relation, unity, sending/mission* and not least *begotten*—can be understood literally, that is univocally, when used of God. Thus calling God "Father," for example, certainly tells us something about the first person of the Trinity, but only the whole of revelation can tell us what this fatherhood is because the divine Father in so many ways is not like a human father. He does not have a father himself, he is not married, he does not impregnate, he does not grow old, and so on. T. F. Torrance says these words "transcend our finite comprehension" because "they point beyond themselves." He then says, "Problems arise immediately we try to understand divine Fatherhood and Sonship, and not least the concept of 'the begotten Son', in terms of what human fatherhood, sonship and begetting mean."[16]

What this means is that the word *begotten*, when used of the divine Son, cannot be understood in terms of human begetting, most obviously because, although he had an earthly birth and a human mother, he also existed before his human birth and incarnation, yet he had no divine mother. The early theologians settled on the term "begotten" (*gennaō*) to speak of the eternal generation of the Son because they found it repeatedly in Scripture; they were nevertheless well aware of its limitations, as we will see. The theological use of this term makes the infinite difference between human begetting and divine begetting explicit by the addition of the word *eternal*.[17] What is temporal is part of

---

[15]See *Decrees of the Ecumenical Councils*, vol. 1, N. P. Tanner, ed. (London: Sheed and Ward, 1990), p. 232.

[16]T. F. Torrance, *The Christian Doctrine: One Being Three Persons* (Edinburgh: T & T Clark, 1996), p. 192.

[17]The questions of what time and eternity involve and how they are to be understood are some of the most difficult that Christian theologians and philosophers have to address. It is agreed that God created (linear) time along with everything else. God, the creator, is thus not bound by time. He is "eternal." But what does this mean? Some argue that God exists continuously without beginning or end; eternal means "everlasting." The more widely held Christian opinion is that God's "eternity" implies existence not bound by temporal succession or temporal location. Everything is simultaneous for God. When the Nicene fathers speak of the Son's begetting as "eternal" we will have to ask what they mean by this.

this world that God created; what is eternal is divine. When God created the world he created time. He himself is not limited or constrained by time. He is the Lord of time. Thus to speak of *the eternal begetting* of the Son is to speak of what takes place within the life of God, of a reality outside of human experience, not definable in human categories, and not bounded by temporal constraints.

In seeking to meet this linguistic challenge in some small measure, I argue that what we are in fact talking about in this study is *eternal self-differentiation within the life of God in eternity,* for which the human words *begetting* and *generation* in relation to the Son, and *procession* in relation to the Spirit, are the best words available to us human beings.

THE CREEDAL BELIEF IN THE ETERNAL BEGETTING OF THE SON

Since the early fourth century, belief in the eternal begetting of the Son has been a foundational Christian doctrine, made evident, for example, by the fact that the Nicene Creed mentions this belief twice. Every Sunday, millions of Christians around the world congregate to celebrate the Eucharist. For most of them, the reciting of the Nicene Creed is part of this assembling.[18] In this creed they confess, "We believe in one Lord, Jesus Christ, the Son of God, eternally *begotten* of the Father, God from God, light from light, true God from true God, *begotten*, not made, of one being with the Father." The "we" in this confession used in church worship[19] makes it plain that this is not simply a confession of the solitary believer, what "I" believe, but rather a corporate confession that places the believer in an ever-extending community: first, in the specific community in which the confession is made, then in a

---

[18]The Nicene Creed is confessed whenever the Eucharist is celebrated in Roman Catholic, Eastern Catholic, Old Catholic, Eastern Orthodox, Assyrian Orthodox, Oriental Orthodox, Anglican and Lutheran churches, with many other Protestant churches ascribing to the creed and often using it. I quote from the Creed as it is given in *A Prayer Book for Australia*, The Australian Anglican Church, 1995. This in turn represents the English Language Liturgical Consultation translation accepted by all the major Western churches.

[19]The words of the 381 creed have come down to us in two variant texts. One is in the first-person singular form which probably reflects a baptismal setting, and the other in a first-person plural form that almost certainly reflects a communal worship setting.

worldwide community of Western and Eastern Christians,[20] and then in a community that spans the centuries from A.D. 325 to the present.

It is therefore somewhat surprising, and very dismaying, to open theological works by contemporary conservative evangelicals who claim to be orthodox Christians and find them advocating the removal of the words from the Nicene Creed, "eternally begotten of the Father," in the clause beginning, "We believe in Jesus Christ, the only Son of God," because they tell us these words have no biblical warrant, or they are of no great importance, or that they open the door to the Arian error.[21] If they are right in making this claim, then the millions of Christians past and present who have confessed these words have been confessing something not warranted by Scripture, at best of no great import and at worst inclined toward Arianism. What is more, if they are right, then the church fathers who argued strenuously to have these words included in the Nicene Creed were misguided, the bishops who in the Athanasian Creed twice affirmed the eternal generation of the Son were misinformed, and the authors of the Reformation and post-Reformation confessions who endorsed the doctrine of the eternal begetting of the Son were mistaken.[22]

On first thought, for many Protestant Christians not versed in theology, omitting a few words from the Nicene Creed may not seem too consequential. And for an evangelical who has been taught that "all we believe comes directly from the Bible," the claim that the eternal begetting of the Son has no biblical grounding is a compelling reason why the words should indeed be set aside. However, the deletion of these words from the creed is a momentous step with huge consequences. To cut out these words from this ecumenical creed is to cut oneself off from the belief of millions of Christians past and present who have confessed Jesus Christ as "eternally be-

---

[20]With one notable exception: the Nicene Creed of 381 speaks of the Spirit as "proceeding from the Father." The third (Western) council of Toledo, in 589, added the Latin word *filoque* ("and the Son"). The Eastern churches have not accepted this change and say the creed in its original form. See further Kevin Giles, *Jesus and the Father: Modern Evangelicals Reinvent the Doctrine of the Trinity* (Grand Rapids: Zondervan, 2006), pp. 156-58.

[21]I will fully document these charges later in this chapter.

[22]For example, the Anglican Thirty-Nine Articles, art. 2; the Second Helvetic Confession, chap. 3; the Westminster Confession of Faith, chap. 2.2 and the Heidelberg Catechism, question 33.

gotten of the Father." It is to break with historic orthodoxy, to move outside the catholic church, and a community that decides to do this becomes a sect. Timothy Larsen, in his introduction to the *Cambridge Companion to Evangelical Theology*,[23] thinks that to reject all or part of the Nicene Creed is even to put oneself outside of the evangelical community of faith. He says an evangelical Christian is first of all an "orthodox Christian"[24] whose "doctrines of God and Christ are in line with the ones articulated at the councils of Nicaea (AD 325) and Constantinople (AD 381)."[25]

Here it needs to be noted that many if not most evangelicals do not see the Nicene Creed and the Athanasian Creed, or their denominational confession of faith, as independent from Scripture, let alone as set over Scripture. Rather, most evangelicals believe them to be accurate summaries of what the Scriptures, read holistically, teach on important matters. In particular, they regard the two creeds mentioned and their particular confessions, as reliable guides for rightly interpreting Scripture on once hotly debated issues and uniting believers who want to grasp correctly what Scripture teaches on key doctrines. Luke Timothy Johnson argues that creeds and confessions are needed more today than ever before.[26] I agree. In an age that celebrates individuality they speak of communal beliefs. In an age that avoids commitment they speak of commitments to certain beliefs. In an age that celebrates innovation and change they speak of long held beliefs that do not change. And, in an age when evangelicals are more divided than ever over what the Bible teaches on fundamental issues, they offer an invitation to read the Bible, not according to their own presuppositions and agendas—a road that leads to disunity rather than unity—but in the light of what those who have gone before have concluded the Bible teaches.

---

[23]Timothy Larsen, ed., *Cambridge Companion to Evangelical Theology* (Cambridge: Cambridge University Press, 2007).

[24]Timothy Larsen, "Defining and Locating Evangelicalism," in *Cambridge Companion to Evangelical Theology* (Cambridge: Cambridge University Press, 2007), pp. 3-4.

[25]Ibid., p. 4.

[26]Luke Timothy Johnson, *The Creed: What Christians Believe and Why it Matters* (London: Darton, Longman and Todd, 2003). In what follows I closely follow his wording on p. 41.

WHAT IS INVOLVED IN DELETING FIVE WORDS FROM THE NICENE CREED?

In the Apostles' Creed, the confession "Jesus Christ, his only Son our Lord, who was conceived by the Holy Spirit, born of the Virgin Mary" speaks entirely of his incarnate ministry. In contrast, in the later Nicene Creed the confession of Jesus Christ as the only or unique Son of God follows with words that speak of the eternal relationship of the Father and the Son: "We believe in one Lord Jesus Christ . . . eternally begotten of the Father, God from God, Light from Light, true God from true God, begotten not made, of one being with the Father. Through whom all things were made." These words were added to categorically exclude Arianism. They speak of the Son's full and eternal divinity apart from and before they speak of what he did in his incarnate ministry for our salvation in history. They make it plain that to be eternally begotten of the Father means that the Son is God in exactly the same way as the Father, but he is not the Father. And his coming down for our salvation (see Phil 2:4-11) in no way diminishes his divine status. J. N. D. Kelly says this whole clause in the creed was added by the bishops at the Council of Nicaea as "a deliberately formulated counterblast to the principal tenet of Arianism that the Son had been created out of nothing and had no community of being with the Father."[27]

Once we recognize the import of this whole clause, we see the far-reaching significance of deleting the words "eternally begotten of the Father." Doing so opens the door to the Arian error and excludes what the Nicene fathers inserted to safeguard the two absolutely essential elements in the Nicene trinitarian doctrine of God: the full divinity of the Son and his distinct personal identity as the Son of the Father.

AND WHERE DO WE STOP?

To argue that just five words, "eternally begotten of the Father" be deleted from the Nicene Creed may at first not seem all that significant, but can the editing of the creed halt at this point? Three lines later, the compilers of the creed speak of the Son as "begotten, not made." Is this

---

[27]J. N. D. Kelly, *Early Christian Creeds* (London: Longmans, 1960), p. 235.

line also to be deleted? But this is the least problematic question. To delete the introductory "eternally begotten of the Father" means that most of the christological confession in this creed would need to be expunged. This second clause in the Nicene Creed begins, "We believe in one Lord Jesus Christ," and then a series of closely connected affirmations follows, all intended to exclude the Arian error.

1. He is the unique (*monogenēs*) Son.

2. He is eternally begotten of the Father (which is then explained by the following words).

3. He is "God from God, Light from Light, true God from true God" (i.e., God in the same way as the Father).

4. He is begotten, not made (not a creature).

5. He is of one being (*homoousion*) with the Father.

If clauses two and four, which speak of the begetting of the Son, are deleted, then clause three must be deleted as well because it explains clause two. And if clauses two, three and four are deleted, then clause five must be deleted because the *homoousios* confession rests on the premise that the Son is not a creature but is of one in being with the Father, "true God." Deleting the confession of the Son as *one in being* is truly a momentous step. It rules out the very term that finally excluded the Arian heresy. Deleting these four affirmations, which explain what it means to confess the Lord Jesus Christ as the unique Son of God, emaciates the creed, removing the barrier to the very idea these words primarily seek to exclude. The door that the church fathers closed in the face of Arianism and all forms of subordinationism, while indelibly differentiating the Father and the Son, is once more thrown open.

As an evangelical and confessional Christian, I thus find this call to delete the words "eternally begotten of the Father" in the Nicene Creed and other confessional statements deeply troubling. I confess this creed gladly because I believe it accurately sums up the teaching of the Bible. I thus hear this call to exclude these words from this creed as both a challenge to my assumptions and as an urgent demand to consider afresh whether or not this doctrine is grounded in Scripture and is theologically sound. I find it hard to believe there is no biblical warrant for this clause, but as an evangelical Christian I must seriously consider this charge.

I found a similar openness to consider the evidence in Samuel Miller's (1769-1850) impressive work defending the doctrine of the eternal generation of the Son, *Letters on the Eternal Sonship of Christ, Addressed to the Rev. Stuart, of Andover.*[28] He eloquently and prosaically writes, "If I do not deceive myself, I hold no opinion which I am not heartily willing to examine to the bottom. No man will ever forfeit my esteem or affection, by kindly and respectfully calling me to re-investigate any article of my creed, however long since I have supposed it to be settled."[29]

THE EVANGELICAL CALL TO ABANDON THE DOCTRINE OF THE ETERNAL GENERATION OF THE SON

I vividly remember in late 1989 reading John Dahms's article "The Generation of the Son" in the *Journal of the Evangelical Theological Society.*[30] At the time I knew very little about the doctrine of the Trinity and even less about the doctrine of the eternal generation of the Son. I was, however, surprised to hear him say that some evangelicals were questioning this doctrine[31] and even more surprised to find him arguing it was to be preserved because it "provides an *ontological* basis for the subordination of the Son of [*sic*] the Father."[32] I had thought the *ontological* subordination of the Son to the Father was the Arian error. His article raised so many questions in my mind that I wrote to him about his essay. I still have his reply on file. From this time on I began to read seriously on the doctrine of the Trinity. His essay made me aware of just how important it is to understand at some depth "our" distinctive Christian doctrine of a triune God. Paradoxically, Dahms's article in defense of the eternal generation of the Son, it would seem, actually

---

[28]Samuel Miller, *Letters on the Eternal Sonship of Christ, Addressed to the Rev. Stuart, of Andover* (Philadelphia: W. W. Woodward, 1823).

[29]Ibid., p. 27.

[30]John Dahms, "The Generation of the Son," *Journal of the Evangelical Theological Society* 32, no. 4 (1989): 493-501. See also Dahms, "The Subordination of the Son," *Journal of the Evangelical Theological Society* 37, no. 3 (1994): 351-64.

[31]Dahms mentions by name the evangelical theologian J. O. Buswell ("Generation," p. 497 n. 20, 498 and 498 n. 25) and the liberal scholar C. C. Richardson (pp. 499-501) as examples.

[32]Ibid., p. 497. Italics added.

encouraged more conservative evangelicals to question this doctrine.

Today, some of the best-known names in the evangelical world advocate the abandonment of the doctrine of the eternal begetting, or generation, of the Son. Those who have put this argument in writing include J. Oliver Buswell,[33] Lorraine Boettner,[34] Walter Martin,[35] Wayne Grudem,[36] Bruce Ware,[37] John S. Feinberg,[38] Millard Erickson,[39] Robert Reymond,[40] Paul Helm,[41] William Lane Craig,[42] and Mark Driscoll and Gerry Breshears,[43] while John Frame admits to "a certain amount of reverent agnosticism on this doctrine."[44] The Korean theologian Jung S. Rhee argues that the Old Princeton theologians Charles Hodge, A. A. Hodge and B. B. Warfield, who questioned the doctrine of the eternal generation of the Son, are to blame for its widespread rejection among contemporary evangelicals today.[45]

---

[33]J. Oliver Buswell, *A Systematic Theology of the Christian Religion* (Grand Rapids: Zondervan, 1978), 1:111-12.

[34]Lorraine Boettner, *Studies in Theology* (Philadelphia: Presbyterian and Reformed, 1947), pp. 121-22. Buswell and Boettner, it is to be noted, wrote before Dahms published his article.

[35]Walter Martin, *The Kingdom of the Cults* (Grand Rapids: Zondervan, 1965), pp. 102-3.

[36]Wayne Grudem, "Appendix 6," in *Systematic Theology: An Introduction to Biblical Doctrine* (Grand Rapids: Zondervan, revised edition, 2000), pp. 1233-34.

[37]Bruce Ware, *Father, Son and Holy Spirit* (Wheaton, Ill.: Crossway, 2005), p. 162 n. 3.

[38]John S. Feinberg, *No One Like Him: The Doctrine of God* (Wheaton, Ill.: Crossway, 2001), pp. 471, 483, 488-92, 498.

[39]Millard Erickson, *God in Three Persons: A Contemporary Interpretation of the Trinity* (Grand Rapids: Baker, 1995), pp. 305-6, 309-10; Erickson, *Who's Tampering with the Trinity? An Assessment of the Subordination Debate* (Grand Rapids: Kregel, 2009), pp. 179-84.

[40]Robert Reymond, *A New Systematic Theology of the Christian Faith* (New York: Nelson, 1998), pp. 326-27.

[41]Paul Helm, "Of God, and the Holy Trinity: A Response to Dr Beckwith," *Churchman* 115, no. 4 (2001): 350-57. In Helm, *John Calvin's Ideas* (Oxford: Oxford University Press, 2004) his wording is more constrained. He speaks of Calvin so "paring down" the idea of the Son's begetting that little content remains.

[42]J. P. Moreland and William Lane Craig, "Christian Doctrines (1): The Trinity," in *Philosophical Foundations for a Christian Worldview* (Downers Grove, Ill.: InterVarsity Press, 2003), p. 594, and in more detail, Craig, "A Formulation and Defense of the Doctrine of the Trinity" (2003), <www.lastseminary.com/trinity/CraigWilliamLTrinity.pdf>, p. 15.

[43]Mark Driscoll and Gerry Breshears, *Doctrine: What Christians Should Believe* (Wheaton, Ill.: Crossway, 2010), pp. 27-28.

[44]John Frame, *The Doctrine of God* (Phillipsburg, N.J.: Presbyterian and Reformed, 2002), p. 713.

[45]On the Web I found five studies, entitled "chapters," on the doctrine of the eternal generation of the Son by Rhee, which I presume are chapters of a thesis. "Chapter 1. A History of the Eternal Generation of the Son and Its Significance in Trinitarianism," <www.jsrhee.com/QA/thesis1.htm>. "Chapter 2. The Doctrine of the Eternal Generation of the Son in Opposition to the Logos Doctrine of the Early Church," <www.rsrhee.com/QA/thesis2.htm>.

Rhee makes a persuasive argument, but he does not tell the whole story.[46] Paradoxically, the longest (295 pages) biblically based, historically informed defense of the doctrine of the Son's eternal gener-

---

"Chapter 3. The Triumph of Ontological Realism and Eternal Generation in the Nicene Creed" <www.jsrhee.com/QA/thesis3.htm>. "Chapter 4. John Calvin and Reformed Theology on the Doctrine of the Eternal Generation of the Son" <www.jsrhee.com/QA/thesis4 .htm>. "Chapter 5. The Significance of the Eternal Generation of the Son Doctrine in the Contemporary Trinitarian Teaching." He has also written the Theopedia web-based article on the doctrine of the eternal generation of the Son <www.theopedia.com/Eternal_genera tion_of_the_Son>. In both "chapter 1" and "chapter 3" he accuses the Princeton theologians of introducing into evangelicalism doubt about the doctrine of the eternal generation of the Son.

[46]On reading for myself the old Princeton theologians I discovered the following.

Charles Hodge (1797-1878), in his *Systematic Theology* (London: James Clarke, 1960), pp. 468-71, does not deny the doctrine, but he raises so many questions and deals with it so inadequately that he undermines the doctrine. For him, "neither the Bible nor the ancient creeds explain" what it means to say that the "Son is begotten of the Father" (p. 468); the Nicene fathers teach that "sonship" means "derivation of essence" (p. 468), and he contrasts "the scriptural fact" that the Son is begotten with "the explanation of that fact, given by the Nicene fathers," which he questions (p. 468).

His son A. A. Hodge (1826-1886), in his *Outlines of Theology* (London: Banner of Truth, 1972), pp. 182-83, follows the trajectory of his father's thinking. He contrasts "revealed truths" about the generation of the Son with "rational explanations" of it (p. 183); he believes that "the early creeds" teach the "subordination [of the Son] as to mode of subsistence and operations" (p. 183) because the Son's generation implies that he "derived" from God, and this belief calls into question the Son's aseity (p. 185). Thus, rather than endorsing the creedal doctrine of the eternal generation of the Son, he concludes, "It should be held in suspense" (p. 183).

B. B. Warfield (1851-1921), in his essay "The Biblical Doctrine of the Trinity" in *Biblical Foundations* (London: Tyndale, 1958), pp. 79-116, presents a complex picture. First, in dealing with the biblical data he reflects classic orthodoxy. He rejects that the designation *Son* implies "subordination and derivation of Being" (p. 109). Rather, he says it indicates "that whatever the Father is the Son is also" (p. 109). He also says rightly that the term "only begotten" (*monogenēs*) "need add only the idea of uniqueness, not of derivation" (p. 109). The only subordination he allows for the Son is in his work of redemption (p. 110). Here his position stands in opposition to that of Charles Hodge and A. A. Hodge, who both endorse the subordination of the Son "in subsistence and operations." However, near the end of this essay, in speaking of how the doctrine of the Trinity developed historically, he argues that the Nicene Creed of 325 got what the Bible teaches wrong. He says this creed is "the vehicle of the Nicene doctrines of the eternal generation of the Son and procession of the Spirit, with the consequent subordination of the Son and Spirit to the Father in modes of subsistence as well as operations." When we turn to his essay "Calvin's Doctrine of the Trinity," in *Calvin and Augustine* (Philadelphia: Presbyterian and Reformed, 1956), pp. 189-284, we find him arguing that "although he [Calvin] taught that the Son was begotten of the Father, and of course begotten before all time, or as we would say from all eternity, he seems to have drawn back from the doctrine of 'eternal generation' as it was expounded by the Nicene Fathers" (pp. 247, 250). Later he adds, Calvin "admitted the facts of 'generation' and 'procession,' [but] he treated them as bare facts, and refused to make them constitutive of the doctrine of the Trinity" (p. 257). Then last, Warfield argues that Calvin rejected the texts "customarily relied upon" to establish the doctrine of the eternal generation of the Son, concluding that "there is little Biblical basis for the doctrine of 'eternal generation' except what might be inferred from the mere terms 'Father,' 'Son' and 'Spirit'" (p. 277).

ation that I know of is given by the earlier Princeton theologian Samuel Miller, in his 1823 work mentioned above, *Letters on the Eternal Sonship of Christ, Addressed to the Rev. Stuart, of Andover.* The later Princeton theologians either did not know this work or chose to ignore it.

These evangelical objectors to the doctrine of the eternal generation or begetting of the Son have not gone unchallenged, but no one in recent times has offered an extended countercase. In published support of the doctrine I can list the contemporary evangelical theologians John Dahms,[47] Roger Beckwith,[48] Andreas Köstenberger and Scott Swain,[49] and in more detail, Jung S. Rhee,[50] Donald Macleod,[51] Robert Letham,[52] Fred Sanders[53] and Keith E. Johnson.[54]

This intramural division among evangelicals over the eternal begetting of the Son, it is important to note, is not correlated with the other major divide among evangelicals over the doctrine of the Trinity, namely, whether the Son is eternally subordinated in authority to the Father.[55] Grudem, Ware, and Driscoll and Breshears support the eternal subordination of the Son, and they advocate abandoning the doctrine of the eternal begetting or generation of the Son. While Erickson and Craig argue for no subordination in the eternal life of God, they too

---

[47]John Dahms, "The Johannine use of *Monogenes* Reconsidered," *New Testament Studies* 29 (1983): 222-32.

[48]Roger Beckwith, "The Calvinist Doctrine of the Trinity," *Churchman* 115, no. 4 (2001): 308-57.

[49]Andreas Köstenberger and Scott Swain, *Father, Son and Spirit: The Trinity and John's Gospel,* New Studies in Biblical Theology (Downers Grove, Ill.: IVP Academic, 2008), pp. 179-85.

[50]See note 45 above.

[51]Donald Macleod, *The Person of Christ* (Leicester, U.K.: Inter-Varsity Press, 1998), pp. 72-74, 131-35.

[52]Robert Letham, *The Holy Trinity: In Scripture, History, Theology and Worship* (Phillipsburg, N.J.: Presbyterian and Reformed, 2004), pp. 383-89.

[53]Sanders, *Deep Things of God,* pp. 83-89, 91-92, 155-56. See also his unpublished lecture, "Relations of Origin in the Eternal Trinity: Biblical Warrant and Systematic Implications," given at the Far West Regional Conference of the Evangelical Theological Society in April 2010. I thank Sanders for sending me a copy.

[54]Johnson, "Augustine's Trinitarian Reading of John 5: A Model for the Theological Interpretation of Scripture," *Journal of the Evangelical Theological Society* 52, no. 4 (2009): 799-811; Johnson, "Trinitarian Agency and the Eternal Subordination of the Son: An Augustinian Perspective," *Themelios* 36 no. 1 (2011): 7-25; Johnson "Augustine, Eternal Generation, and Evangelical Trinitarianism," *Trinity Journal* 32ns, no 2 (2011): 141-63.

[55]On this see Kevin Giles, *Jesus and the Father;* Millard Erickson, *Who's Tampering.*

advocate abandoning the doctrine of the eternal begetting or generation of the Son.

REASONS GIVEN FOR ABANDONING THE DOCTRINE OF THE ETERNAL GENERATION OF THE SON

The most common argument evangelicals put forward for abandoning the doctrine of the eternal generation of the Son is that it has no biblical "warrant," but almost all those who make this case have subsidiary arguments for expunging this doctrine that they think are also important.

Wayne Grudem is a very significant voice in conservative evangelical circles. His *Systematic Theology: An Introduction to Biblical Doctrine* is now the most widely used systematics text in evangelical, Pentecostal, and charismatic Bible colleges and seminaries around the world, with over 300,000 copies in print in the American edition alone. In relation to the doctrine of the Trinity he argues that the Son is eternally subordinated in role, by which he means authority, to the Father. In part he finds support for his doctrine of the Son's eternal subordination in the patristic doctrine of the generation of the Son.[56] However, paradoxically he argues elsewhere that "it would seem more helpful if the words 'begotten of the Father' (signifying the "eternal generation of the Son") were not retained in any modern theological formulations."[57] He makes this assertion because he believes there is no biblical warrant for this doctrine and it does not ground the *eternal distinctions* between the Father, Son and Spirit in any "meaningful" way.[58] His alternative is that *differing authority* between the divine three persons is what primarily, indelibly and eternally differentiates them.[59] The Father commands; the Son obeys.[60]

Bruce Ware holds an almost identical view of the Trinity to Grudem. In his book on the doctrine of the Trinity, *Father, Son and Holy Spirit:*

---

[56]Wayne Grudem, *Evangelical Feminism and Evangelical Belief* (Sisters, Ore.: Multnomah, 2004), pp. 415-18.
[57]Grudem, "Appendix," pp. 1233-34.
[58]Ibid., p. 1234.
[59]For more on this and documentation see chap. 8.
[60]I will document his position more fully in chap. 9.

Relationships, Roles and Relevance, he argues for the eternal subordination of the Son in authority and predicates eternal divine self-differentiation exclusively on the differing authority of the divine persons.[61] The Father is "head over" the Son and the Spirit. He also rejects that divine self-differentiation is grounded in the eternal generation of the Son and procession of the Spirit and that there is any biblical support for such "speculation." He writes, "The conception of both the 'eternal begetting of the Son' and 'eternal procession of the Spirit' seem to me highly speculative and not grounded in biblical teaching. Both the Son as only begotten and the Spirit as proceeding from the Father (and the Son) refer, in my judgments, to the historical realities of the incarnation and Pentecost respectively."[62]

Another highly significant voice arguing for the abandonment of the doctrine of the eternal generation of the Son is Millard Erickson, the doyen of conservative evangelical theologians. He opposes the Grudem-Ware doctrine that the Son is eternally subordinated to the Father in authority,[63] but like them he believes that nowhere in the Bible are there "references to the Father begetting the Son" in eternity. However, he rejects this doctrine not only because he thinks it has no biblical warrant but also because he thinks that speaking of the Son as begotten "as an eternal occurrence, involves the subordination of the Son to the Father."[64]

John Feinberg is yet another well-respected evangelical theologian. In his *No One Like Him: The Doctrine of God,* he argues for a doctrine of the Trinity that does not include the eternal generation of the Son and procession of the Spirit. His arguments for abandoning the doctrine of the eternal generation of the Son are as follows. (1) The "biblical data" does not support this idea.[65] (2) It "makes little sense."[66] Its meaning is "shrouded in obscurity."[67] It is illogical. How can someone

---

[61]Ibid., pp. 45-47, 71-72.

[62]Ware, *Father, Son and Holy Spirit,* p. 162 n. 3.

[63]See Erickson, *Who's Tampering.*

[64]Erickson, *God in Three Persons,* p. 309. See also his *Who's Tampering,* 179-84.

[65]Feinberg, *No One Like Him,* pp. 489-91. In these pages he surveys the biblical arguments and finds them wanting.

[66]Ibid., p. 489.

[67]Ibid., p. 492.

who is eternal have a beginning? (3) It does not safeguard "anything significant in the doctrine [of the Trinity]," particularly, "the notion that there is one God in three persons."[68] In other words, for him the eternal generation of the Son and eternal procession of the Spirit are not necessary doctrines to ensure divine unity in being and divine threefold differentiation. He thus concludes, "It seems wisest to abandon the doctrines of eternal generation [of the Son] and eternal procession [of the Spirit]."[69]

At a more popular level, Mark Driscoll and Gerry Breshears, in their book *Doctrine: What Christians Should Believe,*[70] argue that there is (1) nothing in Scripture to support the idea that the Son is eternally begotten and the Spirit eternally proceeds;[71] (2) the term *begotten* can never be "defined with any clarity" and so it is "of little use";[72] and (3) "*begotten* unavoidably implies a beginning of the one begotten. This would certainly lend support to the Arian heresy that the Son is a created being and not the Creator God."[73] "For these reasons," they conclude, "it is best to omit the creedal terms 'begotten' and 'proceeds' from our definition of the Trinity. Our authority is not in creeds but in scripture."[74]

Large numbers of evangelicals have on their bookshelves Walter Martin's classic study *The Kingdom of the Cults,* which explains and opposes the teaching of most of the modern-day Christian sects or cults. It continues to sell well. In discussing the theology of Jehovah's Witnesses, he argues at length that orthodox Christians should give up the doctrine of the eternal generation of the Son because it has "fed the Arian heresy through the centuries and today continues to feed the Christology of Jehovah's Witnesses."[75] He holds that this doctrine has no biblical warrant because the Greek word *monogenēs*

---

[68]Ibid., p. 495.
[69]Ibid., pp. 492, 498.
[70]Driscoll and Breshears, *Doctrine: What Christians Should Believe.*
[71]Ibid., p. 27.
[72]Ibid., p. 28.
[73]Ibid.
[74]Ibid.
[75]Martin, *Kingdom*, p. 102.

does not mean "only begotten" but "only" or "unique,"[76] and he says the doctrine was first "conceived by Origen in A.D. 230."[77]

Then we have the Christian philosophers Paul Helm[78] and William Lane Craig,[79] who both argue that there is no biblical support for the doctrine of the eternal generation of the Son and that it should be rejected because it implies or necessitates the eternal subordination of the Son.[80] Craig also argues that dropping the doctrine of the eternal begetting of the Son and procession of the Spirit opens the door to a better way of explaining the eternal differentiation of the persons, namely by their differing work in the economy.[81] Helm, for his part, adds the argument that the begetting of the Son and the procession of the Spirit reflect "Neo-Platonism, particularly the idea that from the One emanated Mind and Spirit."[82]

To sum up this section I briefly list the differing arguments contemporary evangelical theologians give for rejecting the doctrine of the eternal generation of the Son.

1. It has no "biblical warrant." This is their first and most important objection.

2. It reflects Neo-Platonic thinking about God more than Christian thinking.[83]

---

[76]Ibid., p. 101.

[77]Ibid., p. 103.

[78]Helm, "Of God," pp. 350-57. We will discuss his arguments in detail in chap. 9.

[79]Craig, "A Formulation"; Moreland and Craig, "Christian Doctrines (I): The Trinity," p. 594.

[80]I will document their views when I come to the specific question in chap. 8, "Does the Eternal Generation of the Son Imply the Eternal Subordination of the Son?"

[81]Craig, "A Formulation," pp. 16-18.

[82]Helm, "Of God," p. 351. The Lutheran theologian Robert Jenson, *The Triune Identity* (Philadelphia: Fortress, 1982), pp. 114-21, makes a similar claim.

[83]This opinion reflects a late nineteenth-century opinion. Edwin Hatch in his Hibbert Lectures of 1888 started the debate about the Hellenization of Christianity. See his *The Influence of Greek Ideas and Usages Upon the Christian Church* (London: Williams and Norgate, 1897). Adolf von Harnack popularized this opinion. See W. Hellman, ed., *Hellenization Revisited* (Lanham, Md.: University Press of America, 1994), pp. 69-98. Ayres, *Nicaea*, pp. 31-32, argues against this idea, as does T. F. Torrance, *The Christian Doctrine of God: One Being Three Persons* (Edinburgh: T & T Clark, 1996), pp. 113, 120, 130. See also, Paul Gavrilyuk, "Harnack's Hellenized Christianity or Florovsky's Sacred Hellenism: Questioning Two Metanarratives of Early Christianity's Engagement with Late Antique Culture," *St Vladimir's Theological Quarterly* 54, nos. 3 and 4 (2010): 325-45.

3. It makes no sense.[84]

4. Nothing theologically important is lost if it is abandoned.

5. There are better ways to eternally differentiate the Father and the Son.

6. It implies or necessarily involves the eternal subordination of the Son, even the Arian heresy.

These objections to the doctrine of the eternal generation of the Son set the agenda for what follows. The book is not structured around these objections, but in what follows I will address them all.

WHERE DO WE GO FROM HERE?

Evangelical theologians who argue that the doctrine of the eternal begetting of the Son should be abandoned because there is no text in the Bible that explicitly teaches it raise the acute question, how should evangelicals "do" theology? Is evangelical systematic theology—or, as it is often called, "doctrine"—simply the reiteration of what is in Scripture, or is it far more? In the next chapter we explore this foundational question for this study. After that, we will examine what in Scripture has lead most of the church to confess, "We believe in one Lord Jesus Christ . . . eternally begotten of the Father"? From then on the book explores how the doctrine of the eternal generation of the Son emerged, gained ever-growing acceptance, and was developed and honed. This process will give us the history of this doctrine, and understanding the history of a doctrine is very often if not always the best pathway to a fuller appreciation and understanding of any doctrine. Put starkly but accurately Khaled Anatolios says, "the [historical] development of trinitarian doctrine is the key to its meaning."[85]

---

[84]Erickson, *Who's Tampering*, p. 182: "It must be acknowledged that for many persons today, the doctrine [of the Son's begetting] does not seem to make much sense." Grudem, "Appendix," p. 1234: "There is no meaningful sense in which we should speak about any one of the persons being a 'source' of these personal distinctions." Feinberg, *No One Like Him,* p. 489: this doctrine "makes little sense."

[85]Khaled Anatolios, *Retrieving Nicaea* (Grand Rapids: Baker, 2011), p. xv. This very important study arrived after the manuscript of this book was submitted to the publisher and is thus not integral to my work.

2

"Doing" Evangelical Theology

◆　◆　◆

This chapter is about how evangelical systematic theology is "done." The now common conservative evangelical opinion that the doctrine of the eternal generation of the Son should be abandoned because it has no explicit biblical warrant acutely raises the question of evangelical theological method and particularly the relationship between Scripture and what is called "the tradition." Much of this chapter will be taken up in exploring what the term *the tradition* means and how it informs the theological interpretation of Scripture. Evangelicals are sharply divided on the question of how evangelical systematic theology, often called "doctrine," is done.[1] Which side of the divide we come down on determines to a large degree which side we come down on with the question, does the Bible warrant the doctrine of the eternal generation of the Son?

EVANGELICAL SYSTEMATIC THEOLOGY

Systematic theology has as its agenda the answering of questions about God and about his relationship with the world and human beings that Christians have asked since the completion of the New Testament. All theology begins with a question. Theologians only start theologizing when a dispute arises in the life of the church as to what is to be believed. For example, what is sin and what are its consequences? What is necessary to be saved? Why did Christ die on the cross? When and how

---

[1]This chapter draws on conclusions I reached twenty years ago and have honed with the passing of the years. See Kevin N. Giles, "Evangelical Systematic Theology: Definition, Problems, Sources," in *In the Fullness of Time: Biblical Studies in Honour of Archbishop Donald Robinson*, ed. D. Peterson and J. Pryor (Sydney: Lancer, 1992), pp. 255-76.

will Christ return? Are women subordinated to men or not? In regard to the subject of this book, broadly put, the question is, how can the biblical teaching that God is one (Deut 6:4; Mk 12:29; 1 Cor 8:4; Eph 4:6; Jas 2:19) and yet three divine persons be understood (Mt 28:19; 2 Cor 13:13)? Or more specifically put, how can the one God be eternally self-differentiated as Father, Son and Spirit without falling into the errors of modalism, tritheism or subordinationism? Anselm (1033-1109) clearly recognized that theology is a question-answering exercise when he described this discipline as "faith seeking understanding."[2] Possibly no better definition of theology could be given.

Evangelical systematic theology seeks to answer such questions by appeal to the Bible. For the evangelical theologian, Scripture is the final authority for determining right belief. However, as we will see in what follows, asserting the ultimate authority of Scripture is the easy part; working out what the Scriptures actually teach on complex theological questions is what is difficult. For this reason, evangelicals are not so much divided over the authority of the Bible as they are over the interpretation of the Bible. Given this agreed evangelical distinctive, the supremacy and authority of the Bible, we find that there are basically two alternative understandings of what is involved in doing evangelical theology.

The Bible alone provides the answers. For many evangelicals, evangelical theology (or doctrine[3]) simply involves the gathering together of what the Bible teaches on any particular topic. The illustration is often given that the Bible is like a forest, where the differing trees, shrubs and plants grow randomly, mixed together, and theology or doctrine is like a botanic garden, where all the species are gathered together and neatly ordered. From this illustration we are supposed to conclude that what is found in the forest is in the botanic garden, and it is obvious to the gardener how the vegetation is to be set out in an orderly way. The theologian adds or subtracts nothing. The nineteenth-century evangelical and Reformed theologian Charles Hodge (1797-1878), one of the most for-

---

[2]See further on this Daniel L. Migliore, *Faith Seeking Understanding: An Introduction to Christian Theology* (Grand Rapids: Eerdmans, 1991), especially pp. 1-3.

[3]I will come back later and explain how these two terms can also be differentiated.

mative influences in late twentieth-century evangelicalism, gave classic expression to this understanding of doing evangelical theology. In the introduction to his three-volume *Systematic Theology*, he writes, "The true method of theology is inductive, which assumes that the Bible contains all the facts or truths which form the content of theology, just as the facts of nature are the contents of the natural sciences."[4]

Today this position is given classic expression in the most widely used evangelical theological textbook, Wayne Grudem's *Systematic Theology: An Introduction to Biblical Doctrine*. He says evangelical theology is "any study that answers the question, *'What does the whole Bible teach us today?' about any given topic*. This definition indicates that systematic theology involves collecting and understanding all the relevant passages in the Bible on various topics and then summarizing their teachings clearly so that we know what to believe about each topic."[5] Given this definition of theology, it is unsurprising that Grudem rejects the doctrine of the eternal begetting of the Son, as we saw in the previous chapter.

The Bible is the ultimate authority in answering theological questions, but doing evangelical theology involves far more than direct appeal to the Bible.[6] In contrast, many other evangelicals argue that doing evangelical theology involves far more than merely organizing and systematizing what is explicitly said in Scripture. They point out that in coming to the Scriptures to find answers, theologians are always confronted with the diversity of scriptural teaching on a given topic, whatever they believe

---

[4]Charles Hodge, *Systematic Theology* (Edinburgh: T & T Clark, 1960), 1:17. See in more detail 1:18-33

[5]Wayne Grudem, *Systematic Theology: An Introduction to Biblical Doctrine* (Grand Rapids: Zondervan, 1999), p. 21.

[6]On the contemporary evangelical debate about the nature of evangelical systematic theology see, among others, Alister McGrath, *Genesis of Doctrine* (Oxford: Basil Blackwell, 1990); John G. Stackhouse Jr., ed., *Evangelical Futures: A Conversation on Theological Method* (Grand Rapids, Baker, 2000); Richard Lints, *The Fabric of Theology: A Prolegomena to Evangelical Theology* (Grand Rapids: Eerdmans, 1993); Stanley J. Grenz, *Revisioning Evangelical Theology: A Fresh Agenda for the 21st Century* (Downers Grove, Ill.: InterVarsity Press, 1993); Stanley J. Grenz and John H. Franke, *Beyond Foundationalism: Shaping Theology in a Postmodern Context* (Louisville: Westminster John Knox, 2001); J. S. Franke, *The Character of Theology: An Introduction to Its Nature, Task and Purpose* (Grand Rapids: Baker Academic, 2005); T. Griggs, *New Perspectives for Evangelical Theology: Engaging with God, Scripture and the World* (London: Routledge, 2010).

about its ultimate unity. Thus evangelical theologians must first of all try to discover the primary and foundational reality to which the varied comments in Scripture on any issue point. In seeking to do this they usually explore what others before them have concluded on the matter in question.

An illustration for this understanding of doing evangelical theology would be a broken-up jigsaw puzzle with no picture provided. By trial and error the people working on the puzzle, often sharply disagreeing, sometimes making mistakes, gradually come to fit the pieces together to form a picture, even if a few pieces do not seem to fit neatly. Subsequent jigsaw-puzzle workers now can see the picture; they never start from scratch, and from time to time they make small corrections that gradually get more pieces to fit, thereby improving the picture.

On this wider understanding, doing evangelical systematic theology is a collective enterprise, not an individualistic one. Each generation learns from the one before. In other words, it is a communal enterprise that develops organically over time.

A conservative evangelical and Reformed example of this wider understanding of evangelical theology appears in the writings of Robert Letham. In the preface to his important 2004 book, *The Holy Trinity in Scripture, History, Theology, and Worship*,[7] he says that in outlining the historic orthodox doctrine of the Trinity, he will interact "with theologians from widely differing backgrounds, from East and West, from Roman Catholicism as well as Protestantism."[8] In other words, he accepts that other Christians provide insights that do not immediately spring from the text of Scripture. He then says that "while our supreme authority is Holy Scripture, we should also listen seriously and attentively to the Fathers, as did Calvin, the Reformers, and John Owen."[9] He is particularly critical of "individualistic religion," which "has led many [evangelicals] to downplay the ecumenical creeds in favour of the latest insights from biblical studies."[10] Then he adds, "Opposition to the orthodox doctrine has often tended to come from those who stress

---

[7]Robert Letham, *The Holy Trinity in Scripture, History, Theology, and Worship* (Phillipsburg, N.J.: Presbyterian and Reformed, 2004).
[8]Ibid., p. ix.
[9]Ibid.
[10]Ibid., p. 5, p. ix

the Bible at the expense of the teachings of the church. These people forget that the church was forced to use extra biblical language because biblical language itself was open to a variety of interpretations—some faithful, others not."[11]

Not surprisingly, given these comments, Letham comes to exactly the opposite conclusion to Wayne Grudem on the doctrine of the eternal generation of the Son. He begins his defense of this doctrine by noting that "since [the time of] Irenaeus, the church has held that the Father begat the Son in eternity. This came to expression in C [the Constantinople-Nicene Creed of 381] and is repeated in later confessions such as the Westminster Confession of Faith."[12] From his basis of trust in the teaching of the church, Letham examines the biblical arguments against this doctrine and finds them wanting. He accepts that there is no text that actually says the Son is eternally generated or begotten but nevertheless finds much in Scripture that suggests this idea and nothing that excludes it.[13] He thus concludes that this long-held and theologically important doctrine should be maintained and supported, because "The doctrine of eternal generation does not depend on the meaning of any one word, not even on strict biblical exegesis alone. It is a theological predicate grounded in the eternal relations of the Son and the Father in the one being of God."[14]

With these two diametrically opposed conclusions on the doctrine of the eternal generation of the Son, predicated on differing understandings of the nature of evangelical theology, we see why this chapter is an integral part of this study. If evangelical theology were simply a reiteration of the explicit statements of Scripture, then there would be no debate. All are agreed: no text in Scripture says, "The Son is eternally begotten or generated by the Father." The problem is that we do not agree on the interpretation of key passages, on the meaning of key

---

[11]Ibid.

[12]Ibid., p. 383.

[13]See ibid., p. 387, where he says at the conclusion of his survey of the Bible's teaching on this matter that it is "impossible to eliminate any reference to begetting when it comes to the Son."

[14]Ibid., p. 384. See also Donald Macleod, *The Person of Christ* (Leicester, U.K.: Inter-Varsity Press, 1998), p. 131, who comes to a similar conclusion. He speaks of the doctrine as "an inevitable corollary of the eternal sonship."

words and on how seemingly contradictory comments in Scripture are to be reconciled. This again brings to our attention the fact that most if not all doctrinal differences among evangelicals, of which there are many, are not disputes over the authority of the Bible but over how the Bible read holistically and prayerfully is rightly to be understood. If this is the case then evangelical theology involves far more than merely re-iterating what Scripture says as if what it said, especially at a macro or doctrinal level, were self-evident.

PROBLEMS WITH THE BIBLE-ALONE VIEW OF EVANGELICAL THEOLOGY

The Hodge-Grudem understanding of evangelical theology implies that, given a concordance, one could accumulate all the texts on any topic and the answer would be clear and precise and indisputable. We would have what the Bible taught on sin, salvation, eschatology, the atonement or whatever. This method conveys the idea that each generation of Christians simply opens their Bibles and finds the doctrines their teachers hold dear clearly spelled out on the pages of Holy Writ. The teaching of the great theologians of the past, the creeds and Reformation confessions, and theologians themselves contribute nothing of importance. The problem with this view is that no doctrine springs directly from the pages of Scripture because the Scriptures do not speak univocally on most topics, and on some important questions that Christians have asked subsequent to the closing of the canon, the Bible says nothing specific at all. Because some will immediately dispute these assertions, I need to illustrate how complex appeal to the Bible is in the doing of theology. I give some examples.

- In some instances, the Bible seems to give two conflicting answers to the one question, and theologians have concluded that both need to be embraced. The doctrine of election is an example. On the one hand, the Bible says that God freely elects to save. He chooses who will believe (e.g., Mt 24:31; Rom 11:5; 1 Cor 1: 27-28; Eph 1:4). On the other hand, the Bible also makes it plain that people are invited to freely respond to the Gospel (e.g., Jn 3:16; Acts 2:38; Rom 10:5-13). The truth, theologians have concluded, is found not by excluding one but by embracing both insights. Salvation is entirely a gift of God to those he loves and chooses, but it must be accepted. Reformed theologians make the added conclusion that grace must always triumph on the premise that God is sovereign. Arminian theologians, in contrast, conclude that it is possible to reject the grace of God on the premise that God has given human beings free will.[15]

- In other cases where the Bible seems to give conflicting information on a specific question, theologians have concluded that one strand should be given priority over the other. The doctrine of justification by faith is an example. Paul makes it plain that he believes we are justified by faith through grace. We do not earn our way into heaven by our good deeds (e.g., Rom 3–4; Gal 4). However, there are many other texts that could suggest that good works do contribute to our salvation or even merit it (e.g., Mt 25:31-46; Mk 10:17-22; Jn 5:29; 1 Tim 2:15; Jas 2:18-26). Protestant theologians, following the six-teenth-century Reformers, in this case give precedence to the Pauline teaching on justification by faith and interpret the other texts that speak of works as speaking of the works that naturally follow from being justified by grace.

- The doctrine of the Trinity also fits this pattern, but in this case there is a major and a minor voice. The majority of texts depict the Father, Son and Spirit alike as coequal and eternal God, or as the confessions put it, eternally one in being and power, yet many rec-ognize that at least two texts seem to suggest otherwise (Jn 14:28; 1 Cor 15:28). Here theologians typically interpret these two texts and any others that might be quoted in support in a way that harmonizes with the dominant perspective of Scripture. In this case orthodoxy represents the prioritizing of the major voice over the minor voice.

- Then we have examples of important doctrines that have no explicit biblical support; the doctrine is based on inferences drawn from what Scripture says. Ordained ministry as we know it today is an example. Most Christians believe that each local church should have

---

[15]See Roger E. Olson, *Arminian Theology: Myths and Realities* (Downers Grove, Ill.: IVP Aca-demic, 2006).

a (chief) pastor, and most evangelical theological textbooks have a section on ordained ministry that assumes and justifies this. However, not one instance of mono-congregational leadership in the apostolic age or a prescriptive comment in the Bible supporting such a model of congregational leadership can be cited. Paul insists that all ministry is Spirit-initiated and authenticated and is plural in number (Rom 12:4-8; 1 Cor 12:4-30), a model of ministry that fits well the little house churches that prevailed for the first three centuries of Christian history.[16]

- And then there is infant baptism. The majority of Christians, including millions of evangelicals, believe that infants of Christian parents may be baptized. For evangelicals this belief is not predicated on any text but on the basis of God's covenantal promises to his people and their children.

- In what is possibly the most difficult example, theologians conclude that one explicit text that prescribes something is not the final word on the question at hand. The Sabbath/Sunday divide is a good example. The fourth commandment rules that the seventh day should be kept holy and that no work is to be done on that day. The emphasis falls on the abstention from labor of any kind. This command is grounded in creation (Gen 1:2-3; Ex 20:8-11) and is one of the Ten Commandments in the moral law. However, in the light of the resurrection of Christ on the first day of the week this command was abrogated (see Rom 10:4). The early Christians began meeting on the first day of the week (Acts 20:7; Rev 1:10), and Paul ruled that one day was no more holy than any other (Rom 14:1-12), saying nothing at all against working on this day.

A historical example of one text leading the church into error is seen in the Arian debate, specifically on the question of the generation of the Son. The Arians of the fourth century constantly appealed to one

---

[16]On the historic realities of leadership in the early church see Kevin N. Giles, *Patterns of Ministry Among the First Christians* (Melbourne: Collins-Dove, 1989); and Giles, "Church Order, Government," in *Dictionary of the Later New Testament and Its Development*, ed. Ralph P. Martin and Peter H. Davids (Downers Grove, Ill.: InterVarsity Press, 1997), pp. 219-26.

text, Proverbs 8:22, in their "authorized version," the Septuagint (the Greek translation of the Old Testament), to prove that the Son, identified with personified Wisdom in this verse, was created in time by God the Father. In Greek the text does speak of the creation of Wisdom in time, but none of the Nicene fathers would allow this interpretation.[17] For them the whole of Scripture made it clear that the Son was not a creature brought forth in time. This one discordant text, they argued, had to be interpreted in the light of what was primary and foundational in scriptural revelation. The renowned Reformed New Testament scholar Oscar Cullman, noting how Christians often major on one text,[18] makes the startling conclusion that "the fountainhead of all false biblical interpretation and of all heresy is invariably the isolation and the absolutising of one single passage."[19]

I conclude from these observations that no doctrine immediately springs from the pages of Scripture. Every doctrine is informed by Scripture, but ultimately it represents a theological affirmation predicated on a synthetic apprehension of what is given in Scripture. In other words, doctrines are not merely the systematizing of what Scripture explicitly says. Determining the correct theological conclusion to draw from Scripture must always be the fruit of long and hard prayerful reflection on Scripture, undertaken while listening attentively to other theologians. It is a collective enterprise. In each case given above, the doctrine is the fruit of centuries of prayerful study of Scripture by the best minds in the church, often in prolonged and painful debate, and it represents an agreed communal conclusion usually spelled out in a creed or confession. Doctrines, therefore, represent what the church past and present has come to agree are the right conclusions to draw from Scripture in answer to specific theological questions. It is always possible to challenge these conclusions by arguing that the church has missed or misrepresented important and weighty biblical teaching, or has drawn the wrong conclusion from the words of Scripture, but until the evidence is so compelling that most

---

[17]The Hebrew Bible does not raise this problem. In the next chapter we will say more on this.
[18]Oscar Cullmann, *The State in the New Testament* (London: SCM Press, 1957).
[19]Ibid., p. 47.

Christians agree that change is needed, the collective mind of the church over centuries should be upheld. It is the best guide we have to a right reading of Scripture and right belief, right *doctrine*.

Prior to this paragraph I have taken the terms *systematic theology* and *doctrine* to mean much the same. In doing this I agree with Wayne Grudem, who titles his systematics, *Systematic Theology: An Introduction to Biblical Doctrine*. However, Alister McGrath, in his book *The Genesis of Doctrine*, argues that the term *doctrine* should be used of the agreed "beliefs of a community" and *theology* of the views of individual theologians.[20] This is a helpful distinction, and I use it in the paragraph above. This terminology makes clear that it is correct to call the eternal generation of the Son "a doctrine" in the narrow sense that McGrath uses the term. It is a theological conclusion that the church has affirmed and publicly endorsed by including it in creeds and confessions. What we are arguing against is a current theological opinion, "the theology," of a minority of individual theologians who are asking that "the doctrine of the eternal generation of the Son" be abandoned.

DOING EVANGELICAL THEOLOGY INVOLVES MORE THAN APPEAL TO THE BIBLE

In the discussion above I have introduced a much broader understanding of evangelical theology than that seen in the Hodge-Grudem approach, one with a strong ancestry and one that is growing in support today.[21] This understanding of evangelical theology finds its roots in the work of the great sixteenth-century Reformers and its immediate antecedents in the writings of late nineteenth- and early twentieth-century Dutch Reformed theologians. This approach gives pride of place to Scripture but insists that in the theological enterprise Scripture must be read in the light of how it has been interpreted by the best of theologians in the past and prescribed in creeds and confessions. On this understanding of evangelical theology, theology is not an individualistic enterprise in

---

[20]McGrath, *Genesis of Doctrine*, pp. 10-13.
[21]See among others mentioned in note 7 above, McGrath, *Genesis of Doctrine;* Stackhouse, ed., *Evangelical Futures;* Lints, *Fabric of Theology;* Grenz, *Revisioning Evangelical Theology;* Grenz and Franke, *Beyond Foundationalism;* Franke, *Character of Theology;* Griggs, *New Perspectives.*

which each theologian alone decides what the Bible teaches on any matter but is rather a communal exercise in which the opinions of others, past and present, are of huge importance. Theologians thus build on the work of those who have preceded them, and each succeeding generation adds something, as new insights emerge and the question in focus changes because an old error has appeared in a new form. In this process the best of theologians with the best of minds objectively advance theological understanding in a number of ways that I will mention below. On this view, evangelical theology is an organically developing and cognitive enterprise predicated on Scripture read holistically and theologically yet drawing on secondary sources as well.

THE SO-CALLED SOURCES OF THEOLOGY

In my paragraph above I allude to what are commonly called the "sources" of systematic theology, Scripture, tradition and reason,[22] arguing that each contributes to evangelical theology. However, speaking of "sources of theology" is problematic. We are not thinking of "buckets" from which we draw in varying quantities. It is more helpful to think of "contributing elements" in the theological enterprise.

The Scriptures. For all evangelicals, charismatics and Pentecostals, the Bible is the supreme authoritative guide to what we should believe and do as Christians. Saying this is the easy part. How Scripture actually informs and directs systematic theology is far more complex than we might first think, as I illustrated earlier.

A great deal has been written on the relationship between Scripture and systematic theology by evangelicals in the last thirty years.[23] However,

---

[22]And sometimes "experience" and "culture" are added. See on this Grenz, *Revisioning Evangelical Theology*, pp. 87-108.

[23]Joel B. Green and Max Turner, eds., *Between Two Horizons: Spanning New Testament Studies and Systematic Theology* (Grand Rapids: Eerdmans, 2000); I. Howard Marshall, *Beyond The Bible: Moving from Scripture to Theology* (Grand Rapids: Baker Academic, 2004); C. J. Scalise, *From Scripture to Theology* (Downers Grove, Ill.: InterVarsity Press, 1996); Markus Bockmuehl and Alan J. Torrance, eds., *Scriptures, Doctrine, and Theology's Bible: How the New Testament Shapes Christian Dogmatics* (Grand Rapids: Baker Academic, 2008); Kevin Vanhoozer, *The Drama of Doctrine: A Canonical–Linguistic Approach to Christian Theology* (Louisville: Westminster John Knox, 2005); E. A. Martins, "Moving from Scripture to Doctrine," *Bulletin for Biblical Research* 15, no. 1 (2005): 77-103. See also the fine study by the Catholic scholars Gerald O'Collins and D. Kendall, *The Bible for Theology: Ten Principles for the Theo-*

I have found most helpful the insights in the writings of the Dutch Reformed theologians Herman Bavinck (1854-1921),[24] Abraham Kuyper (1837-1920)[25] and Louis Berkhof (1873-1957).[26] When I studied at Moore Theological College, Sydney, in the 1960s, Louis Berkhof's *Systematic Theology*[27] was the set text for theology classes from second year onward. On reading this book I very soon recognized that Berkhof was expounding the Reformed faith as defined by the Reformation confessions and then seeking to give biblical support for what he believed. Not once in his book did I find him claiming that what he was teaching was dictated solely by Scripture. His way of "doing theology" was *both inductive and deductive.* He presumed that the great doctrines enunciated in the Reformed confessions were the product of centuries of study and reflection on the Scriptures and thus were to be trusted and believed. His task was to expound these doctrines as clearly and concisely as he could, answer objections that had been raised to them and demonstrate that the Bible backed up what he was saying.

Some years later, I read Abraham Kuyper's *Principles of Sacred Theology,* only to find him sharply attacking the idea that evangelical systematic theology is nothing more than a systematizing of what the Bible teaches. He calls such claims "unscientific," "grotesque" and "utterly objectionable."[28] He says,

> There is, to be sure, a theological illusion abroad . . . which conveys the impression that, with the Holy Scriptures in hand, one can independently construct theology. . . . This illusion is a denial of the historic and organic character of theology, and for this reason is inwardly untrue. No theologian following the direction of his own compass would ever have found by himself what he now confesses and defends on the ground of

logical Use of Scripture (Mahwah, N.J.: Paulist, 1997).

[24]Herman Bavinck, *Reformed Dogmatics,* 4 vols, trans. J. Vriend (Grand Rapids: Baker Academic, 2003), first published in Dutch between 1895 and 1899.

[25]Abraham Kuyper, *Principles of Sacred Theology,* trans. J. Hendrik De Vries (Grand Rapids: Baker, 1980), first published in Dutch in 1898.

[26]Louis Berkhof definitely stands in the Dutch theological tradition. He was born in the Netherlands and came to America with his parents as a boy. He taught at Calvin Theological Seminary for almost forty years and was president of the seminary from 1931 to 1944.

[27]Louis Berkhof, *Systematic Theology* (London: Banner of Truth, 1963), first published in 1939.

[28]Kuyper, *Principles,* p. 574.

Holy Scripture. By far the largest part of his results is adopted by him from theological tradition, and even the proofs he cites from scripture, at least as a rule, have not been discovered by himself, but have been suggested to him by his predecessors.[29]

Kuyper is asserting in this strong language that theology does not spring directly from the text of Scripture and that no theologian independently constructs theology. Rather, theology historically develops and thus has an "organic" character. Theologians may claim that they are getting their doctrine directly from Scripture, but in truth the "theological tradition" in which they stand determines to a large degree what they conclude and claim to be entirely "biblical" and what they think is involved in doing evangelical theology.

More positively, Herman Bavinck in the prolegomena to his four-volume *Reformed Dogmatics* says, "The material for constructing dogmatic theology comes from Holy Scripture, church teaching and Christian experience,"[30] and he adds that "cultural factors" should never be overlooked or denied.[31] He argues that Christian theology, or dogma, as he calls it, develops "organically," being built not on isolated texts but from Scripture taken as "a whole."[32] Later, he argues that Scripture is "the foundation (*principium*) rather than the source (*fons*)" of theology. He rejects the term "source" because it suggests that "the relation between Scripture and theology is a mechanical one, as though dogmas could be drawn from Holy Scripture like water from a well." Rather, he says, theology is "the truth of scripture, absorbed and reproduced by the thinking consciousness of the Christian theologian . . . [who] lives in communion of faith with the church of Christ."[33]

What all these Reformed theologians want to stress is that systematic theology organically develops, building on the foundation of Scripture. Solutions to theological questions emerge as certain texts in Scripture are noted, then other texts are drawn in to help fill out the

---

[29]Ibid., pp. 574-75.
[30]Bavinck, *Reformed Dogmatics*, 1:59, cf. 1:25, 1:60, 1:82.
[31]Ibid., 1:60.
[32]Ibid., 1:60 and 1:93-94.
[33]Ibid., 1:89.

answer, and as the theological enterprise continues theologians see more
and more in Scripture that confirms what the church has come to believe.
I thus conclude that the appeal to Scripture in the ongoing theological
enterprise is *always inductive and deductive.* The work begins with
Scripture, but what we come to believe opens our eyes to find other things
in Scripture that reinforce what we already believe.

At this point we should be able to see that asserting that a doctrine is
"biblical" is not a claim that one or more verses in the Bible explicitly
teaches this or that doctrine. It cannot mean this because the Bible seldom
if ever answers complex theological questions univocally and indeed often
does not address the question asked directly. It is rather a claim that after
a long period of debate and careful and prolonged study of the Scriptures
the church has come to agree that one particular answer seems to best
capture all of what is central and fundamental to all that Scripture says or
infers on the question in contention. In this process individual theologians
each make their own contribution to the debate but what we rightly call
doctrine is the answer the Christian community endorses. The wider and
more unanimous this communal endorsement is of the "biblical" answer
to the theological question asked, the greater authority this doctrine has
in the life of the church. One of the most important communal voices of
the church comes from those who have preceded us. To this voice called
"the tradition" we now turn.

The tradition. What is handed down from the past is called "tradition." It is not always clear what Christians are talking about when
they use this term, but from the time of Heiko Oberman's 1963 seminal
book *The Harvest of Medieval Theology,*[34] informed theologians have
recognized that in Western theology we must distinguish between
what he calls "tradition 1," "the exegetical tradition," and "tradition 2,"
teachings authorized by the church that are independent of Scripture.[35]
The sixteenth-century magisterial Reformers highly valued tradition 1,
whereas for them tradition 2 had no authority at all. It should be the

---

[34]Heiko A. Oberman, *The Harvest of Medieval Theology* (Cambridge, Mass.: Harvard University
Press, 1963).
[35]Ibid., pp. 371-75.

same for evangelicals today.[36] Tradition 1, the exegetical tradition, should be highly valued because it reflects how the best of theologians from the past have understood the Scriptures on disputed issues and because it sums up what is prescribed as biblical teaching in creeds and confessions. In other words, tradition 1 represents in the theological enterprise the communal dimension of theology. It is nothing less than the collective wisdom of the past. It is the church in the past speaking to the church in the present. Karl Barth in one of his profound asides says that to denigrate or dismiss the tradition in this sense is to break the fifth commandment, "Honor your father and mother."[37]

Tradition 1, what is commonly called today "the tradition," or in my case, "the theological tradition," is not a second source of revelation alongside the Bible, let alone something standing over the Bible. It is always subordinate to the Bible. The premise is that if we listen carefully to how the great theologians of former days came to understand the Bible on much-debated, complex issues, such as on the Trinity and the eternal generation of the Son, we will learn how best to understand the Bible today in our context. One of the foundational insights provided by the study of hermeneutics in the last thirty years has been that everyone comes to the text of Scripture with beliefs that they have inherited. These beliefs can be informed by all sorts of influences, some good and some bad. The surest and most trusted, and therefore the best, beliefs to bring to our theological reading of Scripture are those informed by the ecumenical creeds and the Reformation and post-Reformation Protestant confessions.

A high estimation of tradition 1 is well illustrated in the First Helvetic Confession of Faith of 1536. Article 2 says that "divine scripture

---

[36]All the books listed in note 7 above have good discussions on the evangelical understanding and misunderstanding of "the tradition." See in addition D. H. Williams, *Retrieving the Tradition and Renewing Evangelicalism: A Primer for Suspicious Protestants* (Grand Rapids: Eerdmans, 1999; Williams, *Evangelicals and Tradition: The Formative Influence of the Early Church* (Grand Rapids: Baker Academic, 2005); Williams, ed., *Tradition, Scripture, and Interpretation: A Sourcebook of the Ancient Church* (Grand Rapids: Baker Academic, 2006); Christopher H. Hall, *Learning Theology with the Church Fathers* (Downers Grove, Ill.: InterVarsity Press, 2002); Vanhoozer, *Drama of Doctrine*, considers this issue at the greatest depth.

[37]Karl Barth, *Church Dogmatics* (Edinburgh: T & T Clark, 1956), p. 585; and Barth, *The Humanity of God*, trans. J. N. Thomas and T. Weiser (London: Collins, 1961), p. 12.

is to be interpreted in no other way than out of itself and is to be explained by the rule of faith and love." Article 2 continues, "Where the Holy Fathers and early teachers, who explained and expounded scripture, have not departed from this rule, we want to recognize and consider them not only as expositors of scripture, but as elect instruments through who God has spoken and operated."[38]

On the Reformer's rejection of nonbiblical "church traditions," tradition 2, and on their valuing of the exegetical tradition, tradition 1, Alister McGrath says, "Although it is often suggested that the Reformers had no place for tradition in their theological deliberations, this judgment is clearly incorrect. While the notion of tradition as an extra-scriptural source of revelation is excluded, the classic concept of tradition as a particular way of reading scripture is retained. . . . The suggestion that the Reformation represents the triumph of individualism and the total rejection of tradition is a deliberate fiction propagated by the image-makers of the Enlightenment."[39] Unfortunately, many conservative evangelicals today also propagate this myth.

None of the magisterial Reformers took the slogan *sola scriptura* ("Scripture alone") to literally mean *solo scriptura* ("Scripture only").[40] Scripture was their primary and ultimate authority, but they were committed to reading it in the light of how the church had understood it across the centuries. On the central doctrines of the faith they argued that what they were teaching was what the best of theologians from the past had taught and how they had understood the Scriptures. There was nothing novel, they insisted, in what they were teaching on the central doctrines of the faith. Only when it was crystal clear that what the medieval church believed and practiced patently contradicted the plain meaning of Scripture did they reject any doctrine or practice.

What we must recognize is that there is no reading of Scripture apart from a communal understanding of it, apart from tradition. The

---

[38]See A. Cochrane, *Reformed Confessions of the Sixteenth century* (London: SCM, 1966), pp. 100-101.

[39]McGrath, *Genesis of Doctrine*, pp. 130-31.

[40]Vanhoozer, *Drama of Doctrine*, p. 156. On this idea see also N. G. Award, "Should We Dispense with *Sola Scriptura*? Scripture, Tradition and Postmodern Theology," *Dialog* 47, no. 1 (2008): 64-79.

question is not, do I accept that my communally held beliefs inform my exegesis or not?—they unquestionably do—but, which communal beliefs will I prioritize? The sixteenth-century Reformers, the late-nineteenth and early twentieth-century Dutch Reformed theologians, and evangelicals today who advocate a return to "the theological exegesis of scripture"[41] in the theological task all hold that the best tradition to inform our interpretation of Scripture is what the best of theologians across the centuries have taught, especially when it is codified in the creeds and confessions of our church. Speaking of the relationship between Scripture and tradition, Kevin Vanhoozer says that twentieth-century hermeneutics has shown that "exegesis without tradition—apart from participation in the history of the text's reception—is impossible."[42] Similarly, the English evangelical theologian A. N. S. Lane writes, "It is impossible to read scripture without tradition, save in the rare example of those with no prior contact with the Christian faith who pick up a portion of scripture. We bring to the Bible a pre-understanding of the Christian faith that we have received from others, thus by tradition."[43]

The special authority of the Nicene and Reformation tradition. The patristic scholar and theologian Lewis Ayres, in his important book, *Nicaea and Its Legacy*,[44] is highly critical of much contemporary work on the Trinity, seeing it as fundamentally at odds with Nicene theology. He believes that too many contemporary theologians have recast the Nicene faith in terms of their own agendas.[45] In reply he argues that Nicene theology should be "an authority within modern Christian thought"; it should be assumed to be "normative."[46] He

---

[41]I will explain what this involves below.

[42]Vanhoozer, *Drama of Doctrine*, p. 113.

[43]A. N. S. Lane, "Tradition," in *Dictionary for the Theological Interpretation of the Bible*, ed. Kevin J. Vanhoozer (Grand Rapids: Baker Academic, 2005), p. 811.

[44]Lewis Ayres, *Nicaea and Its Legacy: An Approach to Fourth-Century Trinitarian Theology* (Oxford: Oxford University Press, 2004). For a similar conclusion from an evangelical perspective see the collection of essays, T. George, ed., *Evangelicals and the Nicene Faith: Reclaiming the Apostolic Witness* (Grand Rapids: Baker, 2011).

[45]Ibid., pp. 384-429.

[46]Ibid., p. 385. Exactly the same argument is put by Khaled Anatolios, *Retrieving Nicaea* (Grand Rapids: Baker, 2011), p. 1 and repeatedly. This book arrived after the manuscript of this book was submitted to the publisher.

admits that his work is predicated on this belief. "Throughout this investigation I understand pro-Nicene theology to be functioning as an authority when its basic principles are treated as foundational for subsequent theological reflection and its theologians as a constant point of departure in the articulation of Trinitarian belief in subsequent periods and cultural contexts."[47]

Ayres's argument that the Nicene tradition, summed up in the Nicene Creed, should function as a norm for evaluating later work on the Trinity and as the "grammar" to a right reading of the Scriptures has much to commend it. However, as an evangelical I also want to listen carefully to the Reformation theological tradition of which I am an heir. In the sixteenth and seventeenth centuries, Protestants were sharply divided over the doctrine of the Trinity in general and the doctrine of the eternal generation of the Son in particular.[48] The conclusion of those debates is now enshrined in the Reformation and post-Reformation confessions. These documents doctrinally mandate what those who confess them should believe and how they should interpret the Bible on disputed doctrinal issues

The theological interpretation of Scripture. Before moving to discuss the contribution of "reason" in the theological enterprise I must say something about the "theological interpretation of Scripture." This is a very important way the tradition contributes to the doing of evangelical theology. The meaning of this phrase, "the theological interpretation of Scripture," needs explanation because it is only in the last few years that this topic has come onto the evangelical agenda and because no broadly agreed definition can be quoted.[49]

---

[47]Ibid., p. 386. So also T. F. Torrance, *The Christian Doctrine of God: One Being Three Persons* (Edinburgh: T & T Clark, 1996), for a very similar argument.

[48]See Richard A. Muller, *Post-Reformation Reformed Dogmatics: The Triunity of God*, vol. 4 (Grand Rapids: Baker Academic, 2003).

[49]For good introductions to this topic see Daniel J. Treier, *Introducing the Theological Interpretation of Scripture: Recovering a Christian Practice* (Grand Rapids: Baker Academic, 2008) and Stephen E. Fowl, *Theological Interpretation of Scripture* (Eugene, Ore.: Cascade, 2009). See also, David C. Steinmetz, "The Superiority of Pre-Critical Exegesis," in *The Theological Interpretation of Scripture*, ed. Stephen E. Fowl (Malden, Mass.: Blackwell, 1997), pp. 26-38, and in the same volume David S. Yeago, "The New Testament and the Nicene Dogma: A Contribution to the Recovery of Theological Exegesis," pp. 87-102; Kevin J. Vanhoozer, "What Is Theological Interpretation of the Bible?" in Vanhoozer, *Dictionary*. The entire issue of *The*

For long centuries Christian theologians and exegetes read the Bible as one unfolding account of God's saving work in the world. For them, the theological message of the Bible, not its historical meaning, was primary. They believed the Old Testament spoke of Christ as much as the New Testament did. On this matter they were perfectly in line with both Christ himself and the New Testament writers, who consistently read Old Testament texts that had a specific historical application to be speaking primarily of him (e.g., Mt 2:15; 1:23; Mk 12:10-11, 35-37; Acts 2:21; Rom 15:12; 1 Cor 10:1-5; Heb 1:5-14). However, from the 1960s evangelicals began giving primacy to a historical and critical approach to the reading of the Scriptures. They rejected a naturalistic, liberal "historical-critical methodology," but they agreed that the Bible should be interpreted using critical methodologies to seek the historical meaning of what was written. All scholarly evangelical commentaries today use this methodology. It is now generally believed that this way of studying Scripture provides the best avenue for discovering both what the author was saying and what his readers understood him to be saying. However, this methodology creates other problems, especially for evangelical systematic theologians. It highlights diversity in Scripture; it sharply divides the Old and New Testaments; it often ignores or denies the prophetic and christological implications of Old Testament texts; it emphasizes the gulf between the historical and cultural world of the biblical writers and that of contemporary readers; and it discounts how Christians have interpreted the Scriptures across the ages. As a consequence, by the 1980s evangelicals began thinking about what might supplement and complement the historical and critical approach to interpreting Scripture, which had created as many problems for them as it had solved. Out of this discussion many evangelicals have come to believe that *in addition* to the historical and critical interpretation of Scripture, a theological interpretation of the Bible is demanded.

Kevin Vanhoozer says, "It is much easier to say what theological interpretation of the Bible is *not* rather than what it is."[50] First, he says, it

---

Southern Baptist Journal of Theology 14, no. 2 (2010) is on this topic. See also, *Evangelicals and the Nicene Faith: Reclaiming the Apostolic Witness*, ed. T. George (Grand Rapids: Baker, 2011).
[50]Vanhoozer, "What Is Theological Interpretation?" p. 19.

"is not an imposition of a theological system or confessional grid onto the biblical text."[51] In other words, it is not a reading of Scripture presupposing evangelical beliefs, or Anglican, Lutheran or Presbyterian doctrinal commitments. Second, it "is not an imposition of a general hermeneutic or theory of interpretation onto the biblical text."[52] It is not a "new hermeneutic." And third, it "is not a form of merely historical, literary, or sociological criticism preoccupied with (respectively) the world 'behind,' 'of,' or 'in front of' the biblical text."[53] What then is it? What we can say is that it is an interpretative way of reading Scripture seeking to reflect in a contemporary form how the Scriptures were read before historical and critical methods became dominant. I found a number of summaries in the literature of the key elements in this approach, many of which used convoluted language. I thus decided to develop my own summary in the light of what others suggest and on the basis of my own reading of the historical writings of the church fathers and the Reformers. I suggest the following assumptions in a theological reading of Scripture.

1. The Bible must be read canonically, on the premise that the overall teaching of Scripture must determine and inform the meaning of individual and isolated texts.

2. The Old Testament is to be read in the light of the New Testament.

3. The historical meaning of a biblical text does not exhaust the meaning of a text.

4. The best guide to a right interpretation of the Scriptures in relation to any historically developed doctrine is the theological tradition, especially given in creeds and confessions.

It is on the basis of such a theological reading of Scripture that I will explore the question in the next chapter: is there biblical warrant for the doctrine of the eternal generation of the Son?

Reason. "Reason" is the most nebulous of the so-called sources of theology because it can mean different things to theologians from dif-

---

[51]Ibid.
[52]Ibid.
[53]Ibid.

fering traditions. Thomas Aquinas held that reason can discover basic theological truths such as the existence of God but that the higher truths such as the doctrine of the Trinity are known only through revelation. The Enlightenment thinkers who gave rise to "liberalism" went even further. They argued that reason can provide all that we need to know about the world, ourselves and God. In direct opposition to such views, evangelical theology insists that what we know of God and his ways can be known only through revelation. In other words, what we know about God is revealed by God, not discovered by human reason.

Nevertheless, evangelicals should accept that reason makes an important contribution to the theological enterprise in many ways. For example, it makes possible the understanding and analysis of what is revealed in the text of Scripture. It is also the facility that makes theology possible in the first place. If evangelical theology is far more than the reiteration of the contents of Scripture, then able minds that can see coherence in the diverse comments in Scripture and draw appropriate inferences are going to be invaluable in the doing of theology. Systematizing in this way is the constructive contribution of reason to theology. The great advocate for the inerrancy of the Bible, B. B. Warfield, speaking of the contribution of reason in the formulating of doctrines said, "The mind brings to every science something which though included in the facts, is not derived from the facts considered in themselves alone, or as isolated data."[54] Modern discussions on the theological enterprise often call this constructive contribution of reason in theology "model-building" or "paradigm-building," drawing on the use of these terms in the philosophy of science to explain what is involved in theory construction. A model or paradigm in this usage is a way of seeing all the data in a unified way that makes sense of the parts.

The generative and creative contribution of theologians who have listened long and hard to the Scriptures and to how they have been understood in the past should be fully appreciated. Athanasius as much as anyone illustrates what one exceptional theologian can give to the progress of theological clarification and understanding. He stands out

---

[54]B. B. Warfield, "The Idea of Systematic Theology," in *The Necessity of Systematic Theology*, ed. J. J. Davis (Grand Rapids: Baker, 1978), p. 131.

head and shoulders over most other theologians because of his numerous innovative and breathtaking theological insights that objectively advanced the theological enterprise.[55] These include the following:

- God could and did take human flesh. He really became man in Jesus of Nazareth. In contrast to the Arians, who believed, following Greek ideas, that God could have no contact with matter let alone human flesh, Athanasius argued that God could become human because we humans are made in the image of God. The creaturely can be assumed into communion with God the Creator through whom the human was made. God can thus have fellowship and communion with his creation.

- What the Bible says of the Son is only rightly understood when we recognize that the whole "scope" of Scripture contains a "double account" of the Son, one as God and one as the *kenotic* (self-emptying) God in the flesh. All texts that speak of Christ in all might, majesty and power speak of him as God as he is; all texts that speak of Christ as subordinate, submissive and obedient to the Father speak of him as the incarnate God. He argued that this interpretative key, or we would say "hermeneutic," is suggested in John 1:1 and John 1:14 and Philippians 2:4-11.

- The one God revealed in Scripture is eternally triune (Mt 28:19). God is not to be understood as a Monad who becomes a Triad.

- Because the Father and the Son are each true God, they must be confessed as "one in being" (*homoousios*).

- The name "Father" implies a son, a "true offspring" of the same nature/being as his father: like begets like. The Bible suggests this divine generative act should be called a "begetting," and given that it is a divine begetting, it must be an *eternal* begetting. What is created by God is temporal; what is divine is eternal.

---

[55]On Athanasius's contribution to the formulation of the doctrine of the Trinity, see more fully my *Jesus and the Father*, pp. 83-84, 97-99, 134-44, 179-85, 216-20. I am not suggesting that Athanasius in all the examples I am about to give was the first to reach this conclusion—although in several cases he was—but rather that he was the first to see the foundational importance of each insight and develop it.

- Divine begetting should not be equated with human generation but rather be understood in terms of "God from God, light from light."

- The divine three are the one God, yet one is Father, one is Son and one is Holy Spirit. This is undeniably and indelibly established by the fact that the Father is "unbegotten," the Son "begotten" and the Spirit "proceeds" from the Father, and he would add, "through the Son."

Athanasius's breathtaking theological conclusions are not predicated on explicit verses of Scripture; nevertheless, once those conclusions had been articulated, other theologians agreed that they captured what Scripture read holistically *implies* better than any other suggestions. In other words, they accurately reflect what the Bible seems to be indicating. This tells us that sanctified and biblically informed reason can objectively progress theological understanding by making affirmations on the basis of what is revealed yet can go beyond what Scripture actually says.

CONCLUSION

Once we fully recognize that evangelical systematic theology involves far more than finding one or more texts that says explicitly what we are to believe on any specific matter some two thousand years after the Bible was completed, we see that judging whether or not a doctrine is "biblical" or "warranted by Scripture" is more complicated than we might at first think. Yes, making such a judgment on any doctrine will demand the critical examination of the Scriptures, seeking the historical meaning of relevant texts, but this approach *on its own* is insufficient to reach a verdict. We need, in addition to a historical and critical reading of Scripture, both a theological reading of Scripture that is informed by the theological tradition and an understanding of theology which recognizes that systematic theology develops organically and conceptually as it inductively and deductively draws on and is directed by Scripture.

When we turn to consider in the next chapter what in Scripture "warrants" the specific doctrine of the eternal generation of the Son, we will see that while no text in the Bible explicitly speaks of this, much in Scripture nevertheless suggests the idea. This explains why the church fathers came to formulate this doctrine and vigorously defended it. They thought it was a "biblical" doctrine even if they had no text that specifically spoke of the eternal begetting or generation of the Son.

In my discussion of tradition earlier in this chapter, I did not mention one of the very important contributions that the theological tradition (tradition 1) makes to systematic theology. The study of the Scriptures does not explain why a doctrine emerged, how it was developed or what problem or question it sought to resolve. The history of the doctrine provides this information. For this reason most books on doctrine or systematic theology include sections on the historical development of each doctrine, and in addition there are many books on the history of the great doctrines.[56] Those who write on the historical development of doctrines are convinced that the information they supply helps Christians deepen their understanding and comprehension of each doctrine they discuss. Given that it is important and helpful to know why a doctrine emerged, how it developed and what problem or question it sought to resolve, we see why we should explore the specific historical development of the doctrine of the eternal generation of the Son. It will help us understand why the church fathers, the Reformers and post-Reformation theologians spent so much time thinking and writing about this doctrine and why it was so important to them. From this we may see why it is still a very important doctrine to uphold today. Robert Letham is of much the same opinion on what I have said in this paragraph. He says, "To think clearly about the Trinity, we must grapple with the history of discussion in the church."[57]

In the chapter immediately following we consider what in Scripture warrants the doctrine of the eternal generation of the Son. Then in the rest of the book we study how this doctrine emerged and was developed by the best of theologians across the centuries, constantly seeking to

---

[56]For example, Louis Berkhof, *A History of Christian Doctrines* (London: Banner of Truth, 1937); Bernhard Lohse, *A Short History of Christian Doctrine* (Philadelphia: Fortress, 1966); J. N. D. Kelly, *Early Christian Doctrines* (London: Adam & Charles Black, 1968). Virtually all substantial works on systematic theology have sections on the development of each doctrine discussed.

[57]Letham, *Holy Trinity*, p. 2.

understand at greater depth through this historical work what truth this doctrine conveys about God, and then finally we will explore how contemporary mainline and (some) evangelical theologians deal with this doctrine. In pursuing this agenda I am seeking to illustrate how in fact theology is done and confirmed as doctrine by the church and how doctrine answers the deepest questions that human beings can ask about God.

3

No Biblical Warrant?

◆ ◆ ◆

In this chapter I respond specifically to the most common and most telling argument evangelicals have made against the doctrine of the eternal generation of the Son, namely that this doctrine has no biblical warrant. In the previous chapter we explored what is involved in "doing" evangelical systematic theology. We concluded that while Scripture has ultimate authority for evangelicals, doctrines represent human attempts to answer profound theological questions that arise in the ongoing historical life of the church. These doctrines emerge and are developed through the careful study of and listening to the whole of Scripture, the critical consideration of what others in the past have concluded on this or that question, and by thinking hard and long about the issues that specific questions raise.

If this is how theological work is done, and how doctrines emerge in the ongoing life of the church, then to ask, does this or that doctrine have "biblical warrant"? is not to ask, is there at least one text that explicitly teaches this doctrine? It is rather to ask, what has the Christian community come to agree is the overall teaching of Scripture on this particular question and is this justifiable in the light of what we now believe Scripture is saying? Thus we are asking in this chapter, has the church been right in warranting the doctrine of the eternal generation of the Son by claiming that this doctrine is taught in Scripture? As we have already noted, some evangelical theologians today believe the church was wrong to draw this conclusion. In what immediately follows, I will outline their case. I will then seek to restate the case in support of this doctrine by drawing on both the historic communal reading of Scripture summed up in creeds and confessions and a contemporary critical and historical reading of Scripture, listening carefully and critically to both.

NO BIBLICAL WARRANT?

The widespread evangelical opinion that the doctrine of the eternal generation of the Son has no biblical warrant finds its contemporary[1] origin and basis in a 1953 journal article, "The Translation of John 3:16 in the Revised Standard Version," by the evangelical Dale Moody, longtime professor of theology at Southern Baptist Seminary.[2] Virtually every evangelical who questions this doctrine appeals to this article. Moody's case is as follows. (1) The translators of the 1952 Revised Standard Version of the Bible were right in translating *monogenēs* in the Johannine literature as "only Son" rather than "only begotten Son" (see Jn 1:14, 18; 3:16, 18; 1 Jn 4:9).[3] Their motive was entirely linguistic, not an attempt "to water down a Bible doctrine." Indeed, he says, this translation of *monogenēs* is to be commended because it "gives greater emphasis to the uniqueness and deity of Jesus Christ."[4] (2) The RSV translators render the Greek word this way because linguistic study in the twentieth century has shown that the word *monogenēs* is related not to *gennaō* ("beget") but to *genos* ("class or kind"). It thus means "one of a kind," "special" or "unique." (3) In our earliest Latin translation of John's Gospel, *monogenēs* in John 1:14, 18; 3:16, 18 is translated *unicus* ("only"), not *unigenitus* ("only begotten"). The translation *unigenitus* first appeared in the late fourth century and was adopted by Jerome. His use of this Latin word to translate *monogenēs* led the translators of the Authorized Version of 1611 to render this Greek word into English as "only begotten." (4) He also

---

[1]Arius and the later Arians would not allow that the Bible spoke of the eternal generation of the Son, as have many others across the centuries. The point I am making is that in contemporary evangelical literature the appeal is almost always to Moody's article. Probably the influence of the Old Princeton theologians who all questioned this doctrine should also be noted but it seldom is. See the comment on this in chapter 1.

[2]Dale Moody, "The Translation of John 3:16 in the Revised Standard Version," *Journal of Biblical Literature* 72 (1952): 213-19.

[3]In ibid., p. 218, Moody points out that in John 1:18 the best manuscripts speak of the Son as "only begotten God."

[4]Ibid., p. 213.

notes that in one of two creeds Epiphanius gives at the end of his work *Anacoratus,* of A.D. 374, *monogenēs* qualifies *gennaō*.[5] The point he is seeking to make in mentioning this wording is difficult to see. *Monogenēs* may qualify *gennēthenta* ("begotten") but the two words are not given as synonyms.[6] What the creed seems to be implying is that the Son is unique because he alone is eternally begotten of the Father. (5) Finally, in relation to the Greek term *gennaō,* Moody notes first that it "is used in the Johannine writings to designate the relationship between [God] the Father and all his children," and second that the New Testament "never uses *gennaō* to designate the relationship between the [divine] Father and the Son."[7] To complete his case, he points out that Psalm 2:7, which speaks of God's Son as "begotten" (*gennaō*), alludes to a "coronation idea not a conception idea," and when this text is quoted in Acts 13:33 and Hebrews 1:5; 5:5 it alludes to the Son's resurrection or his exaltation.

WHAT MOODY SAYS AND WHAT HE DOES NOT SAY

Moody begins his article by stating clearly that he believes in the "preexistent deity of Christ" and the virgin birth and that his only motive for writing is to "simply correct an error" in translation of a Greek word.[8] He never questions *the doctrine of the eternal generation* of the Son, and he does not conclude that theologians have erred in speaking of the "eternal begetting of the Son." The primary intent of his article is to argue that *monogenēs* does not mean "only begotten" but rather "one of a kind," "unique" or "only." He does not argue, as Grudem does, that the Greek-speaking Nicene fathers "had a misunderstanding of" the word *monogenēs,* and mistakenly gave it the meaning "only begotten."[9]

---

[5]Moody does not seem to realize that Epiphanius in this second creed is giving his received wording of the 325 Nicene Creed. If he does, he says nothing on this.

[6]The word order in this sentence is difficult, and so there is some debate how best to translate the Greek. I discuss the options later in this book considering what the fourth-century creeds say.

[7]Ibid., p. 219.

[8]Ibid., p. 213.

[9]Wayne Grudem, "Appendix 6," in *Systematic Theology: An Introduction to Biblical Doctrine,* rev. ed. (Grand Rapids: Zondervan, 2000), pp. 1233-34. Similarly, R. L. Reymond, *A New Systematic Theology of the Christian Faith* (Nashville: Thomas Nelson, 1998), p. 325, says, "The Nicene and post-Nicene" fathers thought *monogenēs* indicated that "the father begat the Son."

Moody's arguments definitely do not invalidate the doctrine of the eternal generation of the Son. His essay tells us that this doctrine is not supported by appeal to the word *monogenēs*, and no text in the Old or New Testaments explicitly speaks of the "eternal" begetting or generation of the Son. From the perspective of a historical and critical reading of the Scriptures, his conclusions, I believe, cannot be disputed. They have gained wide scholarly support and should be accepted as conclusive.[10] Nevertheless, many well-informed scholars have made the point in reply that to translate *monogenēs* as "only begotten" is theologically justifiable.[11] An only son is begotten like all offspring; for John the Evangelist the Son of God is *monogenēs* ("unique") because he is "from the bosom of the Father" (*eis ton kolpon*) (Jn 1:18), a comment that indicates he existed before he became incarnate, and as we will see, for the Nicene fathers he is *monogenēs* ("unique") because he alone is eternally begotten. To say this is not to deny that the primary meaning of the word *monogenēs* is "one of a kind" or "unique," or to suggest that John's use of the word *monogenēs* gives support for the doctrine of the eternal begetting of the Son. It is simply to make the point that in profoundly theological contexts the word *monogenēs* may imply that what is unique about the Son is his pre-existence as God yet other than God the Father (Jn 1:1), something explained in terms of his eternal begetting or generation.

THE ARIAN BIBLICAL ARGUMENT AGAINST
THE ETERNAL GENERATION OF THE SON

At this point I briefly digress to observe that in the fourth century "the Arians"[12] had a quite different "biblical" basis for rejecting the

---

[10]F. W. Danker, *A Greek-English Lexicon of the New Testament and Other Early Christian Literature*, 3rd ed. (Chicago: University of Chicago Press, 1979), p. 658. See also Craig S. Keener, *The Gospel of John: A Commentary* (Peabody, Mass.: Hendrickson, 2003), pp. 412-15. See most recently, M. Peppard, "Adopted and Begotten Sons of God: Paul and John on Divine Sonship," *Catholic Biblical Quarterly* 73, no. 1 (2011): 92-110.

[11]See, J. M. Buhlman, "The Only Begotten Son," *Calvin Theological Journal* 16, no. 1 (1981): 56-79, and Robert Letham, *The Holy Trinity in Scripture, History, Theology, and Worship* (Phillipsburg, N.J.: Presbyterian and Reformed, 2004), pp. 383-89. Both refer to other scholars who make the same point. Letham points out that all the uses of *monogenēs* in the Johannine literature are in contexts discussing birth.

[12]This is the name the Nicene fathers gave to all those who could not confess that the Son was "one in being" with the Father. On this fundamental matter the so-called fourth-century

doctrine of the eternal begetting or generation of the Son than that of evangelicals today. The meaning of the word *monogenēs*, as we will show, was not an issue. They rejected this doctrine because they were convinced that one text explicitly spoke of the Son, identified as divine Wisdom, as created in time, and if he was created in time, they concluded, he must be God in second degree. The text they quoted ad infinitum was Proverbs 8:22, "The lord created [*ktizō*] me at the beginning of his works."[13] Given their high view of Scripture the Greek-speaking Nicene fathers gave this text much attention. As we will see, Athanasius gave more space to exploring the force of Proverbs 8:22 than any other Scripture the Arians quoted. It was a particularly difficult text for the Greek-speaking Nicene fathers because, like the apostolic writers, the Septuagint was authoritative Scripture for them. In reply, Athanasius and the Cappadocians argued that one text should not be interpreted to counter what "the whole scope" of Scripture indicated, namely that the Son is eternally true God, not a creature brought into existence in time; thus another interpretation was demanded. Their solution was that Proverbs 8:22 spoke not of the *eternal begetting* of the Son in "the form of God" but of his begetting in time in "the form of man" in his incarnation.[14] Proverbs 8:25, however, they agreed did speak of his eternal generation.

Contemporary supporters of the doctrine of the eternal generation, in contrast, find no problem with Proverbs 8:22, and evangelicals opposed to this doctrine do not quote it in making their case. They do not because for all evangelicals today the Hebrew text is authoritative Scripture. In the Hebrew, the word in contention is *qānānî*, which is

---

Arians were of one mind, but on many other matters they differed. The identity of and differences between those the Nicene Fathers called Arians is today much discussed by historical theologians. See for example, D. M. Gwynn, *The Eusebians: The Polemic of Athanasius of Alexandria and the Construction of the "Arian Controversy,"* (Oxford: Oxford University Press, 2007).

[13]This assertion will be fully documented in the next chapter. On this text and its usage in Arian exegesis see Gordon D. Fee, *Pauline Christology: An Exegetical-Theological Study* (Peabody, Mass.: Hendrickson, 2007), pp. 595-97, 597 n. 4.

[14]We will study in some detail both Athanasius's and the Cappadocians' treatment of this text in what follows.

best translated as "brought me forth."[15] It does not mean "create." Bruce Waltke says on this word, "The metaphor 'brought me forth' signifies that Solomon's inspired wisdom comes from God's essential being; it is a revelation that has an organic connection with God's very nature and being, unlike the rest of creation that comes into existence outside of him and independent from his being."[16]

THE BIBLE READ CRITICALLY, HISTORICALLY AND THEOLOGICALLY

Moody's conclusions can be accepted, but they leave the question unanswered: Does proving that *monogenēs* etymologically explained and lexically defined does not mean "only begotten" and that Psalm 2:7, Acts 13:33, Hebrews 1:5 and Hebrews 5:5, interpreted critically and historically, do not speak of the eternal begetting of the Son prove that the *doctrine of the eternal generation of the Son* is without biblical basis? I for one think not. I think not because I am writing in defense of *the doctrine* of the eternal generation of the Son, which I take to be a human attempt to understand the eternal and immutable self-differentiation that constitutes the first person of the Trinity, "the Father," and the second, "the Son," by appeal to what the Bible as a whole says and infers. Whether there is one or more verses that speak of the eternal begetting of the Son and what the Greek word *monogenēs* may mean when used in reference to the Son are important questions, but *the doctrine* of the eternal generation of the Son does not stand or fall on the answer to these two questions. Specific biblical words or one or two texts seldom if ever are the basis for any doctrine.

Before I give in full what I believe in Scripture warrants the *doctrine* of the eternal generation of the Son, I give a brief summary of my case to help my readers know where I am going on this fundamental issue.

• The Bible reveals God as eternally triune. The one God is the Father, the Son and the Holy Spirit. Scripture thus raises for us the question, how is God eternally triune? He is eternally self-differentiated; this

---

[15]See Bruce Vawter, "Prov. 8:22: Wisdom and Creation," *Journal of Biblical Literature* 9 (1980): 205-16.

[16]Bruce Waltke, *The Book of Proverbs*, vol. 1 (Grand Rapids: Eerdmans, 2004), p. 409.

is not in dispute. What is in dispute is the best way to explain this in terms of what is revealed.

- The doctrine of the eternal generation of the Son arises and is predicated *primarily* on the biblical revelation that the "first" and "second" persons of the Trinity are eternally and indelibly identified and related as "the Father" and "the Son." A father-son relationship presupposes begetting. Fathers beget children.

- The primary meaning of the Greek word *monogenēs,* "unique" or "only," is significant because it highlights the uniqueness of Christ. He is the *only* Son of the Father. The Greek-speaking fathers, as we will show, understood the word in this way. They did not appeal to it to support the doctrine of the eternal generation of the Son. When they quote the Johannine texts that use this word, they do so to make the point that Jesus Christ is the *monogenēs*/unique Son because he alone is eternally begotten, not made. All else in the world is created in time; the Son is "eternally begotten, not created," along with the Holy Spirit, who eternally proceeds.

- Designating the eternal Father-Son act of self-differentiation "the begetting of the Son" is justified because Psalm 2:7 and Proverbs 8:25, which both use the term "beget" (*gennaō*) are interpreted christologically in the New Testament. Calling this an *eternal* begetting is justified because these texts ultimately refer to Christ, who is God. What is created is temporal; what is divine is eternal.

- Besides Psalm 2:7 and Proverbs 8:25, many other texts in Scripture imply an eternal act of divine self-differentiation. This biblical teaching may be taken to confirm the conclusion that the Son is begotten and as such "true God from true God."

Before expanding on what in Scripture warrants *the doctrine* of the eternal generation of the Son, I must reiterate a point I made in the last chapter. In the theological enterprise, the historical and critical interpretation of Scripture and the theological interpretation of Scripture are complementary. The former is the best way to discover the historical meaning of individual biblical texts, and the latter is the best way to discover how the great theologians from the past, asking specific theological questions, came to understand individual texts in the light of the whole Bible. I definitely do not consider these two ways of understanding the Bible to be mutually exclusive.[17] Both are needed in the doing of evangelical theology. In exploring whether Scripture warrants *the doctrine* of the eternal generation, I will draw on both. I will outline how the church fathers came to believe that the Bible taught the eternal generation of the Son and on what basis, and I will evaluate their appeal to Scripture in the light of contemporary historical and critical exegetical conclusions.

In deciding to utilize both ways of reading Scripture, I was interested to find Andreas Köstenberger, a Southern Baptist, and Scott Swain, a conservative Presbyterian, taking much the same approach in their exposition of John's Gospel in their book *Father, Son and Spirit: The Trinity and John's Gospel.*[18] They say their aim is to read John's Gospel historically, critically and as a narrative yet also "within the salvation-historical context of the canon" and "with the *church* because Jesus promised to lead the body of lectors into all truth (16:13)."[19] In other words, they are saying, we will interpret John's Gospel historically and critically *and* also in the light of the whole Bible and the theological tradition. They say specifically in relation to the doctrine of the Trinity,

> In keeping with an increasing body of literature we believe there is a strong and natural link between the canonical books of the Old and New Testaments and later trinitarian formulations and terminology (e.g., the Nicene Creed, *trinitas, hypostasis, homoousios,* etc.). Simply put, John's portrayal of the Father, Son and Spirit (along with the rest of the Bible) put "pressure" on fourth-century discussions about the nature of

---

[17]As I have made clear in the previous chapter, where I discuss the difference between historical and critical exegesis and the theological interpretation of Scripture.

[18]Andreas Köstenberger and Scott Swain, *Father, Son and Spirit: The Trinity in John's Gospel* (Downers Grove, Ill. InterVarsity Press, 2008).

[19]Ibid., p. 23. Unfortunately, when they come to discuss the Johannine theme that the Son is "sent" by the Father they break with the Nicene tradition, arguing that this language speaks of the Son's eternal subordination and obedience to the Father (pp. 71-72, 88-90, 120-21). In Augustine, as I will show later, the language of sending speaks of the eternal Father-Son distinction while at the same time upholding the full coequality in being and authority of the Son. At this point these authors follow the Knight-Grudem-Ware "tradition," not that of the church fathers, especially Augustine.

God in such a way that later formulations and terminology should be viewed less as evolutionary developments beyond the NT data and more as attempts "to describe" and analyze the way in which Jesus Christ and the Spirit were "intrinsic to" Scripture's way of speaking about God. In other words, the creeds represent the "descriptive grammar" of the Bible's own intrinsically trinitarian discourse.[20]

Like Köstenberger and Swain I too "believe there is a strong and natural link between the canonical books of the Old and New Testaments and later trinitarian formulations and terminology." Or to say much the same in my own words, I am persuaded that what the Christian community has concluded is the teaching of the Scriptures on the major doctrines of the faith, and has codified in creeds and confessions, reflects accurately what the Bible teaches when read holistically. Thus in what immediately follows I will not come to Scripture as if I were reading it for the first time, seeking to find out what it says on the eternal generation of the Son. Rather, I will come to Scripture having first studied carefully how and why the great theologians of the past concluded that the Bible speaks clearly of the eternal generation of the Son, and then I will consider whether or not their conclusions can stand in the light of a historical and critical interpretation of Scripture.

THE CASE IN DEFENSE OF THE DOCTRINE OF THE ETERNAL GENERATION OF THE SON

The doctrine of the eternal generation of the Son, like all doctrines, seeks to answer a profound *theo-logical* question. If the one God is triune, as Scripture indicates, how can this be so? Or to put it another way, how is the one God eternally self-differentiated as Father, Son and Holy Spirit? This question arose in the century immediately following the apostolic age. I reiterate the story I told in the first chapter because it helps us understand and appreciate the complexities and challenges of appealing to the Bible to answer profound doctrinal questions that it does not explicitly answer, as is often the case.

• First, the so-called monarchical modalists argued that God is one, a

---

[20]Ibid., pp. 21-22.

monad, who simply appears in three successive modes. This preserved divine unity, but it was rejected because it denied the eternal personal distinctions of Father, Son and Spirit.

- Justin Martyr, Irenaeus and Tertullian agreed that God is one, but they argued he has eternally within himself his Word (*Logos*) and his Spirit, whom he brings forth in time for the works of creation and redemption. This explanation of divine self-differentiation was rejected because the Son and the Spirit were depicted as "second" and "third" God, not the one God for all eternity, and because identifying the Son almost solely as the *Logos* was not reflective of what the whole of Scripture said of him.[21]

- Arius then developed another explanation. God is a monad who *creates in time* a Son and the Spirit, who are above all other creatures but less in being and power than the Father. This answer was rejected because particularly the Son according to Arius is not God in the same sense as the Father. The Son is a creature and thus subordinated God.

- Finally, building on the insights of Origen and his mentor Bishop Alexander, and in opposition to the Arians, Athanasius argued that God is eternally triune. He does not simply reveal himself as triune or become triune for the work of creation and redemption; he is a triad for all eternity. In history and in Scripture the one God is revealed as three "persons," and God's own revelation of himself is to be trusted and believed.

The idea that God is eternally triune has been so compelling for Christians that from the time of Athanasius it has been the foundational premise of trinitarian orthodoxy. By the time Augustine published *The Trinity* (*De Trinitate*), early in the fifth century, the triune nature of God was a catholic axiom. In his wonderful summary of the doctrine of the Trinity in book one he says that he is writing on "the

---

[21]I make the point again that the orthodox doctrine of the Trinity developed historically. This means early answers often gave way to better answers that came later. It is anachronistic to judge second-century theologians on the basis of later theological formulations that in all or most cases emerged out of debates they never envisaged.

Trinity which God is."[22] Believing that the one God is eternally triune makes more sense of what the New Testament says than any other suggestion; it corresponds with what is revealed in the economy, and it avoids completely the very difficult postulate that God changes from a solitary monad to a triad in history. Athanasius found the idea that God changes in time, as the Arians argued, abhorrent. He wrote, "If the Word is not with the Father from everlasting, the Triad is not everlasting; but a Monad was first, and then afterwards by addition it became a Triad. . . . What sort of religion then is this, which is not even like itself, but is a process of completion as time goes on, and now not thus, and then again thus?"[23]

What Athanasius saw with great clarity and logic is that if the Son (and the Spirit) are not eternal, then God is a God who changes. He would first be a monad who later became a triad; the Son and the Spirit would then simply be afterthoughts, we might say.

In arguing for the eternity and full divinity of both the Father and the Son, Athanasius not only appealed directly to the Scriptures that spoke of the preexistence of Christ but also to two other arguments. First, the names "the Father" and "the Son" are correlatives. There can be no Father without Son and vice versa. Therefore, first, if the Father is eternal, so too is the Son. And second, if the Son is true God, one in being with the Father, as Athanasius was certain the Scriptures indicated, then the Son, like the Father, is eternal. For him what God creates is temporal; what is truly God is eternal.

The Bible nowhere explicitly says, "The one God is eternally triune," but I suspect most of my readers, including those well-grounded in contemporary scholarly methods of studying the Bible, would believe this to be what the Scriptures teach for the following reasons and possibly others.

The one God is revealed as triune in Scripture (Mt 28:19; 1 Cor 12:4-6; 2 Cor 13:13) and as unchangeable in his eternal existence (Ex 3:14; Ps 102:26-28; Is 41:4; Rom 1:23; Heb 1:11-12; Jas 1:7). If we agree

---

[22]Augustine, *The Trinity* 1.2.7 (trans. Edmund Hill [New York: New City Press, 1991], p. 69). Subsequent references to Augustine are from this translation.

[23]Athanasius, *Discourses Against the Arians* 1.6.17 (*The Nicene and Post-Nicene Fathers*, ed. Philip Schaff and Henry Wace, vol. 4, series 2 [New York: The Christian Literature Company, 1982], p. 316). Subsequent references to Athanasius are from this translation.

that what God reveals of himself is to be trusted, then it seems conclusive that God is not only triune but also eternally triune. The eternal triunity of God is also indicated by the fact that in the New Testament the Son and the Spirit exist outside of human space and time before they appear in the economy. Speaking of the Son as coming into the world (Mk 10:45; Lk 12:49; Jn 6:38) and as sent by the Father (Jn 3:17; 8:42; 17:3; Gal 4:4) presupposes that the Son existed before his incarnation, and speaking of him as the co-creator presupposes that he existed before the world was made (Jn 1:3; Col 1:16; Heb 1:2).[24] The Spirit likewise is depicted as existing prior to the incarnation and Pentecost. In the Old Testament God's Spirit is active in creation (Gen 1:2; Ps 33:6; 147:18) and in empowering leaders in Israel. To this we may add the conclusion that if the Son and the Spirit are truly God then they are both not only pre-existent but also eternal. What is created is temporal; what is divine is eternal. John indicates that it is an appropriate deduction to make of the Son when he says, "In the beginning was the Word, and the Word was with God, and the Word was God" (Jn 1:1).

On the basis of this biblical teaching we may safely conclude that God's eternal threefoldness, made manifest in the incarnation and in the bestowal of the Spirit (the historical "missions" of the Son and the Spirit), does not constitute God's triunity but rather make it manifest. So we can rightly say that the immanent triunity of God is revealed in the economy, and the economy reflects what is true in eternity.[25]

If, then, we are to believe that the one God is eternally triune, we must presuppose eternal self-differentiation. The one God for all eternity is Father, Son and Spirit, and cannot be otherwise. Thus in seeking to answer the question, is the doctrine of the eternal generation

---

[24]On the preexistence of the Son see D. McCready, *He Came Down From Heaven: The Preexistence of Christ and the Christian Faith* (Downers Grove, Ill.: InterVarsity Press, 2005); Larry W. Hurtado, *Lord Jesus Christ: Devotion to Jesus in Earliest Christianity* (Grand Rapids: Eerdmans, 2003), pp. 118-26; S. Gathercole, *The Preexistent Son: Recovering the Christologies of Matthew, Mark, and Luke* (Grand Rapids: Eerdmans, 2006), Fee, *Pauline Christology*, pp. 500-512. K.-J. Kuschel's, *Born Before All Time* (London: SCM, 1992), is a very different kind of book. It is a scholarly reflection on what it means to believe in the preexistence of Christ today, written by a liberal Roman Catholic scholar.

[25]This should not be read as an unqualified endorsement of Rahner's so-called rule: "The economic Trinity is the immanent Trinity and vice versa." On this see my *Jesus and the Father*, pp. 242-74. My wording gives what I think is true in Rahner's Rule.

of the Son warranted by Scripture? the first thing to be said in support is that in revealing the one God as eternally three persons, the Bible assumes eternal divine threefold self-differentiation. The question of whether or not divine eternal self-differentiation should be called *the eternal begetting of the Son* and *the eternal procession of the Spirit* is a second and subsequent question. In other words, I am arguing that belief in threefold eternal divine self-differentiation is not only "warranted" by Scripture but also prescribed by Scripture. What is in dispute is the validity of understanding and designating the eternal self-differentiation of the Father and the Son as *the eternal begetting or generation of the Son*. I now address this question.

Again I begin with Athanasius, one of the greatest theologians to have ever lived.[26] We noted above that he argues that the revealed names Father and Son are correlative. God the Father could not be a father unless he had a son, and God the Son could not be a son unless he had a father. Then he takes three further steps. First, he argues that to call God "the Father" implies a son. He says, "He who calls God Father, thereby conceives and contemplates the Son."[27] Then, second, he reasons that to be a son implies "begetting." Fathers beget children. This inference he takes to be correct because the Bible speaks of God "begetting" an elect son (Ps 2:7) and of "begetting" divine Wisdom (Prov 8:25), texts he interprets christologically. Third, he concludes that to speak of God the Father as unbegotten God and the Son as begotten God indelibly and eternally differentiates the Father and the Son, allowing for no confusion or coalescing of the persons. Speaking of the Son as "eternally begotten," he finds, is particularly helpful in refuting the Arian argument that all sons are other than and subordinate to their father. In reply, he points out that in fact fathers *beget* children of one and the same *nature* or *being*. The doctrine of the eternal generation of the Son, therefore, safeguards both divine unity of being/nature and eternal self-differentiation.

Thus for Athanasius the doctrine of the eternal generation of the Son

---

[26]This and other comments on Athanasius's teaching will be more fully explained and documented in my summary of his views in the following chapter.

[27]Athanasius, *Discourses Against the Arians* 1.5.16 (p. 316).

is first of all a theological inference, or deduction, based on the biblical revelation that the one God is Father and Son (and Spirit). He concludes that the Bible, in differentiating the first two persons of the Trinity by the names Father and Son, implies that the best word available to us human beings to understand and speak of their self-differentiation is the word *begotten*. The use of this term is appropriate and compelling, he argues, because it is found in the Bible in christological texts that speak of the begetting of God's Son and of divine Wisdom.

Augustine follows in Athanasius's steps. He too concludes that the Bible, in designating the one God as Father, Son and Holy Spirit, takes us right to the heart of the doctrine of the Trinity. From this it follows, first, that the names "Father" and "Son" in particular disclose that the divine persons are of one divine substance yet are not to be identified. What indelibly distinguishes them, notwithstanding their oneness in substance, is that "The Father has begotten the Son, and therefore he who is Father is not the Son; and the Son is begotten by the Father, and therefore he who is the Son is not the Father; and the Holy Spirit . . ."[28] Second, in naming the first two persons of the Trinity "Father" and "Son," the Bible infers an eternal begetting. To be a son means to be begotten. Fathers beget children. He writes, "When we say begotten we mean the same as when we say "son." Being son is a consequence of being begotten, and being begotten is implied by being son."[29]

In a moment we will see that Augustine, like Athanasius, appeals to a number of texts to confirm this deduction, but here we note that again like Athanasius, his primary reason for holding to the doctrine of the eternal generation of the Son is that the names "father" and "son" imply begetting. And in the case of "the Son" the begetting is eternal because like the Father, he is God without any caveats; God exists outside of time.

Modern critical study of the Bible confirms that Athanasius and Augustine were right in recognizing the primacy and importance of the names Father and Son. Every one of Paul's epistles begins with a greeting or opening blessing in which God is designated as "our Father"

---

[28]Athanasius, *Discourses Against the Arians* 1.5.16 (p. 316).
[29]Augustine, *The Trinity* 5.1.8 (p. 193).

or "the Father" or "the Father of our Lord Jesus Christ." The last of these, "the Father of our Lord Jesus Christ," is particularly common (e.g., Rom 1:7; 1 Cor 1:3; 2 Cor 1:2; Gal 1:3). It is a phrase that identifies both parties and relates them intimately together as a father and a son. For Paul the name Father is not simply an equivalent for the term God (Greek, *theos*); it names one divine person, the Father, in distinction to the Son. Father-Son language is pervasive in John's Gospel, where Jesus is depicted as the unique Son (Greek, *monogenēs*) of the Father.

Identifying Jesus Christ as the eternal Son of the eternal Father does not necessitate the language of birth or generation, but it certainly makes it appropriate and turns our mind to this possibility. Athanasius, the Cappadocian fathers, Augustine and Aquinas, as I will show, all saw this clearly. For them the divinely revealed names of Father and Son imply an eternal begetting. They reason that if the Son is the eternal Son of the Father, then to say he is the eternal Son is virtually the same as saying he is eternally begotten of the Father. Unfortunately, most Reformation and post-Reformation discussions of this doctrine did not adopt or note this reasoning in seeking biblical justification for the doctrine of the eternal generation of the Son. Most followed a proof-text approach in seeking biblical support for the doctrine of the eternal generation of the Son. However, we find that those who have thought the deepest about the doctrine of the eternal generation of the Son clearly recognize that this doctrine is rooted primarily in the revealed and correlated names "Father" and "Son." Athanasius, the Cappadocian fathers, Augustine and Aquinas all came to this conclusion and, after them, John Gill (1697-1771),[30] Samuel Miller (1769-1850),[31] Louis Berkhof (1873-1957)[32] and in our day Donald Macleod, who concludes that "the idea of the eternal generation of the Son is an inevitable corollary of the eternal sonship [of the Son]."[33] Samuel Miller deserves quoting as well. In putting forward his case for the eternal generation of the Son he says, "My *first argument* in favour is the eternal

---

[30]John Gill, *Body of Divinity* (Grand Rapids: Sovereign Grace, 1971), p. 147.

[31]Samuel Miller, *Letters on the Eternal Sonship of Christ; Addressed to the Rev. Professor Stuart, of Andover* (Philadelphia: W. W. Woodward, 1823), p. 47.

[32]Louis Berkhof, *Systematic Theology* (London: Banner of Truth, 1958), p. 95.

[33]Donald Macleod, *The Person of Christ* (Leicester, U.K.: Inter-Varsity Press, 1998), p. 131.

Sonship of Christ is drawn from the correlate names, *Father* and *Son*,"[34] and he adds, "The terms b*egotten* and *generation*, are intended by the Spirit of God to refer to the same *relation* which the names Father and Son express."[35]

These theologians are to be commended for primarily basing the doctrine of the eternal generation of the Son on the fact that the Bible names the first two persons of the Trinity the Father and the Son, placing them in an eternal relationship. Nevertheless, some term is needed to speak of this eternal "relation" between the Father and the Son, or in my terminology of "the eternal self-differentiation" that constitutes them as the Father and the Son. First Justin Martyr in the second century, and then Origen and the Nicene fathers agreed that no better word can be found than the one the Bible suggests, "begotten" (*gennaō*) (in the Septuagint, Ps 2:7; 110:3 [109:3 LXX]; Prov 8:25; Is 53:8).

Here we might recall that Augustine faces the same challenge when designating the divine three as "persons." He clearly sees the limitations of this human word when applied to the Father, Son and Holy Spirit, who are not three separated individuals. However, he concludes, if we are not to be "reduced to silence," a word must be chosen. The word "person," he concluded, is the best available.[36] In reference to the eternal generation of the Son, the term "begetting" is not simply the best word available, it is suggested by Scripture.

THE TEXTS QUOTED IN SUPPORT OF THE DOCTRINE OF THE ETERNAL GENERATION OF THE SON

I have just made the case that belief in the eternal triunity of God implies an eternal act of self-differentiation, and the correlated revealed divine names Father and Son imply a generative act in eternity that the Bible suggests is best termed an "eternal begetting." Now I consider the scriptural texts to which theologians generally appeal to warrant this deduction.

---

[34]Miller, *Letters*, p. 47. Italics added.
[35]Ibid.
[36]Augustine, *The Trinity* 7.3.7 (pp. 224-25).

It seems that the first Christian theologian to conclude that the divine Father-Son relation implies a generative act called a "begetting" was Justin Martyr. In support he appeals to Psalm 2:7, which speaks of the begetting of God's royal son, and to Proverbs 8:25, which speaks of the begetting of divine Wisdom, texts he interprets christologically.[37] Athanasius follows him but adds that the generative act these and other texts speak of is eternal; he does so on the premise that what is created is temporal and what is divine is eternal. Athanasius's conclusion became the teaching of the church, "the tradition."

The church fathers' christological interpretation of Psalm 2:7 and Proverbs 8:25, along with other Septuagint texts that use the word "beget" (*gennaō*) (Ps 110:3 [109:3 LXX]; Is 53:8), should be endorsed. It is true that Psalm 2:7 *read critically and historically* does not speak of *the eternal begetting of the Son of God*. Nor does Acts 13:33, in which Paul takes the words of Psalm 2:7 to be fulfilled in the resurrection of Christ, or Hebrews 1:5 and 5:5, which understands the words of this Psalm to be fulfilled in the Son of God's exaltation. However, we learn from these New Testament appeals to Psalm 2:7 that the apostolic authors read this Psalm christologically. They did not assume that the words of Psalm 2:7 were limited or constrained to their historical meaning and application. They assumed, rather, that these passages spoke not just of a royal son who reigns temporally but ultimately of the divine Son of God, who reigns eternally. Justin, Athanasius and other church fathers take their lead from these inspired apostolic authors when they read Psalm 2:7 christologically, but in their case in reference to the begetting of the Son. They reason that when speaking of a historical royal son, this text speaks of a temporal begetting, and when applied to Christ it speaks of an eternal begetting.

Proverbs 8:25 is another text the church fathers frequently quote in support of the Son's eternal begetting. The verse reads, "Before the mountains had been shaped, before the hills, I was begotten." Indeed, this was Athanasius's favorite text in support of the doctrine of the eternal generation of the Son.[38] He understood this text to identify the

---

[37]Again for documentation see the discussion on Justin in the next chapter.
[38]Athanasius, *Discourses Against the Arians* 2.22.80 (p. 392).

Son with divine Wisdom and thus speaking of the Son's begetting before creation and thus before time. He concludes that the Son's begetting must be eternal, not only because what is divine is eternal but also because the Scriptures speak of Wisdom as the co-creator.[39]

We can again endorse the church fathers' identification of the Son of God with divine Wisdom because the writers of the New Testament do the same thing. Contemporary critical scholars generally agree that the New Testament writers make this identification. For example, John depicts the preexistent *Logos*, or Son, in terms of the Jewish understanding of personified divine Wisdom. Like Wisdom he is from the beginning (Jn 1:1; cf. Prov 8:22-23; Sir 24:9; Wis 6:22); the agent of creation (Jn 1:2; cf. Prov 8:27-30; Sir 1:4; 24:9; 43:26); descended from heaven to dwell among people (Jn 3:17; cf. Prov 8:31; Sir 24:8; Bar 3:3; Wis 9:10); to reflect the glory of God (Jn 1:14; 2:11; cf. Wis 7:25); to be the light that comes into the world (Jn 8:12; cf. Wis 7:26); and to be born of God (Jn 18:37;[40] cf. Prov 8:25).[41]

Paul also identifies the Son with divine Wisdom.[42] In 1 Corinthians 1:24, 30, Paul explicitly calls Christ "the Wisdom of God," and in Colossians 1:15-20 he designates Christ as "the image of God," "the firstborn over all creation" (Col 1:15 TNIV), "the agent of creation (Col 1:16), "the beginning" (Col 1:18) and the "fullness of God" (Col 1:19), all attributes or activities predicated of divine Wisdom. In Hebrews 1:1-3, the author of the epistle similarly speaks of the Son in terms of divine Wisdom to develop a christological argument reflecting Psalm

---

[39]Athanasius, *Discourses Against the Arians* 2.22.73 (p. 388). He quotes in support Prov 3:19: "The Lord by Wisdom founded the earth" and alludes to Hebrews 1:2: "through whom he created the worlds."

[40]Only once in John's Gospel does Jesus speak of his birth; he says to Pilate, "For this I was born [*gegennēmai*, perfect continuous tense], and for this I came into the world" (Jn 18:37). Leon Morris, *The Gospel According to John* (Grand Rapids: Eerdmans, 1971), p. 771, says, "It is difficult to see how the implication is to be avoided that Jesus is [here] claiming pre-existence."

[41]See further on the Synoptic Gospels and John, F. W. Burnett, "Wisdom," in *Dictionary of Jesus and the Gospels*, ed. Joel B. Green, Scot McKnight and I. Howard Marshall (Downers Grove, Ill.: InterVarsity Press, 1992), pp. 873-77.

[42]E. J. Schnabel, "Wisdom," in *Dictionary of Paul and His Letters*, ed. Gerald H. Hawthorne, Ralph P. Martin, Daniel G. Reid (Downers Grove, Ill.: InterVarsity Press, 1993), pp. 967-73. However, I note that Gordon D. Fee, *Pauline Christology: An Exegetical-Theological Study* (Peabody, Mass.: Hendrickson, 2007), pp. 594-619, is not convinced.

2:7 and Psalm 110:3 (109:3 LXX).[43] Here the Son is again depicted as the agent of creation (Heb 1:2) and the "reflection of God's glory and the exact imprint of God's very being" (Heb 1:3; cf. Wis 7:26).

In arguing that the Bible supports the use of the word "begotten" to speak of the eternal generation of the Son, I must comment on the five Johannine texts that designate the Son as *monogenēs* (Jn 1:14, 18; 3:16, 18; 1 Jn 4:9). As we have seen, there is now general agreement that the correct translation of this word is "unique" or "only," rather than "only begotten." The use of this word in reference to the Son is, however, still relevant to any study of Scripture investigating the eternal begetting of the Son. The Greek-speaking church fathers saw these texts that use the word *monogenēs* as highly significant, not because they thought the word meant "only begotten" and thus spoke of the Son's eternal generation, but because they understood it to mean "unique."[44] This designation set Jesus Christ apart from all others. What made him utterly unique, they concluded, was that he alone is eternally begotten, not made. All else in the world is created in time; the Son is "eternally begotten, not created," along with the Holy Spirit, who eternally proceeds.

At this point I need to reiterate the fact that while the semantic meaning of the word *monogenēs* is "unique" or "only," it implies begetting because all children are begotten. And in the case of the Son it speaks of a unique begetting, because the Son alone is eternally begotten of the Father and as such is the unique Son. Robert Letham, in seeking to support the conclusion that John the Evangelist understood *monogenēs* as a unique begetting, notes that all five passages in the Johannine writings that designate Jesus as the *monogenēs* Son, the unique Son, the verb *gennaō* ("to beget, to give birth") is used in close proximity. What is more, one text in which John designates the Son as the *monogenes* Son speaks of him as "from the bosom of the Father" (*eis ton*

[43]W. L. Lane, *Hebrews 1–8* (Dallas: Word, 1991), p. 9.

[44]In the chapters following, in which I outline the teachings of Greek-speaking fathers, I explore carefully how each of them understood the word *monogenēs*. I find that they do not use it or the texts in which it is found as textual support for the eternal generation of the Son. For them, as we would expect if modern discussions on the meaning of this word are correct, the word was understood to mean "unique" or "only."

kolpon) (Jn 1:18).[45] He existed before his incarnation. This certainly makes the Son of God unique.

Another text demanding comment is Colossians 1:15-16, where Paul speaks of the Son as "the image of the invisible God, the first*born* of all creation; for in him all things . . . were created"[46] (italics added). Both Arius and the Nicene fathers appealed to this text.[47] Arius quoted it to prove that the Son was born in time. He understood the Greek to be speaking of the Son as "the firstborn of creation." In reply, Athanasius insisted that Christ was not created in time but was the co-creator and the Lord over the creation. As such he was the unique Son, eternally begotten of the Father.[48] To make his case he linked the title *prōtotokos* with John's designation of the Son as *monogenēs*, arguing that the Son is designated "the firstborn" because "he alone is *from* him" (the Father).[49] Modern critical commentators agree that in Colossians 1:15 Christ is depicted as unique, not because he is the *monogenēs* Son, but because he is called the *prōtotokos*. This word literally means "firstborn,"[50] a title indicating his unequalled preeminence, not birth order as such. In the Old Testament, Israel is called God's firstborn (Ex 4:22; Jer 31:9) and so too is the Davidic messianic king (Ps 89:27). Paul almost certainly had this messianic Psalm in mind when he designated the glorified Christ *prōtotokos*, not only because he uses the same title as that found in the Psalm but also because in Colossians 1:12-14 he speaks of Christ in kingly, messianic terms. In saying the *prōtotokos* is "the image of the invisible God," Paul seems also to identify Christ with personified divine Wisdom, who is also said to be the "image of the invisible God." Thus the New Testament scholar Peter T. O'Brien concludes that the title *prōtotokos* "belongs to Jesus Christ not only as the Messiah of David's line, but also as the Wisdom of God."[51]

---

[45]I have already noted that there is some textual uncertainty with the wording of this text, but whether or not the Son is called God at this point does not detract from my point.

[46]I follow the TNIV translation of the Greek. This takes the genitive construction, *pasēs ktiseōs*, to be speaking of Christ the co-creator, not he who is created first.

[47]For a history of the interpretation of this text, see A. Hockel, *Chrisrtus der Estergeborene: Zur Geschichte der Exegese von Kol. 1:15* (Dusseldorf: Patmos, 1965).

[48]Athanasius, *Discourses Against the Arians* 2.21.62-64 (pp. 382-84).

[49]Athanasius, *Discourses Against the Arians* 2.21.63-64 (p. 383). Italics added.

[50]The noun is derived from the Greek *prōtos*, "first," and the aorist root *tek-*, "born."

[51]Peter T. O'Brien, *Colossians and Philemon* (Dallas: Word, 1982), p. 44.

Finally, in discussing scriptural support for naming the eternal act of self-differentiation between the Father and the Son an eternal begetting, or generation, I mention two often-cited New Testament texts. Neither serves as weighty evidence because the interpretation of both texts is disputed. First, I mention 1 John 5:18, which interpreters from the time of Bishop Alexander of Alexandria, in the early fourth century, have often taken to speak of the begetting of the Son outside of time.[52] Those who follow this interpretation understand John to contrast those born of God (believers), where the participle (*gennētheis*) is in the perfect tense, with the birth of him who protects them (the Son), where the participle (*gennētheis*) is in the aorist tense. The second text is found in John's Gospel. In a cryptic reply to Pilate, Jesus says, "For this I was born [*gegennēmai*, perfect tense] and for this I came [*elēlytha*, perfect tense] into the world" (Jn 18:37). John's wording suggests the preexistence of the Son.[53] He was born and existed before he came into the world.

These texts speaking of the begetting of the Son of God, especially Psalm 2:7 and Proverbs 8:25, give biblical justification for designating the eternal self-differentiation between the Father and the Son as *the eternal begetting of the Son*, but much more in Scripture supports *the doctrine* of the eternal generation of the Son. From the time of the Council of Nicaea, in 325, the New Testament teaching that Jesus is "from" the Father has been taken to suggest and support this doctrine. Sons are "from" their fathers because they are begotten, or generated, by their father and as such are of the same nature or being as their father. Thus in his discussion of Colossians 1:15, Athanasius says that the Son is designated "the first born" because "'he alone is *from* him" (the Father).[54]

Athanasius tells us that the bishops at the Council of Nicaea hotly disputed the meaning of the biblical passages that spoke of the Son as "from" God the Father.[55] The Arians, led by Eusebius of Nicomedia, tried to convince the assembled bishops that "from" in these contexts

---

[52]Raymond E. Brown, *The Epistles of John* (New York: Doubleday, 1982), p. 620, gives a list of those who have argued for this interpretation.

[53]So Morris, *Gospel According to John*, p. 771.

[54]Athanasius, *Discourses Against the Arians* 2.21.63-64 (pp. 382-83). Italics added.

[55]Athanasius, *Defence of the Nicene Definition* 19 (p. 162).

meant that the Son was like human beings, created by God "from nothing." Athanasius says that, perceiving "their craft and cunning," the bishops "were forced to express more distinctly the sense of the words, 'from God.' Accordingly, they wrote 'from the essence (*ousia*) of God,' in order that 'from God' might not be considered common and equal in the Son and in things originate. . . . For though all things be said to be from God, yet this is not the sense in which the Son is from him."[56]

Then, seeking to exclude the thought that the Son is "from the Father" like a human son is from his father, Athanasius says that the bishops at Nicaea likened the Son's begetting to "light from light" to banish "every corporeal inference" and to make the point that the Father and the Son are "one in essence" (*ousia*). Thus it can be said with confidence, "Truly the light and the radiance are one, and one is manifested in the other."[57]

In Augustine's articulation of the doctrine of the Trinity, the fact that the Bible speaks of the Son as "from" the Father is of great importance. He made a very important doctrinal advance when he concluded that in speaking of the Son as "from the Father," the Bible envisages an eternal *and* a temporal "from the Father." The Son is eternally "from" the Father by his eternal generation and temporally "sent" by the Father on mission into the world to save. A number of Johannine texts that speak of Jesus as coming down from heaven and "from" the Father (e.g., Jn 1:1-14; 8:14, 23, 42; 13:3; 16:28) suggest this distinction. For example, in John 7:29 Jesus says, "I am from [*para*] him, and he sent [*apostello*] me." These words seem to imply two moves.[58] On the basis of this twofold "fromness," Augustine concludes that the temporal missions of the Son and the Spirit are antecedently grounded in the eternal processions of these persons within the Godhead but do not constitute them as divine persons, as he explains toward the end of his long discussion of the missions in book four of *The Trinity:* "As being born means for the Son being *from* the Father, so being sent means for the

---

[56] Athanasius, *Defence of the Nicene Definition* 19 (p. 162).
[57] Athanasius, *Defence of the Nicene Definition* 24 (p. 166).
[58] B. de Margerie, *The Christian Trinity in History* (Petersham, Mass.: St. Bede's, 1981), p. 153.

Son being known to be *from* the Father. And as being the gift of God means for the Holy Spirit proceeding *from* the Father, so being sent means for the Holy Spirit his being known to proceed *from* the Father."[59]

Again this appeal to the Bible by the church fathers in support of the doctrine of the eternal generation of the Son has great weight. Frequently, John the Evangelist speaks of the Son as "coming from" God or the Father, and of the Son coming down from or out of heaven (*ek tou ouranou*) (Jn 3:13, 31; 6:33, 38). Using three closely related prepositions, John says the Son is "from God": *ek tou theou* (Jn 8:42), *para tou theou* (Jn 6:46; 7:29; 9:33; 16:27; *apo tou theou* (13:3), or "from the Father" [*para tou patros*], Jn 16:28).[60] Paralleling this imagery of the Son as "from" heaven and "from" the Father is the Johannine imagery of the Son being "sent" on mission by the Father to reveal and to save (Jn 3:17, 5:30, 7:29, 8:42, 17 3, 23). The language reflects the Jewish concept of *shaliach,* in which the one sent has the same authority as the one who sends.[61] In all these metaphors, John assumes the Son's pre-existence, and so it is understandable that the church fathers took a step further and spoke of his eternal "fromness" in reference to his eternal begetting.

In providing biblical support for the doctrine of the eternal generation of the Son, Augustine quotes the well-established proof texts Psalm 2:7, 45:1, Proverbs 8:25 and Wisdom 7:24-27, but he also finds important biblical validation for this doctrine in John 5:26.[62] Indeed, for Augustine this is one of the most important texts indicating the eternal generation of the Son. Here Jesus says, "For just as the Father has life in himself, so he has granted the Son also to have life in himself."[63] For Augustine these words speak of the divine life that the Father has given to the Son in his eternal generation; "he begot the Son to be un-

---

[59]Augustine, *The Trinity* 4.5.29 (p. 174). Italics added.

[60]On John's use of these prepositions, see C. H. Dodd, *The Interpretation of the Fourth Gospel* (Cambridge: Cambridge University Press, 1970), pp. 259-60.

[61]See further Giles, *Jesus and the Father,* pp. 119-21. In contrast Köstenberger and Swain, *Father, Son and Spirit,* pp. 71-72, 88-90, 120-21, argue that the *shaliach* concept speaks of the eternal subordination of the Son in authority.

[62]For a fuller treatment of Augustine's appeal to the Bible in support of the doctrine of the eternal generation of the Son, see chap. 6.

[63]See further on Augustine's appeal to this text, Keith E. Johnson, "Augustine's Trinitarian Reading of John 5: A Model for the Theological Interpretation of Scripture," *Journal of the Evangelical Theological Society* 52, no. 4 (2009): 799-811.

changeable light, that is to say eternal life."[64] The contemporary evangelical exegete D. A. Carson, commenting on this verse, says,

> Like God he [the Son] has life-in-himself. God is self-existent; he is
> always the "living God." Mere human beings are derived creatures . . .
> but to the Son, and to the Son alone, God has imparted life-in-himself.
> This cannot mean that the Son gained this prerogative only after the
> incarnation. The Prologue has already asserted of the pre-incarnate
> Word, "In Him was life" (1:4). The impartation of life-in-himself to the
> Son must be an act belonging to eternity. . . . Many systematicians have
> tied this teaching to what they call "the eternal generation of the Son."
> This is unobjectionable.[65]

I would speak more positively. To conclude that John in this verse is speaking of the full and perfect bestowal or sharing of the divine life from the Father to the Son, as Augustine first argued, is not only unobjectionable but is implied by the wording of this Scripture.

I sum up my case. I have argued that the Bible, in giving the names "the Father" and "the Son" to the first and second persons of the Trinity, eternally differentiates and relates them analogically in terms of a human father-son relation. These names supplied by divine revelation strongly suggest that no better human word can be found to speak of the eternal self-differentiation of the Father and the Son than the words "generation" or "begetting." The choice of the word "begetting" to speak of a divine generative act can be justified because the psalmist speaks of God begetting a royal son, who in the New Testament is identified with Jesus Christ, the divine Son, and because the writer of Proverbs speaks of the begetting of divine Wisdom before creation, who again in the New Testament is identified with Jesus Christ, the divine Son. Furthermore, in speaking of the Son as "from" the Father,

---

[64] Augustine, *The Trinity* 1.5.26 (p. 85). For the same argument see also 1.5.29 (p. 87), 1.5.30 (p. 88), 2.2.3 (pp. 98-99). In greater detail see Augustine, *Tractates on The Gospel of John* 11-17 (J. W. Rettig, trans., *St. Augustine's Tractates on The Gospel of John*, Fathers of the Church [Washington, D.C.: Catholic University of America Press, 1988], pp. 152-53).

[65] D. A. Carson, *The Gospel According to John* (Grand Rapids: Eerdmans, 1991), pp. 256-57. For a similar conclusion see also Carson, "God Is Love," *Bibliotheca Sacra* 156 (1999): 139. For very similar conclusions see also R. Schnackenburg, *The Gospel According to John* (New York: Crossroad, 1990), 2:112.

the New Testament implies the language of begetting, or generation, and in speaking of him as both the eternal Son and the temporally incarnate Son, it implies an eternal and a temporal "fromness." Finally, in speaking of the Father as "having life in himself" and yet granting the Son to "have life in himself," John implies an eternal communicative act that results in the Son having the same divine life as the Father.

CONCLUSION

Given this evidence I am convinced that the church fathers and the creeds and confessions were right to conclude that on the basis of Scripture the best explanation of divine self-differentiation is summed up in the doctrines of the eternal generation of the Son and the eternal procession of the Spirit. For this reason I will continue to confess with a good conscience, along with millions of other Christians of the same mind, "We believe in one Lord Jesus Christ, the only Son of God, eternally begotten of the Father . . . begotten not made."

Having reached this point we are ready to explore in greater detail how the doctrine of the eternal generation of the Son emerged in church history, why it became such an important doctrine, and how it was developed and honed across the ages. This is by far the longest section of the book because we are covering, albeit selectively, almost two thousand years of the history of this doctrine. I include it because I am convinced that only a historical study of this doctrine will enable us to understand it at some depth. However, before we outline this story I want to say something, as an addendum to this chapter, about the doctrine of the eternal procession of the Spirit.

THE ETERNAL PROCESSION OF THE SPIRIT

In this book I mention the doctrine of the eternal procession of the Spirit only in passing, not because I am uninterested in the Holy Spirit: far from it. I focus on the doctrine of the eternal generation of the Son because in the early church and today this is the more disputed doctrine. True, most of those today who argue for the rejection of the doctrine of the eternal begetting, or generation, of the Son also argue for the rejection of the doctrine of the eternal procession of the Spirit, but for them their questioning of the second of these doctrines logically follows from their questioning of the first. Samuel Miller, in his masterful 1823 defense of the doctrine of the eternal generation of the Son,[66] recognizes this fact. He says, "Those who deny the eternal generation of the Son, will naturally, and almost unavoidably, deny the eternal procession of the Spirit."[67] For this reason, he adds, the two doctrines "must stand or fall together."[68]

This is certainly true, but there is another reason why in this book the doctrine of the eternal generation of the Son fills the horizon. For Christians trying to think through the doctrine of the Trinity, "Jesus is always the problem." It seems that somehow Christians do not see that divine oneness is compromised by thinking of God (the Father) and of his Spirit. It is Jesus who calls into question divine oneness—he claims to perfectly reveal God (Jn 14:9) and to be one with God (Jn 10:30; 17:11), he does the things that only God can do and rules as the Lord and is worshiped as God (Phil 2:10-11; Rev 5:9-14). Thus the protracted and painful debate over the doctrine of the Trinity in the fourth century was primarily about how Jesus could be true God if in fact God is one. Once this question had been answered and codified in the Nicene Creed of 325, the question of the Spirit's status was more easily resolved. The church concluded that if Jesus is "true God from true God," "one in being" with the Father, and the Father, Son and Spirit are the one God (Mt 28:19; 2 Cor 13:13), then whatever is true of the Son is true of the Spirit. He too is "true God from true God."

The most common evangelical objection to the doctrine of the eternal procession of the Spirit, as in the case of the doctrine of the eternal generation of the Son, is that there is no biblical warrant for it. Again it has to be admitted that no text says, "The Spirit eternally proceeds from the Father." To say this, however, is not conclusive. Hints and inferences of the doctrine in Scripture may suggest that this doctrine is the best way to understand eternal self-differentiation between the Father and the Son and the Spirit. The text to which interpreters

---

[66]Miller, *Letters.*
[67]Ibid., p. 21.
[68]Ibid.

have most frequently appealed in support is John 15:26. Here Jesus speaks of the Spirit, "whom I will send to you from [*para*] the Father, the Spirit of truth who comes from the Father [*ho para tou patros ekporeuetai*]." Most commentators today take these words to refer to one coming of the Spirit, the historical coming of the Spirit. However, Letham is not convinced. He argues that John uses the future tense (*pempsō*) to refer to the Spirit's sending in time and the present tense (*ekporeuetai*) of his eternal procession from the Father. He says, "The Spirit's sending at Pentecost, of which the Son is the sender, is distinct from the Spirit's procession, which is continuous, and for which the Father is the spirator."[69]

Notwithstanding this biblical support it must be admitted that the doctrine of the eternal procession of the Spirit is a corollary doctrine complementing the doctrine of the eternal generation of the Son. As mentioned earlier, all Christians agree that God is eternally triune, eternally self-differentiated. The doctrine of the eternal generation seeks to explain this self-differentiation in reference to the Son; the doctrine of the eternal procession of the Spirit seeks to explain this in reference to the Spirit.

At this point, mention must be made of the *filioque* controversy.[70] In the Creed of Nicaea (325) and the Nicene Creed of Constantinople (381), the Holy Spirit is said "to proceed from the Father." This wording represents the majority opinion of the Eastern bishops that the Father is the *monarche*—the sole source—of the being of the Son and the Spirit. Due to the continuing threat of Arianism, the third council of Toledo, in 589, in Spain, added the words "and the Son" (these three English words translate one Latin word, *filioque*) to the Nicene Creed to exclude any possibility of subordinating the Son to the Father. In the eighth century this addition to the Nicene Creed was accepted by the French Church. In 1014 Pope Benedict VIII ruled that this wording represented the teaching of the Catholic Church. This addition reflects the Western belief that the Father and the Son are inseparably one, and

---

[69]Letham, *Holy Trinity*, p. 389.
[70]I discuss this matter more fully in my *Jesus and the Father*, pp. 156-58. See also Letham's excellent discussion, *Holy Trinty*, pp. 202-20.

it disallows any disjunction between the Son and the Spirit contrary to passages of Scripture such as Acts 16:6-7, in which the Spirit is called "the Spirit of Jesus" (cf. Rom 8:9; Gal 4:6). However, neither the Western nor the Eastern conceptions of the procession of the Spirit can be considered satisfactory. In an eternally coequal Trinity, the Spirit proceeding from the Father alone or from the Father and the Son is unsatisfactory. Neither view is adequately trinitarian. In his extended discussion of this issue, Robert Letham argues that the best solution is to speak of the Spirit proceeding "from the Father in the Son."[71]

To discuss the *filioque* debate more fully or say more on biblical support for and against each position would demand a full chapter, which is unnecessary for this book.

In speaking of the eternal self-differentiation of the Father and the Son, no better metaphors than "begetting" or "generation" are possible. Father's beget or generate children, who are of the same nature. However, the primary metaphor regarding the Spirit, "procession," is less than ideal. The word Aquinas gave to the Roman Catholic Church, *spiration*, is far better.[72]

The Spirit is self-differentiated in eternity by being "breathed out" within the life of God. Why "breathed out" or "spirated" are not more widely used is perhaps related to two factors. The creeds have not been translated this way. And the idea of "spiration" has less direct biblical support than does "procession," a word used in many English translations of John 15:26. These two factors likely have reciprocally influenced each other.

---

[71]Ibid., p. 219. For a similar conclusion see T. Smail, "The Holy Spirit in the Holy Trinity" in *From Nicea to Christianity: The Future for a New Ecumenism*, ed. Christopher Seitz (Grand Rapids: Brazos, 2001), pp. 149-65.

[72]I outline Aquinas's teaching on the Trinity and document it in chap. 6.

4

The Eternal Generation of the Son

From the Apologists to Athanasius

◆ ◆ ◆

Having shown that there is wide-ranging and solid biblical and theological warrant for the doctrine of the eternal generation of the Son, I now begin the major part of this book where I trace the emergence and development of this doctrine in the early church, its analytical articulation by Aquinas, clarification by Calvin and embrace by post-Reformation theologians. History, in this case the history of a doctrine, is always instructive and enlightening. With the doctrine of the eternal generation of the Son, the more we know of how and why this doctrine emerged, developed and became so important, the better and more adequately we will understand this doctrine today. The church fathers studied in this chapter are the Apologists (mainly Justin Martyr), Irenaeus, the monarchical modalists, Tertullian, Origen, Arius and Athanasius. In the subsequent chapters I will consider the Cappadocian fathers, Augustine, Aquinas, Calvin, and other important Reformation and post-Reformation theologians.

It may be helpful at this point to inform my readers what I have concluded from carefully reading the second- to fourth-century sources. In doing this I hope I will make it much easier to understand and comprehend what follows. At least from the time of Justin in the second century the language of "begetting" was used to speak of the self-differentiation of the Father and the Son with monotheism taken as an axiom. In the prolonged and heated fourth-century dispute between the supporters of the Creed of Nicaea and those who opposed it because they could not confess Jesus Christ as "one in being" (*homoousios*) with the Father, the focal issue that divided the warring sides was whether the Son was *temporally created* or *eternally begotten*. If the Son's "begetting" alluded to his creation in time, as all the so-called Arians of the fourth century argued,[1] then the Son was a creature, no matter how elevated, and thus subordinate to God. If, however, his begetting implied an eternal generative act in which the Father shared his being with the Son, as Athanasius and those who followed him argued, then the Son was "true God from true God," *one in being* with the Father, "coeternal" and "coequal" God.[2] Athanasius and all the Nicene theologians saw clearly that to speak of the Son of God as "eternally begotten" not only safeguarded his full divinity but also indelibly distinguished him from the Father. If the Son is true God, then he is not subordinate in "being and power" to the Father,[3] and if he is "begotten God" and the Father "unbegotten God," then the two divine persons cannot be identified and confused. This grounding of the *two essential elements* of the Nicene faith, divine unity/equality and divine differentiation/threeness, is what made this doctrine so theologically important for the Nicene fathers.[4]

In this debate we are going to see that the key categories are temporality and eternity. The Arians insisted that the Son was created in

---

[1]One caveat needs to be made. In the 340s, when confusion reigned, we find a number of very ambiguous affirmations of the Son's begetting "before the ages" emerging from the so-called Dedication Council of Antioch in 341. In the second of these creeds, often thought to be the most important, the Son is confessed as "begotten of the Father before the ages." However, this statement of faith does not say that the Son is "from the Father's *ousia*," as does the Creed of Nicaea, or that he is one in being (*homoousios*) with the Father, and it does not anathematize the doctrine's association by the bishops at Nicaea with Arius. On this confusing period see D. M. Gwynn, *The Eusebians: The Polemic of Athanasius of Alexandria and the Construction of the Arian Controversy* (Oxford: Oxford University Press, 2007).

[2]"Coequal" is the term the Athanasian Creed uses.

[3]Many think that Arianism involved solely the eternal subordination of the Son in being/nature/essence. This is not so. All the Arians subordinated the Son in being *and* authority. The two were correlated by the Arians, who advocated both, and by the Nicene theologians, who rejected both. Both sides agreed they were two sides of one coin. If the Son is subordinate in being, he is subordinate in authority; if he is one in being with the Father, then he is one in authority. Lewis Ayres, *Nicaea and Its Legacy: An Approach to Fourth-Century Trinitarian Theology* (Oxford: Oxford University Press, 2004), p. 271, says, "It is fundamental to all Pro-Nicene theologies that God is one power, glory, majesty and rule, Godhead, essence and nature."

[4]Much on this matter has been written. See William Lane Craig, *Time and Eternity: Explaining God's Relation to Time* (Wheaton, Ill.: Crossway, 2001).

time, temporally, the Nicenes that he is begotten outside of time, eternally. For the debaters on both sides the temporal characterizes God's creative work; the eternal characterizes God in his unchanging being.

THE LATE SECOND- AND EARLY THIRD-CENTURY THEOLOGIANS

In the second and early third centuries the primary concern of Christian theologians was to safeguard the unity of God. Their challenge as ardent monotheists was to show, without falling into tritheism, how the Son and the Holy Spirit could be confessed as God alongside God the Father, who for them was God in the absolute sense. These theologians saw John the Evangelist's identification of the divine Son with the *Logos* (Jn 1:1) as the best way to understand how the Father and the Son could both be designated God and yet distinguished. They assumed, first, that the *Logos* of John 1:1 was to be identified with the Stoic understanding of the *Logos* as God's reason or rationality and, second, that the Stoic distinction between the *Logos endiathetos* ("the immanent Word") and the *Logos prophorikos* ("the expressed Word") was to be identified with the preexistent Word and the incarnate Word spoken of by John.[5] Because they all focused on what took place in the economy, what was revealed of God's triunity in history, they are designated "economic trinitarians."

THE APOLOGISTS, AND JUSTIN MARTYR IN PARTICULAR

Justin Martyr (ca. 100-165) is usually taken to be the most important of the Apologists. More than any of the others, he introduced ideas that later theologians would develop. For Justin and the other Apologists, God the Father is a monad who becomes triune for the purpose of creation and redemption. The *Logos* for him is eternally with the Father but not *eternally begotten* or *generated*.[6] He thus speaks of the *Logos* "in the

---

[5]Cf. R. Holte, "*Logos Spermatikos:* Christianity and Ancient Philosophy According to St Justin's *Apologies*," *Studia Theologica* 12 (1958): 109-68.

[6]Justin, *Dial.* 129 (*The Ante-Nicene Fathers*, ed. A. Coxe and A. Roberts, vol. 1 [Buffalo: Christian Literature Publishing, 1885], p. 264). Hereafter this series is referred to as *ANF*. All citations of Justin are from this volume. *Dialogue with Trypho* is abbreviated as *Dial.* and the *First Apology* and *Second Apology* are abbreviated as *1 Ap.* and *2 Ap.* respectively. However,

beginning" with God yet also of his coming forth as the first of God's
creative acts. He says, "The Son was begotten of the Father before all
creatures."[7] The generation of the *Logos*, Justin believes, is to be likened
to the manner in which the rational mind (*logos*) expresses itself in a rational word (*logos*). So the begetting of the Word (*Logos*) occurs when
God "speaks" and "sends him forth."[8] Then, anticipating the Nicene
imagery of "Light from Light," Justin likens the begetting of the Son to
"the light from the sun," which is "indivisible and inseparable from the
sun in the heavens."[9] Following scriptural language, Justin most frequently speaks of the generation of the Son or *Logos* in birth terminology. He is "begotten" (*gennaō*) of the Father,[10] God's "offspring"
(*gennēma*),[11] his "first begotten" (*prōton gennēma*),[12] his firstborn
(*prōtotokos*),[13] his "child" (*teknon*),[14] and his unique (*monogenēs*) Son.[15]
And then, as the Nicene fathers would later do, he argues that the Father's begetting and the Son's begottenness is the very thing that distinguishes the Father and the Son. For him, the Father is "unbegotten"
(*agennētos*) God[16] and the Son, or *Logos*, is "begotten" (*gennētos*) God, or
the "first begotten [*prōtotokos*] of an unbegotten [*agennētos*] God."[17]

Justin unquestionably presupposes Stoic ideas, but his intent is always
to speak and argue in terms of Scripture. For him the *Logos* is not the
impersonal Logos of stoicism; the *Logos* revealed in Jesus Christ is the
Son of God. Thus in seeking to understand the generation of the *Logos*
he commences with what John says about the Word (*Logos*): "In the
beginning was the Word, and the Word was with God, and the Word
was God" (Jn 1:1). In speaking of the generation of *the Logos* he notes

---

E. Fortman, *The Triune God* (Grand Rapids: Baker, 1972), pp. 44-46, points out that some
have found in Justin the doctrine of the eternal generation of the Son.
[7]Justin, *Dial.* 129 (1:264).
[8]Justin, *Dial.* 61 (1:227); *1 Ap.* 46 (1:178); *2 Ap.* 13 (1:193).
[9]Justin, *Dial.* 128 (1:264).
[10]Justin, *1 Ap.* 23 (1:251); *Dial.* 62 (1:229), 105 (1:251).
[11]Justin, *1 Ap.* 21 (1:170); *Dial.* 62 (1:228), 129 (1:264).
[12]Justin, *1 Ap.* 21 (1:170), 22 (1:170); *Dial.* 103 (1:250).
[13]Justin, *1 Ap.* 33 (1:174), 46 (1:178).
[14]Justin, *Dial.* 125.3 (1:262).
[15]Justin, *Dial.* 105.1 (1:251).
[16]Justin, *1 Ap.* 6 (1:126); *Dial.* 114 (1:256), 126 (1:262).
[17]Justin, *1 Ap.* 53 (1:180); *2 Ap.* 6 (1:164).

that the Bible uses generative human language; the Son, or *Logos,* is "begotten," "first begotten," "offspring" and so on.[18] And following Paul and the writer to the Hebrews he identifies God's Son, the *Logos,* with divine Wisdom, quoting Proverbs 8:25: "Before the hills be begat me."[19] Positively, he finds biblical warrant for speaking of the Son's generation in terms of begetting in Psalm 2:7, "Today have I begotten you,"[20] and Isaiah 53:8, "His generation who shall declare,"[21] texts the Nicene fathers would also quote. From this evidence we should conclude that Justin was not seeking to construe the Trinity in terms of Stoicism but rather to give Christian and biblical content to inadequate, yet what he considered to be insightful, ideas in Stoicism. Fourth-century Nicene theologians, in distinction to Justin, would begin with the premise that God is triune for all eternity and make central the Father-Son relationship, but they would all follow him in speaking of the self-differentiation of the Father and the Son in terms of begetting, but for them this was unambiguously an eternal begetting.[22]

IRENAEUS

Irenaeus (130-200) is often described as the first "biblical theologian." He writes primarily to refute the Gnostics of his day, so most of his comments on the Trinity or on the generation of the Son are made in passing. Irenaeus's trinitarian beliefs come through most clearly when he is echoing "the tradition" he has received.[23] What he believes, he maintains, is what his trusted teachers taught him, and this teaching reflects the teaching of the apostles. He is not independently and creatively appealing to the Scriptures, as the heretics do. In reflecting on God's triune life Irenaeus concentrates on what is revealed in the economy, and so like the Apologists before him and Tertullian after him he is called an economic trinitarian.

---

[18]On this birth language in Justin, see J. N. D. Kelly, *Early Christian Doctrines,* 5th ed. (London: Adam and Charles Black, 1977), p. 97.

[19]Justin, *Dial.* 61 (1:227-28), 72 (1:264).

[20]Justin, *Dial.* 89 (1:244), 103 (1:251), 122 (1:261).

[21]Justin, *1 Ap.* 51 (1:179).

[22]Maurice Wiles, "Eternal Generation," *Journal of Theological Studies,* n.s. 12 (1961): 284-91, outlines the development of the doctrine of eternal generation from Justin to Origen.

[23]See, e.g., Irenaeus, *Against Heresies* 1.10 (*ANF* 3:330).

Like the Apologists, he begins by assuming that God the Father is a monad, who "in the beginning" brings forth his Son, whom, following John the Evangelist, he identifies with the *Logos*, God's immanent reason, yet he favors the name "the Son." He rejects any attempt to understand how the generation of the Son, or *Logos*, occurred in human terms. He takes his cue from Isaiah 53:8, "Who shall explain his generation?" He writes, "If anyone, therefore says to us, 'How then was the Son produced by the Father?' we reply to him, that no man understands that production or generation . . . but the Father only who begat, and the Son who was begotten."[24] He stresses the *Logos*'s coexistence with the Father for all eternity, but this is not to say he taught the *eternal generation* of the Son or Logos. "He is the Father of our Lord Jesus Christ, through his Word, who is his Son, . . . the Son co-existing with the Father, from of old, from the beginning."[25]

THE MONARCHICAL MODALISTS

Justin criticizes those who cannot accept that the *Logos* "is something numerically other" than the Father.[26] However, the first theologian known by name to have articulated what would later be called "modalism" was Noetius of Smyrna (ca. 200-225).[27] Appealing to the Bible, he insists that God is one, the divine monarch; the Father, Son and Spirit are simply differing manifestations of the one God. The presbyters of Smyrna condemned his teaching. Nevertheless, one of his students, Epigonus, brought the case to Rome. Hippolytus tells us he believed in one identical Godhead, which could be designated indifferently, Father, Son or Spirit. The names did not stand for real distinctions but were merely names given to the one God at different times. This teaching was taken up by Praxeas, a shadowy figure against whom Tertullian writes. His name literally means "busybody." Tertullian says, "He did a twofold service for the devil at Rome: he drove out prophecy [speaking of his opposition to the Montanists] and brought in heresy. He put to flight the

---

[24]Irenaeus, *Against Heresies* 2.28 (*ANF* 3:401).
[25]Irenaeus, *Against Heresies* 2.30 (*ANF* 3:406).
[26]Justin, *Dial.* 128.3 (p. 264).
[27]In what immediately follows I am largely dependent on Kelly, *Early Christian Doctrines*, pp. 119-23.

Paraclete, and crucified the Father."[28] A more sophisticated form of this teaching was given by Sabellius, who came to Rome toward the end of Pope Zephyrinus's pontificate (198-217). Sabellius regarded the Godhead as a monad who expressed himself in three operations. He used the analogy of the sun, a single subject, which radiates both warmth and light. The Father is, as it were, the form or essence, and the Son and the Spirit his modes of self-expression. In the West this error was known as monarchianism, in the East as Sabellianism.

It is absolutely essential for the case we are developing that this story be told because modalism excludes essential and eternal divine self-differentiation. The primary question, how can God be eternally one and yet three persons? is solved by denying that God is intrinsically and eternally three persons. He just appears in three modes or roles. In modalism there is no *eternal* generation of the Son or eternal procession of the Spirit, only differing *temporal* manifestations of the one undifferentiated God.

TERTULLIAN

Tertullian (160-225) is numbered among the Apologists, but he has a wider agenda. Like both them and Irenaeus, he believes that the God of the Bible is a monad who becomes tripartite for the purposes of creation and redemption. Tertullian, writing in Latin, repeatedly speaks of the generation of the Son, or *Logos,* in terms of begetting. For example, he says, "He [God the Father] made him [the Son] equal to him: By proceeding [*procedendo*] from himself, he became his first-begotten [*primogenitus*] Son, because he is begotten [*genitus*] before all things."[29] Like Justin, Tertullian believed that God the Father and his *Logos* were eternal, but it seems, as this quote indicates, that he thought the begetting of the Son took place "before all things," that is, before the world was created.

Tertullian clearly also saw that to speak of the Son as generated or begotten by the Father indelibly differentiates him from the Father. He writes, "The Father is distinct from the Son. He who generates [*gen-*

---

[28]Tertullian, *Against Praxeas* 1 (*ANF* 3:597).
[29]Tertullian, *Against Praxeas* 7 (*ANF* 3:601).

erator] is one, and he who is generated [*generatus*] is another. He who sends is one, and he who is sent is another."[30] And in ridiculing Praxeas's identification of the Father and the Son he writes, "If you want me to believe him to be both the Father and the Son, show me some passage where it is declared, 'I the Lord said to himself, I am my only Son, today have I begotten myself' [cf. Ps 2:7], or again, 'Before the morning did I beget myself' [alluding to Ps 110:3 (LXX 109:3)], and likewise, 'I the Lord possesses myself, the beginning of my ways for my own works, before all the hills, too, did I begat myself' [Prov 8:25]."[31] As positive evidence for the generation of the Son, Tertullian most often cites Psalm 2:7 and Proverbs 8:25.[32]

Finally, Tertullian's understanding of divine rule demands a comment. He argues that God the Father shares his rule with his Son and the Spirit without ever compromising his unity. He says, "I am sure that *monarchia* (or monarchy) has no other meaning than single and individual rule."[33] Nevertheless, he adds, the rule or monarchy of the one God does not exclude the idea that this rule can be shared with others, especially with a Son: "I contend no dominion so belongs to one only, as his own, or is in such a sense singular, or is in such a sense a monarchy [Latin, *monarchiam*], as not also to be administered through other persons most closely connected with it, and whom itself has provided as officials to itself. If moreover, there be a son belonging to him whose monarchy [Latin, *monarchia*] it is, it does not forthwith become divided and cease to be a monarchy."[34]

According to Athanasius and the Cappadocians, divine rule (in Greek the *monarchia*) is triune. The divine three rule as one. I mention this matter because so many books confuse the terms *monarchia*, which is used to speak of divine rule, and the cognate term *monarche*, which is used to speak of the Father as the sole source or origin of the Son and the Spirit.

---

[30]Tertullian, *Against Praxeas* 7 (*ANF* 3:604). I have changed the English translation in this quote. The *ANF* translation renders, *generator* as "he who begets." I give "generates." And it renders *generatus* as "he who is begotten." I give "generated."

[31]Tertullian, *Against Praxeas* 10 (*ANF* 3:604).

[32]Tertullian, *Against Praxeas* 6 (*ANF* 3:601), 7 (*ANF* 3:601), 11 (*ANF* 3:605).

[33]Tertullian, *Against Praxeas* 1.3 (*ANF* 3:599).

[34]Tertullian, *Against Praxeas* 1.3 (*ANF* 3:599).

ORIGEN

Origen of Alexandria (185-254)[35] is unquestionably one of the greatest theologians in Christian history, even if as a theological pioneer he often did not get it right. His *On First Principles* (Greek title, *Peri Archōn;* Latin title, *De prinicipiis*) gives the most extensive account of Origen's thinking on the Trinity, but unfortunately we possess it in its entirety only in the fourth-century Latin translation by Rufinus of Aquileia, which reflects more the ideas and language of Latin-speaking Nicenes in the 390s rather than that of Greek-speaking Alexandrian Christians in the 220s.[36] For Origen God is triune for all eternity.[37] Thus Origen concluded, in contrast to the later Arius, that there never was a time when the Son "was not."[38] The Son, like the Father, is eternal. In *On First Principles,* he begins by discussing God, whom he identifies with the Father. Reflecting both Platonic and biblical premises, Origen stresses that God is "incorporeal," and as such he speaks of him as "spirit" and "light."[39] The Son is God's *Logos* or Wisdom,[40] a second divine *hypostasis,* and the Spirit a third divine *hypostasis.* He cannot allow that the Son and the Spirit are other than God in nature/being; to do so would admit the existence of three Gods. However, the way in which Origen differentiates the Father and the Son and the Spirit leads him to subordinate them. Bryan Liftin says that Origen made "the Son subordinate to the Father, not just as an obedient Son carrying out the Father's will but by actually ranking the Son at a lower level"[41]—in other words, by hierarchically ordering them in divine being, power and majesty. For Origen, the Father, whom he

---

[35]On Origen see Kelly, *Early Christian Doctrines*, pp. 128-32; Peter Widdicombe, *The Fatherhood of God from Origen to Athanasius* (Oxford: Clarendon, 1994), pp. 7-92; R. P. C. Hanson, *The Search for the Christian Doctrine of God* (Edinburgh: T & T Clark, 1988), pp. 60-70.

[36]J. W. Trigg, *Origen,* (London: Routledge, 1998), p. 18.

[37]Widdicombe, *Fatherhood,* pp. 10-92.

[38]Ibid., p. 68 and 68 n. 14.

[39]The Greek term is certainly *asōmatos.*

[40]On Origen's use of Wisdom Christology and in particular on his distinctive appeal to the Wisdom of Solomon 7:25-26, see A. H. B. Logan, "Origen and Alexandrian Wisdom Christology," in *Origeniana Terta: The Third International Colloquium for Origen Studies,* ed. R. Hanson and J. Crouzel (Rome: Edizioni Dell'Ateneo, 1985), pp. 123-29.

[41]Bryan Litfin, "Origen," in *Shapers of Christian Orthodoxy,* ed. B. G. Green (Nottingham, U.K.: Apollos, 2010), p. 137.

calls "the Unbegotten" (*agennētos*), is "the fountainhead of deity" (*pēgē tēs Theotētos*)[42] and as such is the origin or source (*archē*) and cause (*aitia*) of the Son and the Spirit. He almost certainly called the Son a "creation" (*ktisma*)[43] and certainly spoke of his being "willed" into existence by the Father.[44] Thus for him the Son and the Spirit are contingently and derivatively God, not God in the fullest sense of the word. In his *Commentary on John* he says the Father alone is *autotheos*, God himself, true God.[45] At this point his Middle Platonic presuppositions come to the fore. Because the Son and the Spirit are derived from and contingently caused by the Father, they must be less than the Father. In Middle Platonism a cause is always superior to what is caused because what is caused does not *participate* fully in the being of the ultimate cause. What this means is that for Origen derivation implies diminution in divine being and thus diminution in divine power.

When Origen comes to speak of the origination of the Son, *Logos* or Wisdom in eternity, he speaks of his being "generated" and "born."[46] He writes, "His only-begotten [Latin, *Unigenitus*, the Greek almost certainly *monogenēs*] was born of him, and derives from him what he is, but without any beginning, not only as may be measured by any divisions in time, but even that which the mind alone can contemplate within itself, or so to speak, with the naked powers of understanding. . . . And therefore we must believe that Wisdom was generated [Latin, *generare*] before any beginning that can be either comprehended or expressed."[47] And he adds, "His generation is as eternal and everlasting as the brilliancy which is produced from the sun."[48]

---

[42]Origen, *On First Principles* 2.3 (p. 20). All quotes from Origen are taken from *The Writings of Origen, The Ante-Nicene Library*, vol. 10, ed. A. Roberts and J. Donaldson (Edinburgh: T & T Clark, 1895).

[43]For the evidence see Widdicombe, *Fatherhood*, pp. 89-90.

[44]Origen, *On First Principles* 2.6 (p. 248).

[45]Origen, *Commentary on the Gospel of John* 2.16-17 (Ronald E. Heine, trans., *Origen: Commentary on the Gospel of John, Books 1-10* [Washington, D.C.: Catholic University of America Press, 1989], p. 99).

[46]An excellent account of Origen's teaching on eternal generation is given by John Behr, *The Way to Nicaea*, Formation of Christian Theology (Crestwood, N.Y.: St Vladimir's Seminary Press, 2001), 1:191-97.

[47]Origen, *On First Principles* 2.1.2 (p. 246).

[48]Origen, *On First Principles* 1.2.4 (p. 247). See also J. C. Smith, trans., *Origen's Homilies on Jeremiah and 1 Kings 28* (Washington, D.C.: Catholic University of America Press, 1998), on Jer 9:4.

This last quotation indicates what is basic to Origen's understanding of the generation of the Son. It is eternal in the sense that it is a continuous generation.[49] Peter Widdicombe says, "The idea of the eternal generation of the Son is central to Origen's understanding of the tenor of the relationship between the Father and the Son. [This is] a dynamic relationship, characterized by continuous activity."[50] Origen's depiction of the generation of the Son as "eternal," in the sense of continuous and atemporal, reflects the Platonic understanding of eternity, but Panayotis Tzamalikos argues that Origen's doctrine of time and eternity has come to be the dominant Christian position.[51] For Origen, time, like everything else in the world, was created by God, but God himself is not bound by time. The world is temporal; God is atemporal or, better, supra-temporal.

Origen develops his doctrine of the eternal generation of the Son to ensure that God the Father and God the Son are not separated in nature/being.[52] He speaks of the "absurdities" of those who "divide the divine nature into parts, and who divide God the Father," as if the Son were other than "the image" of the Father.[53] For him the Son is uniquely "Son by nature."[54] He thus shares God's nature/being, yet in lesser measure. In his *Commentary on John* he says those who hesitate to call the Son "God, deny the divinity of the Son, making his particularity and essence [*ousia*] as an individual to be different from the Father."[55] At this point Origen's teaching is again to be contrasted with that of the later Arius. For Arius, the Son does not share the divine nature/being/*ousia* of the Father.

We also note that Origen would not allow that the eternal generation of the Son should be likened to human begetting in any way: "It is monstrous and unlawful to compare God the Father, in the generation [Latin, *generationem*] of his only-begotten [in Greek almost cer-

---

[49]Widdicombe, *Fatherhood*, p. 90.

[50]Ibid.

[51]Panayotis Tzamalikos, *Origen: Cosmology and Ontology of Time* (Leiden: Brill, 2006).

[52]Widdicombe, *Fatherhood*, p. 78.

[53]Origen, *On First Principles* 1.2.6 (p. 248).

[54]Origen, *On First Principles* 1.2.4 (p. 247), and Widdicombe, *Fatherhood*, pp. 91-92.

[55]Origen, *Commentary on the Gospel of John* 2.16 (Heine, *Origen: Commentary*, p. 99).

tainly *monogenēs*], and in the substance of the same, to any man or living thing engaged in such an act.[56]

Origen, following 1 John, repeatedly says that "God is light," and he speaks of the Son as the Father's "brilliance."[57] So we are not surprised that he likens the eternal begetting of the Son to brightness proceeding from the sun.[58]

In designating the eternal origin of the Son as his "eternal generation," Origen firmly cemented this way of speaking of divine Father-Son self-differentiation in eternity into the Alexandrian theological tradition, and for that matter into historical orthodoxy. However, it would be for others to eliminate completely the subordinationist elements in his theology.

ARIUS

In contrast to Origen, Arius (250-336) believed that God is an eternal monad who creates a Son in time.[59] His key text in support of his view is Proverbs 8:22 (LXX): "The Lord created me at the beginning of his works." For him the language of begetting spoke of God's willed act in time to *create* the Son. This foundational element in Arius's teaching, and for the later so-called Arians of the fourth century, raised the absolutely central issue of contention in this historical period. Is the Son of God a creature, *created in time* by God the Father, albeit unlike any other creature made by God, and as such *monogenēs*—a unique creature—or *eternally begotten* of the Father, one in being and power with the Father and thus the *monogenēs*—the unique Son, "true God from true God"?[60]

---

[56]Origen, *On First Principles* 1.2.4 (p. 247).

[57]Origen, *On First Principles* 1.2.7 (p. 245), 1.2.4 (p. 247).

[58]Origen, *On First Principles* 1.2.4 (p. 247).

[59]Once it was assumed that Athanasius was opposing the teaching of a historical Arius and a few of his immediate followers. Today the situation is taken to be far more complex. It is argued that Athanasius lumped together all those opposed to the Nicene settlement of 325 and collectively called them "the Arians." In this book I do not intend to enter this debate. For my theological purposes Athanasius's teaching on the eternal begetting of the Son and his theological method are my concerns. Of the many discussions of this issue I judge M. DelCogliano and A. Radde-Gallwitz, introduction to *St. Basil of Caesarea: Against Eunomius* (Washington, D.C.: Catholic University of America Press, 2011), to be the clearest and the best. However see also Gwynn, *Eusebians*.

[60]Athanasius, *The Defence of the Nicene Definition* 7 (p. 154), 9 (p. 156), 11 (p. 157). All quotations from Athanasius's writings are taken from *The Nicene and Post-Nicene Fathers*, ed. Philip

While the oneness in being and power of the Father and the Son was the primary issue in the fourth century trinitarian debates, the specific issue most mentioned and most contested was whether or not the Son was created in time or eternally begotten. The Arians argued that he was created in time and thus was not of the same being and power as the Father. All the Nicene fathers argued that he was *eternally begotten* of the Father and thus one in being and power with the Father and the Spirit.

I need to mention at this point why I have connected *being* and *power*. Everyone knows that the Arians subordinated the Son in *being*, but few realize that they also subordinated him in power: they were two sides of one coin. If he were less than God the Father in being, he was of necessity less in power. In their important study, *Early Arianism*, Robert Gregg and Dennis Groh argue that the eternal subordination of the Son in authority or power was the *primary* element in Arian theology.[61] They say, *"At the center of Arian theology* was a redeemer obedient to his Father's will, whose life of virtue modelled perfect creaturehood and hence a path of salvation for all Christians."[62] And, "The savior who the early Arians discovered in scripture and promulgated in their writings was never far from an obedient servant who followed God's commands."[63]

Similarly Richard Hanson writes that Arius consistently taught that the Son "does the Father's will and exhibits *obedience and subordination* to the Father, and adores and praises the Father, *not only in his earthly ministry but in Heaven.*"[64] And Robert Letham says much the same: "For Arius will is primary, rather than essence [or being]. The Son was an assistant to the Father, operating under orders."[65] In reply Athanasius, and all the Nicene theologians, insisted that the Father and the

---

Schaff and Henry Wace, vol. 4, series 2 (New York: The Christian Literature Company, 1892). Henceforth abbreviated as *NPNF* with the volume number following. What we see here is that both Arius and Athanasius could use the word *monogenēs* to mean unique but in reference to very different things. In quoting from *NPNF* I take some liberties of minor significance—for example, by modernizing the language and if needed by adding the Greek for a key term in brackets.

[61]Robert Gregg and Dennis Groh, *Early Arianism* (Philadelphia: Fortress, 1981).
[62]Ibid., p. x. Italics added.
[63]Ibid., p. 24.
[64]Hanson, *Search*, p. 103.
[65]Letham, *Holy Trinity*, p. 112.

Son (and the Spirit) are one in being and power. The reigning Son is not a servant set under the ruling Father.

What makes the Arian[66] debate particularly confusing is that in the early fourth century no distinction was made between being made or created (*genētos*) and being begotten or born (*gennētos*) and that only one Greek *n* distinguishes the two words used for these two ideas.[67] The Arians took these two words as synonyms. To be generated by the Father was to be created by the Father. The basis for their common assumption was that the generation of the Son was to be understood in terms of human generation: in time, contingent and resulting in an offspring external to the Father and other than the Father. All the Nicene fathers in contrast argued that, regarding the Son of God, there is a vast difference between being created in time and being eternally begotten.

Behind this debate as to whether or not the Son was created in time or eternally begotten stood the central and fundamental divide between the Arians and the Nicene fathers. The Arians all assumed a Greek understanding of God. He was a monad who could not share his divine being with another and so by necessity for them the Son was a creature, albeit more elevated than any other, but not God in the same sense as the Father. In contrast, all the Nicene fathers concluded on the basis of the New Testament that the Son is the exact image of the Father and as such, "true God from true God, one in being [*homoousios*] with the Father."[68]

ATHANASIUS

The most adamant, most persistent and most insightful opponent of Arius and the early Arians was Athanasius (296-373), who continued and perfected the arguments of his predecessor to the bishopric of

---

[66]The designation "Arian" like "Christian" was not a self-chosen title. Athanasius coined this term to denigrate the teaching of Arius and those he associated with him although he acknowledged they differed among themselves. The differences in teaching between these early Arians and between subsequent fourth-century opponents of the creed of Nicaea also called "Arians" by their opponents is very much to the fore today in scholarly discussions on the trinitarian debates of the fourth century.

[67]The words *genētos* ("created") and *agenētos* ("uncreated") both are derived from *ginomai* ("to become"). However, *gennētos* ("begotten") and *agennētos* ("unbegotten") are derived from the verb *gennaō* ("to beget"). On this matter I found the clearest discussion in Catherine LaCugna, *God for Us: The Trinity and the Christian Life* (San Fransisco: HarperSanFransisco, 1991), pp. 32-33.

[68]T. F. Torrance, *The Trinitarian Faith* (Edinburgh: T & T Clark, 1988), pp. 48, 69-75, 117-32.

Alexandria, Alexander (d. 328), had made to Arius's teaching. In reply to Arius they both insisted that the Son is not a creature willed into existence by a monadic God and that Arius misunderstood the Scriptures he quoted in support of his ideas. Athanasius clearly saw that to depict the Son of God as a creature meant he could not perfectly reveal the Father because he was not of the same divine *being* as the Father; he could not save, because only an omnipotent God can save, and he should not be worshiped because only God is to be worshiped. The importance of what was at stake in this sharp division over the Christian doctrine of God cannot be overestimated. The question was, Is Jesus Christ a god created in time, a subordinate God, or is he the eternally begotten Son of the Father, "true God from true God," one in being and power with the Father?

Athanasius's reply to Arius's argument that the Son was created in time and thus contingent and subordinate God is both logical and profound. In his *Discourses Against the Arians* he argues as follows.

- The God revealed in the Bible is not a monad who becomes a triad but is an eternal triad.

- To call God "the eternal Father" implies an eternal Son—no one can be called father without a child. In other words, the names, "Father" and "Son" are correlate terms that indicate an eternal act of self-differentiation within the one God.

- Fathers beget children of the same nature or being, thus the Son has the same divine nature, or being, as the Father. The Father and the Son are "one in being" (*homoousios*). Thus to dishonor the Son by arguing he is other than the Father in being is to dishonor the Father (Jn 5:23).

- It is impossible to separate and divide the Father from the Son. The Father cannot be separated from his "image," or "'Word and Wisdom," any more than the sun can be separated from its radiance or a spring from its water.

- The eternal Father-Son self-distinction is best understood in terms of an eternal begetting, an eternal noncontingent generative act *within* the life of God. It is not an act of "will" that produces something "external" to God.

- Scripture confirms that this act of divine self-differentiation is rightly designated an eternal begetting because it speaks of God as begetting a royal son and divine Wisdom before creation, both identified with the Son in the New Testament.

- However, human language is inadequate in understanding divine begetting. It is an "ineffable" act best likened to "light from light."

- Because the Father and the Son perfectly share one divine nature, the following rule applies: the same things can be "said of the Son which are said of the Father except for calling him Father."[69]

- Nevertheless the Father and the Son are not to be identified together: one is eternally the Father, one eternally the Son; the Father begets, and the Son is begotten.

I now spell out Athanasius's case more fully for the unity of the triune God and the full divinity of the Son, a case predicated squarely on his doctrine of the eternal begetting of the Son.

Greek philosophy had long used the term, "the Unoriginate" (*Agenētos* or *Agennētos*) to designate God. Arius followed this practice because it enabled him to sharply differentiate the one true and eternal God, the originator of all, from the Son, whom he held was originated in time. For him, God took the name Father when he created the Son. Athanasius says that Arius taught, "God was not always Father; but once God was alone, and not yet Father, but afterwards he became Father."[70] Athanasius in reply charges Arius and his followers with "irreligion," first, because they "borrow from the Greeks the term Unoriginate," thereby making the Son a "creature"[71] and, second, for denying that God is always Father. Following his introductory comments in his famous *Discourses Against the Arians*, Athanasius begins his case for the full divinity of the Son and the Fatherhood of God by first ar-

---

[69]Athanasius, *Discourses* 3.4 (p. 395), 3.5 (p. 395), see also 3.6 (p. 396); *The Councils* 3.49 (twice, p. 476).

[70]Athanasius, *Discourses* 1.2.5 (p. 308).

[71]Athanasius, *Defence of the Nicene Definition* 7.28 (p. 169).

guing that the Father and the Son are alike eternal. If both are eternal, he reasons, one cannot be considered unoriginated and the other originated God. It is "slanderous" and "blasphemy," he says, to say that "once the Son was not."[72] If there was a time when the Son was not, then there must have been a time when the Father was not because without the Father there can be no Son and vice versa. For Athanasius the names Father and Son are eternal "correlatives."[73]

In reply to Athanasius's arguments for the eternity of both the Father and the Son, Arius responded by saying that if this is so then there must be two "Unoriginates" and hence two gods.[74] Using a name for God "not in Scripture" is problematic on its own, Athanasius answers, but in this case it is doubly problematic, because the Greeks themselves do not have one agreed meaning for the word "unoriginated." One possibility is that the word means "what is not a work but has always been."[75] Given this meaning, he concludes, both the Father and the Son can be thought of as unoriginate. Another possibility is that unoriginate (*agenētos*) means "existing but not generated [*agennētos*] of any or having a father."[76] If this meaning is assumed, he says, then the term "unoriginated" can only apply to the Father. However, in the end he concludes that to divide and separate the Father and the Son in such a manner "dishonours the Son," and the Scriptures teach that "to dishonour the Son is to dishonour the Father" (Jn 5:23).[77] He thus rejects this "Greek" name for God, saying, "It is more pious and more accurate to signify God from the Son and call him Father, than to name him from his works and call him Unoriginate."[78]

Besides his argument that if the Father is eternal then so too is the Son, Athanasius makes a twofold appeal to the Bible to establish the eternity of the Son.[79] First, he points out that the "Holy Scripture" never uses temporal terms to speak of the Son "but rather [terms such as]

---

[72]Athanasius, *Discourses* 1.4.11 (p. 312).
[73]Widdicombe, *Fatherhood,* p. 160.
[74]Athanasius, *Discourses* 1.9.30 (p. 324).
[75]Athanasius, *Discourses* 1.9.31 (p. 324).
[76]Athanasius, *Discourses* 1.9.31 (p. 325).
[77]Athanasius, *Discourses* 1.9.31 (pp. 325-26).
[78]Athanasius, *Discourses* 1.9.34 (p. 326).
[79]Widdicombe, *Fatherhood,* p. 152.

'always,' and 'eternal' and 'co-existent with the Father.' And, 'in the beginning was the Word.'"[80] Second, he argues that the Arian slogan,
"there was once when he was not," must mean there was a time prior to
the Son's existence. What God has created, he agrees, is created in time
but not the Son; he is eternally begotten, not made. The Bible is adamant that the Son is the co-creator. He cites as proof many Old
and New Testament texts, including Psalm 145:3 (144:3 LXX): "Your
kingdom is a kingdom for ever"; John 1:3: "All things came into being
through him"; Hebrews 1:2: "through whom he also created the worlds
[*aiōnas*]"; and the Johannine "I am" sayings that "signify that the Son is
eternal without beginning."[81] Behind these arguments lies Athanasius's
fundamental premise. If the Father and the Son are both truly God,
neither is defined by time nor constrained by it. The Son has always
been and will always be.[82] Athanasius thus writes, "[When] the sacred
writers say, 'He exists before the ages' [*aiōnes*] and, by whom he made
the ages [*aiōnes*], they thereby clearly preach the eternal and everlasting
being of the Son, while they are designating that he is God."[83] It is this
understanding of eternity as "time before the world was created," time
outside of human time, that was enshrined in the Nicene Creed of 381,
in which the Son is said to be "begotten *pro pantōn tōn aiōnōn*" (before
all ages).

From what has been said, it is clear that Athanasius took as axiomatic that an eternal Father presupposes an eternal Son. He explicitly
makes this conclusion time and time again. For example, he says, "The
word 'Father' is indicative of a Son." And, "He who calls God Father,
thereby conceives and contemplates the Son."[84] He makes this same
point many times by the use of several analogies. Arguing for the
eternity of the Father and the Son, he asks, "When did man see light
without the brightness of its radiance?"[85] or, "Could a fountain be a

---

[80]Athanasius, *Discourses* 1.4.11 (p. 312).
[81]Athanasius, *Discourses* 1.4.12-13 (pp. 313-14).
[82]See further, E. P. Meijering, "*En Pote Ote Ouk en o Uios*: A Discussion of Time and Eternity,"
    Vigiliae Christianae 28 (1974): 161-68, and D. Bradshaw, "Time and Eternity in the Greek
    Fathers," *The Thomist* 70 (2006): 311-66.
[83]Athanasius, *Discourses* 1.4.12 (p. 313).
[84]Athanasius, *Discourses* 1.4.12 (p. 313).
[85]Athanasius, *Discourses* 1.4.12 (p. 313).

fountain without water?"[86] To which he replies, "God is the eternal Fountain of his proper Wisdom; and if the Fountain be eternal, his Wisdom must also be eternal."[87] And he insists that the Father cannot be without his "image."[88]

For Athanasius, the eternal Father-Son relationship implies and suggests an eternal generative act, the eternal begetting of the Son, an act of divine self-differentiation that results in the Son's sharing the same divine nature or being as the Father. This theological conclusion is, for Athanasius, suggested by Scripture and confirmed by Scripture when it speaks of the begetting before creation of divine Wisdom (Prov 8:25)[89] and of the begetting of a royal elect son (Ps 2:7),[90] texts that the New Testament writers read christologically. As additional confirmation of his theological conclusion he also appeals to several other christologically understood Old Testament texts that spoke of begetting: Psalm 110:3 (109:3 LXX)[91] and Isaiah 53:8[92] or of God uttering "a good word," Psalm 45:1.[93] Moreover, he rejects the Arian appeal to Proverbs 8:22 to prove that the Son is created in time, giving more space to refuting the Arian understanding of Proverbs 8:22 than any other text they quoted—thirty-six pages in the Schaff and Wace translation of his *Discourses Against the Arians* in *The Nicene and Post-Nicene Fathers*. His major objection to *their interpretation* of this one text is that in the light of the whole "scope" of Scripture it cannot be correct. For him it is clear the Bible as a whole teaches that the Son is not a creature, created in time. He is the eternal Son, ever with the Father, his very image; he is "the proper offspring" of the Father, "in all things like

---

[86]Athanasius, *Discourses* 1.6.19 (p. 317).

[87]Athanasius, *Discourses* 1.6.19 (p. 317).

[88]Athanasius, *Discourses* 1.6.12 (p. 318)

[89]Athanasius, *Statement of Faith* (p. 85); *Defence of the Nicene Definition* 13 (p. 158), 26 (p. 168); *Discourses* 2.32 (p. 365), 4.23 (p. 442).

[90]Athanasius, *Defence of the Nicene Definition* 13 (p. 158); *Discourses* 2.16.23 (p. 360), 2.21.57 (p. 379), 4.24 (p. 442).

[91]Psalm 45:1, "God utters a good word," is a text Athanasius frequently quotes in support of the doctrine of the eternal generation of the Son. See, for example, Athanasius, *Deposition* 3 (p. 70); *Defence of the Nicene Definition* 23 (p. 164); *Discourses* 2.21.57 (p. 379), 4.24 (p. 442).

[92]Athanasius, *Statement of Faith* 1 (p. 84); *Councils of Ariminum and Seleucia* 27 (p. 466), in this case, quoting others.

[93]Athanasius, *Deposition of Arius* 3 (p. 70); *Defence of the Nicene Definition* 13 (p. 158), 21 (p. 164); *Discourses* 4.24 (p. 442).

him"; "he and the Father work as one"; "he who has seen him has seen the Father."[94] Then, as supporting arguments, he argues more briefly the following three points.

1. The Arian proof text, Proverbs 8:22, is from the book of Proverbs and thus what is said "is not said plainly, but is put forth latently," the sense being "hidden."[95]

2. What is said in Proverbs 8:22 is "not signifying the essence of his Godhead, nor his own everlasting and genuine generation from the Father . . . but his manhood and economy towards us."[96] In other words, the text speaks of his creation of the man Jesus of Nazareth in time and space.

3. The *eternal begetting* of the Son is spoken of in Proverbs 8:25-26: "Before the mountains, and before the earth, and before the waters, and before all the hills, he begets me."[97] This text, he holds, makes it plain that the Son is not "a creature by nature and essence, but as he himself [God the Father] had added an offspring."[98]

Athanasius wants to exclude above all else the Arian idea that the begetting of the Son implies a creature and as such a contingent and subordinate god. Arius could speak of the Son as "begotten" (Greek, *gennētos*) taking this word as a synonym for "created" (Greek, *genētos*), but this was not acceptable to Athanasius. What God created in time is the creation; the Son is eternally begotten.[99] This is what makes the Son "unique" (*monogenēs*). Athanasius says that the Son is called *monogenēs* because "he alone is from him [the Father]."[100] The things God creates are temporal; the Son is the co-creator. The terms "begotten" (*gennaō*) or "offspring" (*gennēma*), which he endorses and uses repeatedly, he argues, speak of a father-son relationship, and in the case of the Father

---

[94]Athanasius reiterates these arguments time and time again in *Discourses* 2.16-22 (pp. 361-93).

[95]Athanasius, *Discourses* 2.19.44 (p. 372).

[96]Athanasius, *Discourses* 2.19.45 (p. 372). See also 2.20.51 (p. 376), 2.20.55, 56 (p. 378).

[97]Athanasius, *Discourses* 2.22.80 (p. 392).

[98]Athanasius, *Discourses* 2.22.80 (p. 392).

[99]Athanasius, *Discourses* 1.6.17 (p. 316), 1.13.56 (p. 56). See also P. Christou, "Uncreated and Created, Unbegotten and Begotten in the Theology of Athanasius of Alexandria," *Augustinianum* 12, no. 3 (1973): 399-409.

[100]Athanasius, *Discourses* 4.24 (p. 443). See also *Defence of the Nicene Definition* 7-11 (pp. 154-57).

and the Son, of an eternal Father-Son relationship.[101] Athanasius insists that the Son is begotten "from the being of the Father," reflecting the wording of the Creed of Nicaea (325). He says, "All things [may] be said to be from God, yet this is not the sense in which the Son is from God." He is "from the being of the Father" and thus he shares the Father's being.[102] And, to finally exclude completely the idea that the Son is a creature, a work of God, Athanasius argues that the Son's eternal begetting takes place *within* the life of God. Nothing is produced or created outside of God. "A work," he says, "is external to the [divine] nature, but the Son is a proper offspring of the essence."[103] Athanasius did not contrast internal and external divine acts using the later Latin terms *ad intra* and *ad extra*, but he certainly made this very important distinction before anyone else had even thought of the idea. The Son's begetting was for him a divine work *ad intra* to be contrasted with the divine works of creation and salvation *ad extra*.

Athanasius repeatedly calls the Son a "proper [Greek, *idios*] Son," by which he means, a son of the same divine being as his Father.[104] He is definitely not suggesting he is like a human son, a subordinate.[105] So he writes, "The Father always is, so what is proper to his essence must always be; and this is his Word and Wisdom."[106] The Son is "not foreign but proper to the Father's *ousia*."[107] And, "The Father always is, so what is proper to his essence must always be; and this is his Word and

---

[101] Athanasius, *Discourses* 1.5.16 (p. 316).

[102] Athanasius, *Discourses* 2.18.32 (p. 365).

[103] Athanasius, *Discourses* 1.8.29 (p. 323).

[104] Athanasius, *Discourses* 1.8.29 (p. 323). On Athanasius's very frequent use of the word "proper" (*idios*) see Widdicombe, *Fatherhood*, pp. 193-98; and A. Pettersen, *Athanasius* (London: G. Chapman, 1995), pp. 145-46. Athanasius uses this term to underline the coessential unity of the Father and the Son.

[105] Contra, M. D. Jones, *Athanasius' Concept of the Eternal Sonship as Revealed in Contra Arianos* (Lewiston, N.Y.: Edwin Mellen, 2006), who argues that Athanasius understands the divine Son to be like a human son, subordinate and obedient to his father. Indeed, he says, "the main focus" of Athanasius's *Discourses Against the Arians* (p. 220) is on the subordination of the Son! The only evidence he offers is to imply that by calling the Son a "proper Son" (Greek, *idios*) this is what he means; he is like a human son in relation to his father. The truth is that for Athanasius to call the Son a "proper Son" signifies the unique status of the sonship of the Son; he alone is one in being and power with the Father.

[106] Athanasius, *Discourses* 1.8.29 (p. 324).

[107] Athanasius, *Discourses* 2.18.32 (p. 365).

Wisdom."[108] The Son is thus "inseparable from the Father."[109] And, "The Godhead of the Son is the Father's; whence it is indivisible, and thus there is one God and none other than he."[110] For Athanasius the triune God is "simple," meaning "not composed of parts."[111] To be otherwise would be "a disparagement of the perfection of his essence."[112]

Because the Father and Son are one in essence/being on the basis of the Son's eternal generation, they are one in power. For Athanasius and all the Nicene fathers, as well as for all those they named "Arians," divine being and power were two sides of one coin. For the Nicene fathers, if the Father and the Son are one in divine being, then they are one in divine attributes, especially power. For the Arians, if the Son is less than the Father in being, he does not possess in full the Father's divine attributes, especially his power. Addressing the Arians, Athanasius says,

> The Father is eternal, immortal, powerful, light, king, sovereign, God, Lord, creator, and maker. These attributes must be in the image . . . the Son. . . . If the Son be not all this . . . he is not a true image of the Father.[113]

> He [Christ] is himself the Father's power and wisdom.[114]

> The attributes of the Father [are] spoken of the Son.[115]

> He is Lord of all because he is one with the Father's Lordship.[116]

For Athanasius divine rule, the *monarchia*, is triune,[117] and he opposes those who limit it to the Father.[118]

Widdicombe says that for Athanasius, "The Son possesses the divine attributes (things) in the same way as the Father possesses them, be-

---

[108]Athanasius, *Discourses* 1.8.29 (p. 324).
[109]Athanasius, *Discourses* 3.26.28 (p. 409).
[110]Athanasius, *Discourses* 3.23.4 (p. 395).
[111]Athanasius, *Discourses* 1.8.28 (p. 322)
[112]Athanasius, *Discourses* 1.8.28 (p. 322).
[113]Athanasius, *Discourses* 1.6.21 (p. 318).
[114]Athanasius, *Discourses* 3.23.1 (p. 394).
[115]Athanasius, *Discourses* 3.23.5 (p. 395).
[116]Athanasius, *Discourses* 3.30.64 (p. 429).
[117]Athanasius, *Discourses* 4.1 (p. 433).
[118]Athanasius, *Defence of the Nicene Definition* 6.26 (p. 167).

cause he is the proper offspring of the Father's being. He possesses them not in a transferred sense, but fully and properly."[119]

To claim that Athanasius actually teaches the subordination of the Son within the Godhead, in being, rank or authority, as many evangelical do today,[120] simply shows that those who make this assertion have either not read Athanasius or, if they have read him, they have not understood him. No one could be more hostile to the hierarchical ranking of the divine persons within the life of God than Athanasius. He has been criticized for many things but never for ambiguity in his opposition to or tolerance of the Arian thesis that the Son is eternally subordinated in being and power to the Father. Wolfhart Pannenberg rightly concludes, "Athanasius vanquished subordinationism."[121]

In support of their thesis that the Son was created in time, and thus contingently God, the Arians said the Son was created by the will of the

---

[119]Widdicombe, *Fatherhood*, p. 204.

[120]For example, Wayne Grudem, *Systematic Theology: An Introduction to Biblical Doctrine* (Grand Rapids: Zondervan, 1995), p. 246; Jones, *Athanasius' Concept*, pp. 33-34, 172-73, 220; M. Badderley, "The Trinity and Subordinationism: A Response to Kevin Giles," *Reformed Theological Review* 63, no. 1 (2004): 41; R. Doyle, "Are we Heretics? A Review of *The Trinity and Subordinationism* by Kevin Giles," *The Briefing* 307 (April 2004): 355; S. Kovach and P. Schemm, "A Defense of the Doctrine of the Eternal Subordination of the Son," *Journal of the Evangelical Theological Society* 42, no. 3 (1999): 465-67. Strangely, Millard Erickson, *Who's Tampering with the Trinity?* pp. 146-49, who opposes the evangelical teaching on the eternal subordination of the Son, thinks Athanasius teaches this. On looking up the five references he gives in support of his assertion I found that in none of them does Athanasius allow or endorse the eternal subordination of the Son. In the case of the first reference, taken from the Newman translation given in Athanasius's *Four Discourses Against the Arians* 2.20.54 in *NPNF* 4, the word "subordination" is found three times in five lines: once in reference to Paul's being made subordinate to the Gospel, once to John the Baptist's being made subordinate to "the Lord" and once to "the Lord, *not* being made subordinate to any reason." In none of these instances is the Greek word *hypotassō* ("to subordinate") or any of its cognates used. "Subordinate" is Newman's translation of the Greek *pro eautou* ("before him"), which can mean "in rank before." What Athanasius is thus saying is the gospel was "before" Paul in some sense, the Lord was "before" John the Baptist in time and rank, but the Lord had *no* one before him in any sense. The "no" (*oux*) before the *pro eautou* is to be carefully noted. While what Athanasius goes on to say about the Lord is convoluted and hard to grasp, he certainly does not even hint that the Son in relation to the Father is any way ranked under him. The four other references Erickson gives are all taken from Athanasius, *Defence of the Nicene Definition* (*De Decretis*), and all of them represent the opinions of the "Arians" Athanasius is opposing. They certainly speak of the eternal subordination of the Son, but Athanasius judges this teaching to be "blasphemous." What Erickson quotes in support of his belief that Athanasius can endorse the eternal subordination of the Son is precisely what Athanasius condemns as heretical.

[121]Wolfhart Pannenberg, *Systematic Theology* (Grand Rapids: Eerdmans, 1991), 1:275.

Father, like all human sons.[122] By saying this they were indicating their
belief that the Son is dependent on the Father's good pleasure to bring
him into existence and is thus less than the Father, like a human son.
Athanasius in reply writes, "For he who says, 'the Son came to be at the
divine will,' has the same meaning as another who says, 'Once he was
not,' and 'he is a creature.'"[123] The idea that the Son came into existence
by divine "will and pleasure" Athanasius finds nowhere in Scripture.
What this argument misses, Athanasius clearly sees, is that the Father is
"generative" or "fruitful" by nature. It is impossible to conceive of him as
a solitary monad. He writes,

> For if the divine essence be not fruitful itself but barren as they [the
> Arians] hold, as a light that lightens not, and a dry fountain, are they
> not ashamed to speak of him as having framing energy? And whereas
> they deny what is by nature, do they blush to place before it what is by
> will? But if he frames things that are external to him and before were
> not, by willing them to be, and becomes their maker, much more will he
> first be Father of an offspring from his proper essence.[124]

Athanasius will not allow that the eternal begetting of the Son should
be understood in terms of human begetting, except that in both cases the
one nature is shared.[125] He does not use the words "analogical" or "metaphorical" to describe human language used of God, but he clearly recognizes that human language used of God should not be taken literally, or
to use the technical term, "univocally." He writes, "The generation of the
Son exceeds and transcends the thoughts of man, that we become father
of our own children in time, since we ourselves first were not and then
came into being; but God, in that he ever is, is ever Father of the Son."[126]

In a similar vein, Athanasius repeatedly warns against speaking or
thinking about God in general—and eternal generation in particular—
in a "material" or "corporeal" (*sōmatikos*) sense.

---

[122]Athanasius, *Discourses* 1.8.29 (p. 323). In book 3 Athanasius devotes six chapters to refuting
the idea that the Son is begotten by the Father's "will and pleasure." See *Discourses* 3.59-66
(pp. 425-31).

[123]Athanasius, *Discourses* 3.30.59 (p. 426).

[124]Athanasius, *Discourses* 2.14.2 (p. 349).

[125]Athanasius, *Discourses* 1.5.27-28 (p. 322).

[126]Athanasius, *Defence of the Nicene Definition* 3.12 (p. 157).

> Further, let every corporeal inference be banished on this subject; and transcending every imagination of sense, let us, with pure understanding and with mind alone, apprehend the genuine relation of Son to Father, and the Word's proper relation towards God . . . for the words "Offspring" and "Son," are meant to bear, no human sense, but one suitable to God. In like manner when we hear the phrase, "one in essence," let us not fall upon human sense, and imagine partitions and divisions in the Godhead, but as having our thoughts directed to things immaterial, let us preserve undivided the oneness of nature and the identity of light.[127]

Athanasius's most favored metaphor to speak in human terms of the Father-Son relationship is that of light and radiance. He writes, "Let us not fall upon human senses, and imagine partitions and divisions of the Godhead, but having our thoughts directed to things immaterial, let us preserve undivided the oneness of nature and the identity of light. . . . The illustration of light and its radiance is the point. Who will presume to say that the radiance is unlike and foreign to the sun? . . . Truly the light and the radiance are one, and the one is manifested in the other."[128] Or again, "He is the expression of the Father's person as Light from Light, and Power, and very Image of the Father's essence."[129] And, "What is generated from the Father is his Word and Wisdom and radiance."[130] For Athanasius God the Father is light, and the Son is "light from light."

This "light from light" imagery, so important to Athanasius, is first found in Justin, next in Origen and Alexander, and enshrined in the Creed of Nicaea (325), where the eternal begetting of the Son is understood in terms of "God from God, light from light, true God from true God." These words affirm that the Son is from (*ek*) the Father, as the Bible teaches, but in divine majesty, being and power he is identical to the Father. His "fromness" in no way implies any diminution of divine being or power. Time and time again Athanasius insists that the Son fully "participates" (the Greek words are *methexis, metousia, metochē*) in

---

[127]Athanasius, *Defence of the Nicene Definition* 5.24 (p. 166).
[128]Athanasius, *Defence of the Nicene Definition* 5.24 (p. 166).
[129]Athanasius, *Discourses* 1.3.9 (p. 311).
[130]Athanasius, *Discourses* 1.5.15 (p. 315), 1.6.20 (p. 318).

the being of the Father.[131] If he participates fully in the one divine being or nature, then he is not less than the Father in any way.

Thomas Weinandy sums up Athanasius's doctrine of the eternal begetting of the Son in these words:

> The "begetting" [of the Son] is not by way of movement or alteration as if God changed from being simply God to being Father of the Son, and so was altered and mutated. Rather what the one God unalterably and eternally is, is the Father begetting the Son. The very begetting of the Son by the Father defines the reality or being of the one God. Again, as radiance from the sun does not sever the sun's *ousia* by way of division, so "we understand in like manner that the Son is begotten not from without but from the Father" [*Discourses Against the Arians* 2.33]. For Athanasius the very nature of the Father demands that he is unalterably the Father of the Son.[132]

Closely allied to the doctrine of the eternal generation of the Son, but not to be identified with it, is the doctrine of the *monarche* of the Father. For Origen the person of the Father is the one origin or source (*archē*) of the Son and the Spirit. This is not the case with Athanasius, who has his own distinctive understanding of the divine *archē* in relation to the Son. He can speak of the Father as the "origin" (*archē*) of the Son,[133] but by the time he came to write book three of *Discourses Against the Arians* we find him arguing that the Father and the Son are the one Godhead. He writes, "The Father is full and perfect, and the Son is the fullness of the Godhead."[134] "They are one, not as one thing divided into two parts."[135] "So also the Godhead of the Son is the Father's . . . and thus there is one God."[136] And making this specifically a

---

[131]Athanasius, *The Councils* 51-52 (pp. 476-78). On these terms see Widdicombe, *Fatherhood*, pp. 189-92.

[132]Thomas Weinandy, *Athanasius: A Theological Introduction* (Hampshire, U.K.: Ashgate, 2007), p. 75.

[133]Athanasius, *Discourses* 1.5.14 (p. 315). We should not, however, equate what Athanasius says on the Father as the *archē* of the Son with the Cappadocians teaching on the Father as the *monarche* of the being of the Son. Athanasius seems to come to believe that the triune Godhead is the *archē* of the three persons.

[134]Athanasius, *Discourses* 3.23.1 (p. 394).

[135]Athanasius, *Discourses* 3.23.4 (p. 395).

[136]Athanasius, *Discourses* 3.23.4 (p. 395).

trinitarian affirmation, he says, "We know of but one origin [*archē*]; and the all-framing Word we profess to have no other manner of Godhead, than that of the only God, because he is born from him. . . . For there is but one form of Godhead, which is also in the Word. For thus we confess God to be through the Triad."[137]

Later, in his *Synodal Letter to the People of Antioch,* he reiterates this point. He says, there is "a Holy Trinity but one Godhead and one beginning [*archē*], and that the Son is co-essential with the Father . . . while the Holy Spirit [is] proper to and inseparable from the essence of the Father and the Son."[138]

T. F. Torrance says that for Athanasius the *monarche* "is identical with the Trinity."[139]

What Athanasius achieved theologically with his doctrine of the eternal generation is quite breathtaking. In this one doctrine he was able to establish the full divinity of the Son yet establish that he is other than the Father as the Son. As a "proper" Son he shares the one nature or being and power with his Father on the premise that like begets like.[140] Thus in direct opposition to Arius's doctrine of Christ Athanasius will not allow that the Son is created in time (temporal subordination) or that he is less in divine being than the Father (ontological subordination) or that he is eternally set under the Father's authority as a submissive and obedient servant (relational subordination). And by this doctrine he was able to establish a theologically safe and sure way to eternally differentiate the divine Father and Son, a way that allows for no separation or division between the Father and the Son. He writes, "The Father is ever Father and never could become Son, so the Son is ever Son and never could become Father."[141] And he sees clearly

---

[137]Athanasius, *Discourses* 3.25.15 (p. 402); cf. *Discourses* 3.23.1 (p. 394); *Synodal Letter* 11 (p. 494); *On Luke 10:22* 6 (p. 90); *Statement of Faith* 1-4 (pp. 84-85).

[138]Athanasius, *Synodal Letter* 5 (p. 484).

[139]T. F. Torrance, *The Christian Doctrine of God: One Being Three Persons* (Edinburgh: T & T Clark, 1996), p. 183. See also Torrance, *Trinitarian Faith,* pp. 78-79, 241-42; John R. Meyer, "God's Trinitarian Substance in Athanasian Theology," *Scottish Journal of Theology* 59 (2006): 81-97; Letham, *Holy Trinity,* p. 145; and E. P. Meijering, *Orthodoxy and Platonism in Athanasius: Synthesis or Antithesis?* (Leiden: Brill, 1974), p. 8. Hanson, *Search,* pp. 434-35, comes to much the same conclusion.

[140]Athanasius, *Discourses* 1.8.27-28 (p. 323).

[141]Athanasius, *Discourses* 1.1.22 (p. 319), 3.27.36 (p. 413).

that the eternal begetting of the Son indelibly distinguishes him from the Father.[142] He writes, "One is Father, and the other Son; one begets, the other is begotten."[143]

Athanasius is rightly judged to be one of the greatest theologians of all time. His grasp of Scripture and theological acumen are amazing. There is a very small difference between the Greek homonyms, *genētos* ("being created") and *gennētos* ("being begotten")—one Greek *n*. However, Athanasius saw with absolute clarity that there is a huge difference, an uncrossable gulf, between speaking of the Son of God as created or as begotten. If he is *temporally created*, then he is a creature other than God the Father, less in being and power. If he is *eternally begotten*, he is of the same being and power as the Father. Nevertheless, because the Father eternally begets and the Son is eternally begotten, the Father is not the Son and the Son is not the Father for all eternity. More than anyone else, Athanasius laid the groundwork for a fully biblical and coherent doctrine of the Trinity. Nowhere is his contribution to this goal more important than his establishing of the doctrine of the eternal generation of the Son as the theologically surest and safest way to guarantee both the full divinity of the Son and his eternal differentiation from the Father, with whom he is one in majesty, being and power. To reject the doctrine of the eternal begetting of the Son, Athanasius concluded, opened the door to either "Sabellianism"[144] (what is today called "modalism") or to "polytheism"[145] (three separated and divided divine persons, in the case of the Arians, hierarchically ranked), which in both cases denies the eternal triunity of God.

THE CREED OF NICAEA

To complete this chapter a brief comment is needed on the "Creed of Nicaea" promulgated in 325, which is to be distinguished from the so-called Nicene Creed of 381, which is used in Western and Eastern churches today[146] and is technically designated "the Nicene-Constanti-

---

[142]Athanasius, *Discourses* 1.1.16 (pp. 315-16), 1.9.31 (p. 325).
[143]Athanasius, *Discourses* 4.24 (p. 443); cf. 1.1.14 (p. 314).
[144]Athanasius, *Discourses* 3.27.36 (p. 413), 4.4 (p. 434).
[145]Athanasius, *Discourses* 3.25.15 (p. 402).
[146]With one notable exception. The Nicene Creed speaks of the Spirit as "proceeding from the

nopolitan Creed."[147] For simplicity's sake, I speak throughout this book of "the Creed of Nicaea" (of 325) and of "the Nicene Creed" (of 381). At the Council of Constantinople in 381 the "faith of Nicaea" was reaffirmed in a creed with different wording at key points and with an additional clause spelling out the full divinity of the Holy Spirit.[148] I will comment on this creed at the end of the next chapter.

The Creed of Nicaea is the faith that Athanasius defended throughout his adult life at great personal cost. For him, it not only defined *what* was to be believed but also *how* the Scriptures were to be rightly interpreted. The Christological clause reads,

> We believe . . . in one Lord Jesus Christ, the Son of God, begotten [*gennaō*] of the Father, the only [*monogenēs*] [Son] of the being [*ousia*] of the Father, God of God, Light of Light, true God of true God, begotten not made; one in being [*homoousion*] with the Father, through whom all things came into existence . . . who for us and for our salvation came down and was incarnate and became man, suffered and rose again.[149]

Like bookends this clause speaks of the "begetting" of the Son at both its beginning and end, making it plain how important this matter was for the bishops at Nicaea. This begetting is defined as "from the being of the Father" and not a creative act (the Son is "not made"). The word "eternal" is not used, as it is in the 381 edition, but it is implied. For the bishops at Nicaea, what God makes or creates, he does in time. If the Son in his begetting is not "made" by the Father but rather is begotten "from the being of the Father," then his begetting is eternal. The begetting of the Son by the Father, the creed goes on to assert,

---

Father." At the third Council of Toledo, in 589, the words "and the Son" were added by the mainly Western bishops present. In Latin this is one word, *filioque*. The Eastern Orthodox churches have never accepted this addition and say the creed without it. See further my *Trinity and Subordinationism*, pp. 50-51.

[147]This creed was ratified again at the Council of Chalcedon in 451.

[148]For a fuller and specific account of the differences see J. N. D. Kelly, *Early Christian Creeds* (London: Longman, Green, 1950), pp. 296-332; Hanson, *Search*, pp. 812-20; and Letham, *Holy Trinity*, pp. 167-75.

[149]I give my own rendering of the Greek. The full text in Greek and slightly differently worded English translations are given by Kelly, *Early Christian Creeds*, pp. 215-16; and by Hanson, *Search*, p. 163.

means that the Son is "God of [*ek*] God, Light of Light, true God of true God." In other words, whatever the Father is, so too is the Son. Then comes the climactic statement, the Son on the basis of his begetting is "one in being [*homoousios*] with the Father." T. F. Torrance says that "an absolutely fundamental step" was made in the Christian understanding of God when the words, "one in being with the Father" (*homoousios to patri*) were included in this creed. It was, he says, "a turning point of far-reaching consequences."[150] These words clearly assert that *on the basis of the Son's eternal begetting* "there is no division between the being of the Son and the being of the Father, but also that there is no division between the acts of the Son and the acts of the Father."[151] They are one in being and power. Similarly, Carl Beckwith says that when the bishops of Nicaea included the term *homoousios* they not only "assert" that "the Father and Son are of the same essence" but also, "Whatever we predicate of the Father's being or essence, so too we predicate of the Son. This means when we say the Father is almighty, we also say the Son is almighty. When we say the Father is all-powerful, good, wise and holy, we also say the Son is all-powerful, good, wise and holy."[152]

In affirming that the begotten Son is "God from God" and "one in being with the Father," the bishops at Nicaea endorsed both divine differentiation and divine unity. What the Father is, so too is the Son; they are alike God, but one is the Father and one is the Son. The Nicene bishops also in this creed confess that while the Son is fully God in all might, majesty and power "for our salvation [he] came down [from heaven] and was incarnate and became man and suffered." The Lord of glory stooped to save. These two affirmations in this christological clause affirm both the eternal and unqualified deity of the Son and his temporal subordination for our salvation, reflecting the teaching of Philippians 2:4-11.

---

[150]Torrance, *Trinitarian Faith*, p. 144. See also pp. 132-45.

[151]Ibid., p. 137.

[152]Carl Beckwith, "Athanasius," in *Shapers of Christian Orthodoxy*, ed. B. G. Green (Nottingham, U.K.: Apollos, 2010), p. 160.

5

The Cappadocian Fathers
and the Nicene Creed

◆ ◆ ◆

Before considering what the Cappadocian fathers say on the eternal generation of the Son, it is important to note that on some important matters they differ from Athanasius. All the Cappadocians show the greatest respect for the great Alexandrian bishop and his work, but none of them derived their theology directly from him. They began as Origenists, having their theological roots in the school of Basil of Ancyra.[1] And they faced different theological opponents than Athanasius faced. Nevertheless, R. P. C. Hanson says that they learned three things from him: "They learnt the necessity of the doctrine of the eternal generation of the Son. They learnt to reject even the slightest approach to a subordination of the Son. And they learnt only by hard experience, the problem of language, the ambiguity of language used of God."[2]

"The necessity of the doctrine of the eternal generation of the Son" was fundamental for both Athanasius and the Cappadocians because they alike saw with absolute clarity that this doctrine ensured that the Son is to be understood as "true God from true God," not subordinate God created in time, yet other than the Father as the Son. In other words, this doctrine was central for them because it upheld what is central to the doctrine of the Trinity, namely, divine unity in being and power and divine threefold differentiation. On this basis they confessed Christ to be

---

[1]R. P. C. Hanson, *The Search for the Christian Doctrine of God* (Edinburgh: T & T Clark, 1988), pp. 677-78.
[2]Ibid., p. 679.

the *monogenēs*/unique Son because he alone is eternally begotten of the Father and thus of the same being (*ousia*) with him. On the foundational importance and implications of the doctrine of the eternal generation of the Son, the Cappadocians and Athanasius cannot be separated.[3]

The Cappadocians agree with Origen that the Father is to be thought of as the origin/source (*archē*) and cause (*aitia*) of the Son, but in contrast to Origen they insist this does not indicate any diminution in the being or the power of the Son. The *archē* of the Father speaks rather of the community of being/nature shared by the Father and the Son. Athanasius certainly insisted that the eternal begetting of the Son resulted in a oneness in divine being/nature between the Father and the Son, and on this basis he excluded any suggestion that the Son was subordinate to the Father in being or power. But it was the Cappadocians who emphatically ruled out, at least in reference to the Trinity, the Neo-Platonic premise, embraced by Origen, that the cause of anything is always superior to what is caused.

THE CAPPADOCIANS AND THE ETERNAL GENERATION OF THE SON

No topic gets more space than the eternal begetting of the Son in the writings of the Cappadocians. Basil (330-379) has a long treatise titled *Against Eunomius* in which the begetting of the Son is the major theme.[4] After Basil's death, Eunomius replied in his *Apology for an Apology*. Not content to let Eunomius have the last word, Gregory of Nyssa (ca. 340-395), Basil's younger brother, composed his own *Against Eunomius*, in

---

[3]In what follows these points will be substantiated. I am giving my conclusions as a road map for what this chapter is all about.

[4]When I began work on this book Basil's *Against Eunomius* had not been translated into English. I spent hours trying to translate some of the text as it is given in J.-P. Migne, *Patrologia Graeca*, vol. 41 (Paris: Migne, 1857) with the summary before me of the argument given by M. V. Anastos, "Basil's *Kata Eunomiou*, A Critical Analysis," in *Basil of Caesarea: Christian Humanist, Ascetic*, ed. P. J. Fenwick (Toronto: Pontifical Institute of Medieval Studies, 1981), pp. 67-136. When my book was at the editing stage the translation by Mark DelCogliano and Andrew Radde-Gallwitz appeared, *St. Basil of Caesarea: Against Eunomius*, Fathers of the Church (Washington, D.C.: Catholic University of America Press, 2011). Gary Deddo, my editor at InterVarsity Press, graciously allowed me to resubmit this chapter in the light of this new source with its superb introduction to Basil's work. All quotes from or references to Basil's, *Against Eunomius* in what follows are taken from this translation.

twelve books, and then when Eunomius made another reply he wrote, *Answer to Eunomius's Second Book.* In the first of these works by Basil's brother, the eternal begetting of the Son is constantly in focus. Finally, Gregory of Nazianzus (329-389), in Oration 29 and 30 of his *Theological Orations,* which he preached in Constantinople, makes the contested understanding of the generation of the Son the primary issue that divides him and Eunomius. Why do the Cappadocian fathers give so much attention to the doctrine of the eternal generation of the Son? On reading Eunomius's writings, one soon discovers the answer.[5] Right at the heart of Eunomius's *theo-logy* is the belief that God is "unoriginate" (*agennētos*) and thus cannot beget one of the same *ousia* as himself. In making this claim he denied what was at the heart of all pro-Nicene theology, namely, that God the Father is generative and that in eternity he begot the Son, who is of the same divine nature/essence/being and power as himself.

Eunomius (ca. 330-394) and his teacher, Aetius (d. 370), are usually designated today as "neo-Arians," or *anhomoians*—those who believe the Father and the Son are "unlike in being" (Greek, *anomoios*). Hanson speaks of them as "the radical left wing of Arianism."[6] Lewis Ayres calls them "the most subordinationist wing" of the so-called Arians.[7] Eunomius's thought can be summarized as follows.

1. God the Father is a monad who alone is eternal and as such is rightly called *ho agennētos,* which may be translated into English either as "the Unbegotten" or "the Ingenerate" or "the Unoriginated." The term *agennētos* for Eunomius was not just one attribute of God or a term human beings use to speak of God but was a definition of his essence/being. This is what makes the one God God. In making this assertion Eunomius claimed that human beings can know and define the essence or being of God.

2. Because God is *agennētos,* he cannot beget that which is generate: *agennētos* cannot produce *gennētos.* He can create something that he

[5]Given in R. P. Vaggione, *Eunomius of Cyzicus and the Nicene Revolution* (Oxford: Oxford University Press, 2002).

[6]Hanson, *Search,* p. 598.

[7]Lewis Ayres, *Nicaea and Its Legacy: An Approach to Fourth-Century Trinitarian Theology* (Oxford: Oxford University Press, 2004), p. 432.

calls "a son," but he cannot strictly speaking beget him. If God's nature is summed up in the term *agennētos*, then his nature is simple and not composite, and he can have no counterpart.

3. The Son for Eunomius must therefore be understood to be begotten in time, in the sense of created in time, by the will of the Father.[8] His proof text for this conclusion is Proverbs 8:22, which he repeatedly quotes. This begetting/creating does not involve the sharing or passing on of the divine *ousia*, which belongs to the Unbegotten alone. What the *Agennētos* causes or creates must be a "product" other in being than himself and external to him.[9] For this reason, the Son is unlike in being (Greek, *anomoios*) with the Father. Nevertheless, the Son is rightly called *monogenēs* ("the unique Son"), "since he alone was begotten and created by the power of the Unbegotten."[10]

4. Because the Son does not share the same *ousia* as the Father, he does not share the same authority as the Father and is ranked lower. He is simply "the perfect minister of the whole creative activity and purpose of the Father."[11] "He [the Son] is subject to him [the Father] both in essence [*ousia*] and will."[12] And speaking of the Father he says, "None inherit his authority with him, none share the throne of his kingdom."[13] And then of the Son he says, he "does not partake of the status of the one who begot him or share with any other the Father's essence [*ousia*] or his kingdom. . . . [He is] obedient in regard to all governance . . . because he is 'Son' and was begotten."[14]

---

[8] *The Apology of Eunomius* 7 (Vaggione, *Eunomius*, p. 41), 8 (p. 43).

[9] *The Apology of Eunomius* 9 (Vaggione, *Eunomius*, p. 43). Michel René Barnes, "Eunomius of Cyzicus and Gregory of Nyssa: Two Traditions of Transcendental Causality," *Vigiliae Christianae* 52 (1998): 62, explains it this way: "For Eunomius the transcendence of God requires that he cannot be understood to generate a product which has the same kind of existence he has, since that kind of existence is to be uncaused or unproduced, and any product will necessarily (i.e. by definition) be caused. The uniqueness of God's kind of existence means that any productivity must exist outside his nature."

[10] *The Apology of Eunomius* 15.3 (Vaggione, *Eunomius*, p. 53).

[11] *The Apology of Eunomius* 15 (Vaggione, *Eunomius*, p. 53).

[12] *The Apology of Eunomius* 26 (Vaggione, *Eunomius*, p. 71). On the indivisibility of divine nature and power, especially in Gregory of Nyssa, see Michel René Barnes, *The Power of God: Dunamis in Gregory of Nyssa's Trinitarian Theology* (Washington, D.C.: Catholic University of America Press, 2001).

[13] Eunomius, *The Confession of Faith* 2 (Vaggione, *Eunomius*, p. 151).

[14] Eunomius, *The Confession of Faith* 3 (Vaggione, *Eunomius*, p. 153).

Before selectively outlining what each of the Cappadocian fathers says on the eternal generation of the Son in reply to Eunomius, I raise two important matters that need to be highlighted if we are to rightly understand them. First, in direct opposition to Eunomius's rationalistic optimism, the Cappadocian fathers argue both that human beings cannot know the essence of God and that rational explanation and logic are not the pathways to understanding God.[15] In his initial response to Eunomius (and the other two Gregories follow him on this) Basil argues that human beings can have true knowledge of God and yet not know his essence, which in the end means that humans cannot know what it is to be God. What can be known about God, the Cappadocians argue, is revealed in the divine activities (*energeias*), works (*poiemata*) and in the particular characteristics of the three divine persons (*idiomata*). The source of this knowledge is the Scriptures and *epinoia*, a difficult-to-translate Greek term. Ayres says it means something like "the activity of reflecting on and identifying the distinct qualities or properties of something."[16] Mark DelCogliano and Andrew Radde-Gallwitz translate it as "conceptualization," taking it "to denote both the act of reflection and the concepts devised from it."[17] From Basil's comments on the name for God, "Unbegotten," we get an illustration of what *epinoia* involves. Basil notes that even though the term "unbegotten" is not found in Scripture, and it is the "primary building block" of Eunomius's "blasphemy," he accepts that God the Father may be rightly called "unbegotten." It is a term that reveals something important about God, and thus it has a contribution to make in seeking to speak accurately of God. The term does not reveal the essence of God, the Godness of God, as Eunomius argues, but

---

[15]On this matter see R. Letham, "The Three Cappadocians," in *Shapers of Christian Orthodoxy: Engaging with Early and Medieval Theologians*, ed. B. G. Green (Nottingham, U.K.: Apollos, 2010), p. 228.

[16]Ayres, *Nicaea*, p. 191. On this term see his extended and very helpful discussion on pp. 191-98. For all the Nicene fathers God's nature or essence is incomprehensible. God cannot be known like everything else in the created order. God is known in other ways.

[17]DelCogliano and Radde-Gallwitz, *St. Basil of Caesarea: Against Eunomius*, p. 48. S. M. Hilderbrand, *The Trinitarian Theology of Basil of Caesarea* (Washington, D.C.: Catholic University of America Press, 2007), p. 51 and 51 n. 7, however, translates *epinoia* as "concept."

through *epinoia* it indicates that God has no beginning—he is "unbegotten."[18] This term on its own does not encompass "the entire nature of God."[19] It does, however, tell us by *epinoia* that the being of God the Father does not depend "on any cause or principle."[20] To call God the Father "unbegotten" says what is "not present" in him; other names such as "just," "good," "Creator," "Judge," tell us "what is present" in him.[21] Second, on reading the Cappadocians one discovers that they make no argument for the begetting or generation of the Son or offer any scriptural support for this idea. The reason for this is that Eunomius and the Cappadocians agree that the Father is unbegotten God and the Son begotten God. Both presuppose a divine generative act that makes one Father and one Son. What they disagree on is whether or not the Son is of different being than the Father because of his begetting. Eunomius's argument for difference in being in effect is a syllogism. The major premise is, the Father is unbegotten God; this defines his being. The minor premise is, the Son is begotten God; this defines his being. And from this the conclusion follows that the Son is of another being than the Father. For the Cappadocian fathers, rational argument and logic are not ways of doing theology, and in any case Scripture, not logic, is the final arbitrator. They are convinced the Scriptures are unambiguous and emphatic; they teach that the Son is true God without any caveats, therefore Eunomius's logic must be wrong. However, on specifics they also disagree profoundly on what the begetting of the Son indicates. For Eunomius it means he is created in time, a "product" or "work" brought into existence by the will of God, exterior to God, other than God in being, less in power and lower in rank. In contrast, for the Cappadocians the Son's eternal begetting means that he is of the same being and power as the Father; he is not ranked below him and not exterior to him. The Father, the Son and the Holy Spirit share the most perfect communion of being.

---

[18]Basil, *Against Eunomius* 1.11 (p. 104).
[19]Basil, *Against Eunomius* 1.10 (p. 105).
[20]Basil, *Against Eunomius* 1.10 (p. 105).
[21]Basil, *Against Eunomius* 1.10 (p. 105).

Basil's *Against Eunomius*

DelCogliano and Radde-Gallwitz say that in Basil's *Against Eunomius,* "We see a clash not simply of two dogmatic positions on the doctrine of the Trinity, but two fundamentally opposed ways of doing theology. Basil's treatise is as much about how theology ought to be done and what human beings can and cannot know about God as it is about the exposition of the Trinitarian doctrine."[22] They also point out that Basil's work is highly rhetorical and polemical.[23] It is a critique not only of Eunomius's theology but also of him as a man, a point that cannot be missed on reading this work. In answering Eunomius, Basil proceeds by quoting a few lines written by Eunomius and then arguing against both the presuppositions and the content of what he has said. This means that Basil's work is not a systematic exposition of the doctrine of the Trinity but rather a reply to Eunomius that is directed by the matters Eunomius raises in his *Apology.*

Although Basil touches on important issues in the early chapters of *Against Eunomius,* much of what he says is invective against Eunomius's character and motives. In chapter five he turns to address the primary question put by Eunomius: if the Son did not come into existence by himself but was begotten, then he must be secondary to his maker.[24] Basil will have nothing to do with this "rational" argument, but at this point he says he will "postpone" his answer until later.[25] In Book two, chapter fourteen, he comes back to this matter, accusing Eunomius of seeking to explain divine begetting "in a human way."[26] For Basil, Eunomius's explanation of divine begetting in human terms involving both time and subordination cannot be correct because in John 1:1 the Word is with God and is God from the beginning. This text, he says, "connects the begetting of the Only-Begotten to the eternity of the Father."[27] The Son's eternity and divine status, Basil argues, is also indicated by the

---

[22]DelCogliano and Fadde-Gallwitz, introduction to *St. Basil of Caesarea: Against Eunomius,* p. 5.

[23]Ibid., pp. 5, 38-46.

[24]Basil, *Against Eunomius* 1.5 (p. 92). All quotations from Basil's *Against Eunomius* are taken from the DelCogliano and Fadde-Gallwitz translation.

[25]Basil, *Against Eunomius* 1.5.

[26]Basil, *Against Eunomius* 2.14 (p. 148).

[27]Basil, *Against Eunomius* 2.15 (p. 151).

Scriptures that speak of him as the light that comes into the world (Jn 1:19), as "the image of the invisible God" (Col 1:15), as "the radiance of the glory of God" (Heb 1:3) and as God's "wisdom" and "righteousness" (1 Cor 1:24-30).[28] God can never be without his image, radiance, wisdom or righteousness. If God the Father is eternal, then so too is the Son, and if the Son is eternally begotten, then he is of the same being and power as the Father.[29] For Basil, "corporeal comparisons" between divine begetting and human begetting that introduce ideas of temporality and subordination only "sully" what is clearly revealed in Scripture.[30]

Basil does not immediately answer Eunomius's question on how the Son can be begotten of the Father and yet eternal, raised in book one, chapter five, because he wants to concentrate first of all on Eunomius's central argument that the term "Unbegotten" (*agennētos*) defines the *ousia* of God. Basil, citing Isaiah 53:8 and Romans 11:33 and other texts in support, will not allow that human beings can define or know God's *ousia*, let alone that one term can do this.[31] For Basil all that the term *agennētos* indicates is that the Father is uncaused; it is not a name for God. In the Bible, Basil notes, God is called "Father" in distinction to the "Son," who is also God, and for this reason it is to be concluded that they are one in *ousia:* "The Father" and "the Son" are the names prescribed by Scripture, not "the unbegotten" and "the begotten." Later in book two Basil says, "I think there is no doctrine in the gospel of our salvation more important than faith in the Father and the Son."[32] The context makes it plain that he is saying these are not optional names for God; they take us to the heart of what the Christian faith is all about. For Basil, the names Father and Son indicate a community of being (*to koinon tes ousias*) between the Father and the Son, and a generative act in eternity whereby the Father and the Son are differentiated but in no way divided in being, power or rank. In support of the full divinity of the Son, he appeals to Colossians 1:15, Hebrews 1:3, Philippians 2:6 and

---

[28]Basil, *Against Eunomius* 2.16-17 (pp. 152-53).

[29]Basil, *Against Eunomius* 2.17 (p. 153).

[30]Basil, *Against Eunomius* 2.16 (p. 152).

[31]Basil, *Against Eunomius* 1.12 (pp. 108-9).

[32]Basil, *Against Eunomius* 2.22 (p. 163).

John 14:9.[33] Later, he likens the eternal begetting of the Son to "light from light." He says, "In as far as they are light from light, no contrariety exists between them."[34] They are one.

For Eunomius the word "order" (*taxis*) when used of the relationship between the Father and the Son indicates ranking in time and in honor. Speaking of the Father and the Son, he says, "One is first the other second."[35] In reply, Basil asks, "In the case of things whose substance is common, why is it necessary for them to be subject to order and to be secondary to time?"[36] There is no reason for this to be so, Basil says, because according to the Scriptures the Father and the Son are alike eternal and of the same divine being and power. To make matters clear he says a distinction must be made between "a natural order," which is "arranged for created beings," setting one before or above another, and a "deliberative order," which is simply conceptual or "logical," like "the kind of order between fire and light." In this case, the fire is the "cause" of the light, but the fire and the light cannot be either separated in time or in rank. The cause can be distinguished from what is caused, but "we do not separate these things from one another by an interval" or make one primary and the other secondary."[37] Eunomius's error, Basil concludes, is to impose human order, which ranks one person above another, onto God. There is, he agrees, an order in triune divine life, but it is "in terms of relation that causes have with what comes from them, not in terms of a difference of nature or a pre-eminence."[38]

Basil is particularly concerned to answer Eunomius's claim that John 14:28, "The Father is greater than I," teaches that the Father and the Son are not the same in being, power and rank. Basil argues that all John is indicating is that "the Father is greater as the cause [*aitia*] and principle [*archē*]" of the Son. "What else," he asks, "does [the name] 'Father' signify other than he is the cause and the principle of the one begotten of him?" Nothing in this text, he says, indicates that Jesus is

---

[33]Basil, *Against Eunomius* 1.18 (p. 118).
[34]Basil, *Against Eunomius* 2.27-28 (quote from p. 174).
[35]Basil, *Against Eunomius* 1.20 (p. 120).
[36]Basil, *Against Eunomius* 1.20 (p. 120).
[37]Basil, *Against Eunomius* 1.20 (p.121).
[38]Basil, *Against Eunomius* 1.20 (p.121).

speaking of the "pre-eminence" of his Father in being, power or rank.[39]
For Basil and the two other Cappadocian fathers the fact that the Son
is "caused" by the Father never indicates the Son's subordination in
being, power or rank. It speaks of divine order, not *sub*ordering. Specifically speaking of *being*, he says that the Son's eternal begetting in no
way indicates the Father's "pre-eminence according to [being] [*ousia*]."[40]
He who is eternally begotten is of the same *ousia* as he who begets and
thus of the same power and rank.

Basil is particularly hostile to Eunomius's view that the eternal begetting of the Son not only indicates he is other in being than the Father
but also less in "authority" and "sovereignty." For Eunomius the Father
and the Son are *not* of the same being (*ousia*) and thus not one in divine
power (*dynamis*); for Basil the Father and Son are of the same being and
thus of the same power. Basil writes, "If power and being are the same
thing [and he argues they are], then that which characterizes the power
will also completely characterize the being."[41] Commenting on John
14:28 Basil emphatically denies that these words indicate that the Son
is "less than" the Father in "power or according to pre-eminence of
dignity."[42] He then quotes 1 Corinthians 1:24, in which Paul calls
Christ "the power of God," and John 10:30, in which Jesus says, "I and
the Father are one." "The Lord," he says, "takes this *one* as equality in
power."[43] This is shown, Basil adds, by the fact that the Scriptures have
the Son sitting at the right hand of the Father in "equal honor" and
"rank."[44] In book two, in a very explicit section, he writes,

> Now there are two realities, creation and divinity; while creation is as-
> signed to rank and service and submission, divinity rules and is sov-
> ereign. Isn't it clear that the one who deprives the Only-Begotten of the
> dignity of sovereignty and casts him down into the lowly rank of ser-
> vitude also by the same token shows that he is co-ordinate with all cre-

---

[39]Basil, *Against Eunomius* 1.25 (p. 127).
[40]Basil, *Against Eunomius* 1.25 (p. 127). In this quote I have altered DelCogliano and Radde-
Gallwitz's translation. They consistently translate *ousia* as "substance." In this instance I have
changed their "substance" to "being."
[41]Basil, *Against Eunomius* 2.32 (p. 180).
[42]Basil, *Against Eunomius* 1.25 (p. 126).
[43]Basil, *Against Eunomius* 1.25 (p. 126).
[44]Basil, *Against Eunomius* 1.25 (p. 127).

ation? Indeed, there is nothing noble about being set at the head of fellow-servants. Rather, unless one confesses that he [the Son] is king and sovereign, and that he accepts submission [in the incarnation] not because of inferiority of his nature but because of the goodness of his free choice, this is objectionable and horrible, and brings destruction upon those that deny this.[45]

Elsewhere in book two, Basil comes to the other text Eunomius frequently quotes to give biblical warrant for his belief that the Son is created in time and thus other than the Father in being and power, Proverbs 8:22: "The Lord created me at the beginning of his work." In reply, Basil argues that this text does not indicate that the Son's begetting is to be understood as a "work" of God in time. He rejects his interpretation for three reasons. First, because only here in the whole Bible do we find such words. Second, because the book of Proverbs is full of parables and obscurities, and so it is impossible to build doctrine on what it says. And third, because the original Hebrew could be translated "he acquired me," instead of "he created me."[46] Athanasius, we should recall, interpreted this text to be speaking of the human birth of the Son. Basil's interpretation of this problematic verse reflects that of his episcopal predecessor, Eusebius of Caesarea.[47]

Although Basil makes constant appeal to Scripture it is important to note that he does not seek to establish the doctrine of the eternal generation of the Son by appeal to Scripture. He only mentions in passing the texts so often quoted by others in support of this doctrine, Psalm 2:7 and Proverbs 8:25, once in each case. For him, the Bible implies the eternal begetting of the Son when it uses the names Father and Son of the unbegotten and the begotten. He says that for Eunomius, "The term 'Father' means the same as 'unbegotten,' yet it has the additional advantage of implying a relation, thereby introducing the notion of the Son."[48] Then later, he says, "The notion of the Son immediately enters

---

[45]Basil, *Against Eunomius* 2.31 (p. 178).

[46]Basil, *Against Eunomius* 2.21 (p. 160). On referring to the Greek text I found that Basil does not give the Hebrew.

[47]Mark Cogliano, "Basil of Caesarea on Proverbs 8:22 and the sources of Pro-Nicene Theology," *Journal of Theological Studies* 59 (2008): 183-90.

[48]Basil, *Against Eunomius* 1.5 (pp. 93-94).

along with the notion of the Father. For it is clear the Father is the Father of the Son."[49] Thus to speak of the Son as "eternally begotten," Basil insists, indicates that the Father and the Son are of the same being (*ousia*). Because the names Father and Son presuppose a *necessary* eternal begetting, Basil consistently and emphatically rejects Eunomius's argument that the Son is begotten "by the will of the Father,"[50] which would mean the same as saying he was created in time and thus a "product" or "work" external to God. Basil does not argue for the eternal begetting of the Son or appeal to Scripture to support this doctrine because for him, if the Father and the Son are alike eternal, and one is rightly understood to be "unbegotten God" and the other "begotten God," then the eternal generation of the Son logically follows. It is a doctrine that arises out of reflection (*epinoia*) on the biblical revelation that God is the Father and the Son, names that suggest a generative act in eternity.

Basil definitely does not base his doctrine of the eternal generation of the Son on the Johannine use of the word *monogenēs*. Basil's understanding of this term comes into view when he disputes Eunomius's use of this word. Eunomius argues that the Son is called "the *Monogenēs*" because "he was begotten and created by the power of the unbegotten, as one from only one."[51] Basil rejects this understanding of the word. He says, "In common usage, *monogenēs* does not designate the one who comes from only one person, but the one who is the only begotten [*alla ho monos gennetheis*]"[52]—a solitary offspring. And then a little later he says that if Eunomius's meaning of the word was accepted, then it would mean that *monogenēs* no longer indicates "a lack of siblings but the absence of a pair of procreators." [53]

Basil does not make the distinction between *ousia* ("being") and *hypostasis* (which may be translated, "existence resulting from an act of

---

[49]Basil, *Against Eunomius* 2.12 (p. 146).
[50]Basil, *Against Eunomius* 2.13 (p. 147).
[51]Basil, *Against Eunomius* 2.20 (p. 159).
[52]Basil, *Against Eunomius* 2.20 (p. 159). Greek added to the DelCogliano and Radde-Galwitz translation.
[53]Basil, *Against Eunomius* 2.21 (p. 161).

generation,"[54] or "person,") but in book three, chapter three, he does speak of three divine *hypostases*.[55] However, in his subsequent writings he does make a clear distinction between *ousia* and *hypostasis*, and it is often said that this was his most important contribution to trinitarian theology.[56] In his more developed thinking, "being" (*ousia*) or "nature" (*physis*) designates what is common to the divine three and *hypostasis* what is distinctive, what makes Father, Son and Spirit divine "persons" of the Trinity.[57]

While Basil will not allow that the Son's eternal begetting diminishes his divinity in any way, he accepts and argues that because the Father is unbegotten God and the Son begotten God, they are indelibly differentiated. He says "Insofar as they are begotten and unbegotten, one observes the opposition between them."[58] However, he adds, this certainly does not "rupture the unity of the substance [*ousia*]."[59] For him, proper names indicate individual distinctive features (*idiotētes*) of a person; they do not say anything about being (*ousia*), as Eunomius argued. Basil was not the first to recognize that the names Father, Son and their synonyms, "begetting" and "begotten" signify divine differentiation, but in his later writings he advanced this argument significantly by developing the idea that these terms speak of differing relations. For him what makes the divine persons distinct from each other, and not just nominally distinct, is their mutual and exclusive relations, which are expressed by their proper names, which in turn indicate their relationships of origin. The name "Father" expresses a relationship having its correlative "Son," and the name "Son" expresses a relationship that has its correlative, "Father." These relationships can never change: they are essential to the person. Basil speaks of the particular originating relations of the three *hypostases* as "paternity" (*patrotēs*), "sonship" (*huiotēs*) and "sanctifying power" (*hagiastike dynamis*).[60]

---

[54]Ayres, *Nicea and its Legacy*, p. 209, quoting another scholar with approval.

[55]Basil, *Against Eunomius* 3.3 (p. 189).

[56]Hanson, *Search*, p. 690.

[57]Ibid.

[58]Basil, *Against Eunomius* 2.28 (p. 174).

[59]Basil, *Against Eunomius* 2.28 (p. 175).

[60]Basil, *Letter* 214.4 (in *The Nicene and Post-Nicene Fathers*, ed. Philip Schaff and Henry Wace, vol. 8, series 2 [New York: The Christian Literature Company, 1892], p. 254). Henceforth abbreviated as *NPNF* with the volume number following.

What is to be noted from this last paragraph is that, like Athanasius, Basil saw clearly the great theological importance of the doctrine of the eternal generation of the Son. This doctrine, rightly understood, affirms two fundamental truths basic to the trinitarian faith: the Father and the Son are one in divine being and power and yet at the same time indelibly differentiated as the Father and the Son; both are God without any caveats but one is "unbegotten God" the other "begotten God."

GREGORY OF NYSSA

In response to Basil's work, Eunomius wrote an *Apology for the Apology*,[61] which appeared after Basil's death. Basil's brother Gregory of Nyssa made a reply in his own book, also titled *Against Eunomius*, a long and discursive treatise, followed by his *Answer to Eunomius's Second Book*.[62] Like Basil, he first of all assails Eunomius's character and motives, in this case in twelve "chapters."[63] Then he goes to the heart of what he calls his "blasphemy," his view that the Father is "the Unoriginate" and thus the sole true God while the Son and the Spirit belong to "a lower order,"[64] and are thus "subject" to the Father.[65] This erroneous reasoning, he says, is predicated on Eunomius's belief that the Son and the Holy Spirit "belong to created existence."[66] Gregory's primary concern in his *Against Eunomius*, is to refute Eunomius's argument that causation and derivation indicate subordination in being and power.[67] In both his *Apology* and *Second Apology* Eunomius argues that God's essence is to be understood as "unbegotten" (*agennētos*), and thus what he causes is produced in time, external to him and subordinated in rank because it is of different essence/being.[68] The Son and the Spirit are "products" (*ergon*) of his power (*dynamis*) and activity (*energeia*). The

---

[61]See Vaggione, *Eunomius*, pp. 79-99.

[62]In all constituting 279 pages in the *NPNF* translation.

[63]Gregory of Nyssa, *Against Eunomius* 1.1-12 (*NPNF* 5:35-49. All further page numbers in reference to Gregory's *Against Eunomius* are to this translation.).

[64]Gregory of Nyssa, *Against Eunomius* 1.13 (p. 50).

[65]Gregory of Nyssa, *Against Eunomius* 1.16 (p. 53).

[66]Gregory of Nyssa, *Against Eunomius* 1.18 (p. 56).

[67]On what follows see Michel René Barnes, "The Background and Use of Eunomius' Causal Language," in *Arianism After Arius: Essays on the Development of the Fourth-Century Trinitarian Conflicts*, ed. M. R. Barnes and D. H. Williams (Edinburgh: T & T Clark, 1993), pp. 217-36.

[68]Ibid., pp. 217-20.

end result of Eunomius's thinking is a threefold hierarchy; the Father is ranked "supreme" because he is caused by none, the Son is ranked second because he is caused by the Father alone, and the Spirit is ranked third because he is caused by the Father and the Son.[69] Gregory will have none of this. The Son is eternally begotten, not created, not a work or product, and he is not "ranked" below the Father in being or power.[70] The Father, he accepts, may be thought of as the "cause" of the Son and the Spirit, but for him this allows for no division or "any unlikeness" in being or power between the three divine persons.[71] "Like the light that shines from the sun," the Son and the Spirit "are coexistent with the sun, whose cause indeed is in the sun, but whose existence is synchronous with the sun, not being a later addition."[72] In reply to Eunomius's assertion in his confession that the Son has "no share in the Godhead of the Father," he says Eunomius has to choose between denying "the Godhead of the Son or to introduce into his creed a plurality of Gods," both of which for Gregory are "impious" ideas.[73]

Next Gregory takes up, following Basil, what he considers to be the two fundamental errors in Eunomius's rationalistic thinking: first, that the *ousia* of the Father is to be defined by the term *agennētos* ("unbegotten, unoriginate"), and second that the divine *ousia* can be known. Gregory in reply argues that the title "Father" can have two meanings, one nonrelative, the other relative.[74] The Father is *agennētos* because he is from no one (the nonrelative sense), but he is also Father in that he generates a Son (the relative sense). Gregory then adds that because the Father exists for all eternity as the Father and the Son as the Son, the Son must always be thought of with the Father; without the Father there can be no Son, and vice versa. The two names are indivisible and correlative. What is more, he points out, the name Father means "having begotten a Son."[75] Here again we have the argument that to

---

[69]This wording reflects accurately the direct quotation from Eunomius's *Apology* given by Gregory in his *Against Eunomius* 1.13 (p. 50)

[70]This is his constant argument beginning in 1.14 (p. 51) and continuing to 1.36 (p. 84).

[71]Gregory of Nyssa, *Against Eunomius* 1.36 (p. 84).

[72]Gregory of Nyssa, *Against Eunomius* 1.36 (p. 84).

[73]Gregory of Nyssa, *Against Eunomius* 2.6 (p. 107).

[74]Gregory of Nyssa, *Against Eunomius* 1.38 (p. 88).

[75]Gregory of Nyssa, *Against Eunomius* 1.38 (p. 89).

name God as Father and Son indicates an eternal generative act. For
him the names Father and Son are correlative terms that imply the
words "unbegotten" and "begotten." Like Basil, Gregory does not argue
for the doctrine of the eternal generation of the Son or make it a dictate
of Scripture. For him, as with Basil, if the Father and the Son are both
eternal, and one is rightly understood to be "unbegotten God" and the
other "begotten God," then the eternal generation of the Son logically
follows. It is a doctrine that arises out of reflection (*epinoia*) on the biblical revelation that God is the Father and the Son, names that suggest
a generative act in eternity.

To claim to know the being of God, or "the manner of his generation," Gregory says, is "blasphemy." In reply to this Eunomian assertion, Gregory first of all returns to the matter of causation. He says,
"There are different modes of existing as the result of a cause."[76] Some
things caused are works of "material and art," as for example "the fabrics
of a house," others of "material and nature," such as the generation of an
animal, and in the case of the divine Son, "immaterial and incorporeal."[77]
The Son's generation is unlike "generation here below."[78] It is unique,
having had no creational parallels. In particular, Gregory completely
rejects the idea that the Son's begetting indicates a beginning in time or
a difference in being between the Father and the Son by way of human
analogy. He says, in speaking of the Son's generation we are to exclude
all human "affections and dispositions and the cooperation of time, and
the necessity of place—and, above all, matter, without which natural
generation here below does not take place. But when all such material,
temporal and local existence is excluded from the sense of the term
Son, community of nature alone is left."[79]

Basil will not concede that Proverbs 8:22 speaks of the begetting of
the Son, understood as a creative act prior to creation. He argues this
verse refers to the Son's incarnation, not to his eternal begetting.[80] The

---

[76]Gregory of Nyssa, *Against Eunomius* 2.9 (p. 114).
[77]Gregory of Nyssa, *Against Eunomius* 2.9 (p. 114).
[78]Gregory of Nyssa, *Against Eunomius* 2.9 (p. 114).
[79]Gregory of Nyssa, *Against Eunomius* 2.9 (p. 114).
[80]Gregory of Nyssa, *Against Eunomius* 3.2 (pp. 137-42). This interpretation of this problematic
verse is that of Athanasius.

eternal generation of the Son, for him, is not a creative act that produces something exterior and other than the Father but rather a Son who is of the "same nature" and "power" as the one who begat him.[81] He finds this clearly taught in Scripture, where the Son is called not only "the Son" but also "Right Hand," "*Monogenēs*," "Word," "Wisdom" and "Power."[82] He says that no "loftier" name than "Son" could be bestowed on him because "by it we learn that he is of the same essence as he who begat him."[83]

Gregory constantly attacks Eunomius's belief that because the Son is other than the Father in being he is other than the Father in power and "ranked" below him. For Gregory, because the Father and the Son are one in being, they are one in power and of equal rank. He says the three persons are not "relatively greater and less."[84] They have an "equality of honour."[85] It is absurd to speak of "less in perfection" in reference to the Son.[86] In line with the other Cappadocian fathers, Gregory argues that the Father and the Son are one in being and they are one in power and of equal rank. Speaking in trinitarian terms he says, "The Father, the Son and the Holy Spirit are alike in position of power to do what they will."[87] He is particularly hostile to Eunomius's claim that "as a result of being begotten that he [the Son] has shown himself obedient in words and obedient in acts" by nature.[88] He cannot be otherwise. In reply, he says the Scriptures attest to his "independent and sovereign power."[89] Then, addressing Eunomius directly, he asks, why ascribe "to the King of the universe the attribute of obedience" when he is coequal God?[90] For Gregory, subordination and obedience characterize the Son's incarnate existence "in the form of a servant" not his life within the eternal Trinity. He appeals to Philippians 2:4-11 in support of this conclusion.[91]

---

[81]Gregory of Nyssa, *Against Eunomius* 3.4 (p. 145), 3.7 (p. 150).
[82]Gregory of Nyssa, *Against Eunomius* 3.7 (p. 150).
[83]Gregory of Nyssa, *Against Eunomius* 3.7 (p. 150).
[84]Gregory of Nyssa, *Against Eunomius* 1.22 (p. 61).
[85]Gregory of Nyssa, *Against Eunomius* 1.24 (p. 66).
[86]Gregory of Nyssa, *Against Eunomius* 1.22 (p. 62).
[87]Gregory of Nyssa, *Against Eunomius* 2.6 (p. 107).
[88]Gregory of Nyssa, *Against Eunomius* 2.11 (p. 122).
[89]Gregory of Nyssa, *Against Eunomius* 2.11 (p. 121).
[90]Gregory of Nyssa, *Against Eunomius* 2.11 (p. 121).
[91]Gregory of Nyssa, *Against Eunomius* 2.11 (p. 121).

For both Basil and Gregory of Nyssa the Son's eternal generation does not produce something external to and other than God. The eternal generation of the Son is a necessary divine act *within the life of* God that results in a Son of the same being as the Father. He says the Son "exists by nature, by generation from him who is not alienated from the essence of him who begat him."[92] Generation, he adds, can be of two kinds: "of things generated from the essence itself, and of the creation of things external to the nature of their maker."[93] The eternal generation of the Son is of the former kind, an internal act, Scripture indicates, by speaking of "Father" and "Son," not of "Creator" and "Work."[94]

Finally, I mention that Gregory of Nyssa like Basil also recognizes that the doctrine of the eternal generation of the Son is of fundamental theological import because it presupposes the two basic premises of the Nicene doctrine of the Trinity: the Father and the Son are of one divine being, yet one is Father and one Son: one "unbegotten God," one "begotten God." After speaking of all the divine attributes Scripture ascribes to the Son, Gregory boldly states that we recognize "difference" between the Father and the Son, "only in respect to originateness."[95]

GREGORY OF NAZIANZUS

Gregory of Nazianzus, in his *Theological Orations*, Hanson says, "stoutly defends the doctrine of the eternal generation of the Son."[96] He begins his discussion of what it means for the Father to be unbegotten and the Son begotten by arguing that we Christians "honour" divine "monarchy" (*monarchia*), the belief that God's rule is unitary. He says, for us, God's rule "is not limited to one person." It is exercised by the "Trinity."[97] He then envisages an "objector" replying that the expressions "he begat" and "he was begotten" introduce the idea of a beginning in time that would chronologically separate the Father

---

[92]Gregory of Nyssa, *Against Eunomius* 4.6 (p.163).
[93]Gregory of Nyssa, *Against Eunomius* 4.6 (p. 165).
[94]Gregory of Nyssa, *Against Eunomius* 4.6 (p. 165).
[95]Gregory of Nyssa, *Against Eunomius* 1.33 (p. 78).
[96]Hanson, *Search*, p. 711.
[97]Gregory of Nazianzus, *The Third Theological Oration* 29.2 (*NPNF* 7:301. All citations of Gregory of Nazianzus are taken from this volume.).

and the Son. In reply to the specific question, "*when* did these things come into being?" he replies, "There never was a time when he was not, and the same is true of the Son and Holy Spirit."[98] The divine three persons are all "eternal." The Son is "from" the Father, "not after him."[99] Gregory then argues that the name "Father" is ascribed in an "absolute sense, for he is not also Son," and the Son is Son "in an absolute sense because he is not also Father."[100] These names indelibly differentiate the Father and the Son and make them eternal correlatives. Without the Father there can be no Son, and vice versa. Then he envisages the objector asking, did the Father beget the Son "voluntarily or involuntarily"; was he generated by an act of "will" or not?[101] Gregory replies that what is created is an act of the divine will; the Son who is eternally begotten is not an act of will. He is Son by nature. For Gregory, therefore, the Son is neither *after* the Father in time nor *less than* the Father in nature.

In reply to the next question, "*How* was he [the Son] begotten?" he says, "The begetting of God must be honoured by silence. It is a great thing for you to learn that he was begotten. But the manner of his generation we will not admit that even angels can conceive, much less you. Shall I tell you how it was? It was a manner known to the Father who begat, and to the Son who was begotten. Anything more than this is hidden by a cloud, and escapes your dim light."[102]

Like Basil and Gregory of Nyssa he believes that human beings cannot comprehend the eternal begetting of the Son or explain it in human terms. He says that the Father as "the begetter begat without passion, of course, and without reference to time, and not in a corporeal manner."[103] Gregory of Nazianzus is the most emphatic of the Cappadocian fathers on the incomprehensibility of God.

Next he considers Eunomius's assertion that "the Unbegotten" and "the Begotten" are not of the same nature or being. He agrees that the

---

[98]Gregory of Nazianzus, *The Third Theological Oration* 29.2 (p. 301).

[99]Gregory of Nazianzus, *The Third Theological Oration* 29.2 (p. 301).

[100]Gregory of Nazianzus, *The Third Theological Oration* 29.4 (p. 302).

[101]Gregory of Nazianzus, *The Third Theological Oration* 29.6 (p. 303).

[102]Gregory of Nazianzus, *The Third Theological Oration* 29.7 (p. 303).

[103]Gregory of Nazianzus, *The Third Theological Oration* 29.4 (p. 302).

"uncreated and the created" are not the same, but for him the Son is not created and thus is not a creature. He is begotten God, one in being with the Father. Thus in reply to Eunomius he says, "If you say that he who begat and he who is begotten are not the same, the statement is incorrect. For it is in fact a necessary truth that they are the same. For the nature of the relation of father to child is this, that the offspring is of the same nature as the parent."[104]

Gregory spends much time rejecting Eunomius's argument that because the Son is begotten and thus not of the same being as the Father that he is less in power and rank. His denial that the Son is "properly God" by his eternal begetting, he says, deprives the Son of his divine status "and makes him subject to the Father and gives him only secondary honour and worship."[105] It denies his "exact equality."[106]

He agrees that "in respect to cause, the Father is greater than the Son," but he rejects that this infers that the Father is greater in nature.[107] Rather, the eternal begetting of the Son infers that the Father and the Son have the same divine nature. They are both God without any caveats. The unqualified "deity of the Son" he finds clearly taught in the "great and lofty utterances" of Scripture that speak of him as God, of his preexistence, of him as "I am," of him as the power and wisdom of God, of him as "the reflection of God's glory and the exact imprint of God's very being," of him as the image of God and as Lord and King.[108] The texts quoted by Arius and Eunomius "in opposition to all these" biblical affirmations, speaking of his ignorance, his servant form, his obedience, his subjection, his prayer and even his death, he says, "may be easily explained." "What is lofty you apply to the Godhead, to that nature in him which is superior to suffering and the incorporeal, but all that is lowly to his human nature" assumed for our salvation.[109] Speaking specifically of his obedience and as-

---

[104]Gregory of Nazianzus, *The Third Theological Oration* 29.10 (p. 304). All the quotes in this paragraph are taken from this section.

[105]Gregory of Nazianzus, *The Third Theological Oration* 29.14 (p. 306).

[106]Gregory of Nazianzus, *The Third Theological Oration* 29.14 (p. 306).

[107]Gregory of Nazianzus, *The Third Theological Oration* 29.15 (p. 306).

[108]Gregory of Nazianzus, *The Third Theological Oration* 29.17 (p. 307).

[109]Gregory of Nazianzus, *The Third Theological Oration* 29.17 (p. 307). The same rule in different wording is also given in 30.1 (p. 309) and 31.2 (p. 310).

sumption of "the form of a servant," Gregory says this does not refer to him as "Lord and Christ."[110] To argue that "God be subject to God," he thinks is absurd.[111] He will not allow that the Son is eternally obedient to the Father. He sums up his case by saying, "To us there is one God, for the Godhead is one, and all that proceeds from him is referred to one, though we believe in three persons. For one is not more and another less God; nor is one before or after another; nor are they parted in will or parted in power; nor can we find here any equalities of divisible things."[112] For Gregory, the Son's eternal begetting is what distinguishes him as "unique" (*monogenēs*): "In my opinion he is called Son because he is identical with the Father in essence; and not only for this reason, but also because he is of him. And he is called *monogenes* not only because he is the only Son of the Father alone, but also because the manner of his Sonship is peculiar to himself and not shared."[113]

For Gregory what ultimately makes the divine persons distinct from each other, and not just nominally distinct, is their mutual and exclusive ontological relations, which are expressed by their proper names. The name Father expresses an ontological relation having its correlative—Son—a name that expresses an ontological relation that also has its correlative—Father. These relations can never change: they are intrinsic to the person. So he says, "Father is not a name of either an essence [*ousia*] or of an action, most clever sirs [Eunomius and his followers]. It is the name of a relation [*schēsis*] in which the Father stands to the Son, and the Son to the Father."[114]

Yet again—this time in Gregory of Nazianzus—we find the pro-Nicene conviction that the doctrine of the eternal generation of the Son affirms both oneness in divine being and indelible differentiation, and it excludes all thought that the Son is subordinate in being or power to, or ranked lower than, the Father.

---

[110]Gregory of Nazianzus, *The Third Theological Oration* 30.3 (p. 310).
[111]Gregory of Nazianzus, *The Third Theological Oration* 30.5 (p. 311).
[112]Gregory of Nazianzus, *The Third Theological Oration* 32.14 (p. 322)
[113]Gregory of Nazianzus, *The Third Theological Oration* 30.20 (p. 316).
[114]Gregory of Nazianzus, *The Third Theological Oration* 29.16 (p. 307).

THE FATHER AS THE CAUSE (*AITIA*) AND ORIGIN/SOURCE (*ARCHĒ*) OF THE SON AND THE SPIRIT

All the Cappadocians following Origen depict the Father as "the cause" (*aitia*) and "the source" or "origin" (*archē*) of the Son and the Spirit. They see this language implied in speaking of the Father as "unbegotten God" and the Son as "begotten God" and of the Spirit as "proceeding" from the Father. However, in contrast to Origen they will not allow that causation in divine life implies or indicates the subordination of what is caused. We have already noticed that Basil argues that fire is the "cause" of light and Gregory of Nyssa that the sun is the "cause" of light, and in neither case can the light be separated or subordinated in time or rank to what caused it. And we have observed that the Cappadocians are united and emphatic that the Son is of the same being, power and rank as the Father. Oneness in divine being is what unites them as equals, and this is predicated on the Father as the *archē* and the eternal begetter of the Son, which results in their oneness in power, inseparable operations, unity of will, and mutual indwelling (*perichōrēsis*).

The Cappadocian fathers' complete rejection of the Eunomian teaching that the Son is created in time, that he is contingent God, and thus subordinated in being and power is almost universally commended, but the way they speak of the Father as the *Monarche* (*mia arche*) of the Son and the Spirit has been criticized widely by Western theologians.[115] The argument is that in speaking of the Father in this way at the very least conceptually gives pre-eminence to the Father. Even one of their number saw this possibility. Gregory of Nazianzus says,

> I am afraid to use the word origin (*arche*), lest I should make him [the person of Father] the origin of inferiors, and thus insult him by precedence of honor. For the lowering of those who are from him is no glory to the source.[116]

---

[115]Prestige, *God in Patristic Thought*, p. 249; Fortman, *The Triune God*, p. 282; Pannenberg, *Systematic Theology*, vol. 1, pp. 279-80; Robert Letham, *The Holy Trinity in Scripture, History, Theology, and Worship* (Phillipsburg, N.J.: P & R, 2004), pp. 7, 179, 377; Torrance, *The Christian Doctrine*, pp. 180-85. On Torrance's criticism see P. Molnar, *Thomas F. Torrance, Theologian of the Trinity* (Surrey, U.K.: Ashgate, 2009), pp. 214-17.

[116]*NPNF*, 7, "Theological Orations," 5.43 (p. 376).

Conceptually the *Monarche* model of the Trinity may have its weaknesses but we need to note that the Cappadocian fathers were totally opposed to any hierarchical ranking in divine life. Basil speaks unambiguously, "Those who teach subordinationism, and talk about first, second and third, ought to recognize they are introducing erroneous Greek polytheism into pure Christian theology. . . . Subordination cannot be used to describe persons who share the same nature."[117] Gregory of Nyssa likewise says, "We do not know of any difference by way of superiority and inferiority in attributes which express our conceptions of the divine nature."[118] Gregory of Nazianzus is even more emphatic. Speaking against the teaching of the long-dead Arius, he says, "For he did not honour the Father, by dishonouring his Offspring with his unequal degrees of Godhead. But we recognise one glory of the Father, the equality of the Only-begotten; and one glory of the Son and the Spirit. And we hold that to subordinate any of the three is to destroy the whole."[119] And again, "The one Godhead and power found in the three in unity, and comprising the three separately, not unequal in substance or natures, neither increased nor diminished by superiorities or inferiorities; in every respect equal, in every respect the same."[120] And, quite explicitly and forcibly Gregory of Nazianzus says, "That which is from such a cause is not inferior to that which has no cause; for it would share the glory of the Unoriginate, because it is from the Unoriginate."[121]

Letham, summing up the contribution of the Cappadocian fathers, says that for them, "All three persons are God in themselves. None is more and none is less God than the others. Hence Kelly comments that "as stated by the Cappadocians, the idea of the twofold procession from the Father through the Son lacks all traces of subordinationism."[122]

Therefore, to argue that in speaking of the Father as the "begetter," "cause" or "origin" of the Son, the Cappadocians introduced an element

---

117In this quote I give the translation by David Anderson, *St. Basil the Great: On the Holy Spirit* (New York: St. Vladimir's Seminary Press, 1980), p. 75. Cf. Basil, *On the Spirit* 47 (*NPNF* 8:30).

118Gregory of Nyssa, *On the Holy Trinity* (*NPNF* 5:327).

119Gregory of Nazianzus, *The Panegyric on St. Basil* 30 (*NPNF* 7:405).

120Gregory of Nazianzus, *Oration on Holy Baptism* 40.41 (*NPNF* 7:375).

121Gregory of Nazianzus, *Fourth Theological Oration* (*NPNF* 7:312).

122Robert Letham, *The Holy Trinity in Scripture, History, Theology, and Worship* (Phillipsburg, N.J.: Presbyterian and Reformed, 2004), p. 165.

of subordinationism or hierarchical ordering in divine life that was mistaken. For all of the three Cappadocian fathers, speaking of the Father as the "cause" and "origin" of the Son, on the basis of the Father's eternal generation of the Son, affirms that the Father and the Son share perfectly the one divine being and are thus one in power and equal in rank and divine dignity.

To Sum Up

For the Cappadocian fathers, like Athanasius, the doctrine of the eternal generation of the Son was foundational and central in their quest to articulate the Christian doctrine of God in the light of scriptural revelation. Working somewhat independently of Athanasius, they concluded that the Father's eternal begetting of the Son is a noncontingent divine act within the life of God that results in the Father and the Son sharing perfectly the one divine being and power. They spoke of the Father as the "cause" and "origin" of the Son, but they excluded completely any suggestion that to be caused indicated any subordination. Ayres, summarizing the "pro-Nicene" doctrine of the Trinity as expressed in the latter part of the fourth century, says it is characterized by three elements.

1. A clear version of the person-and-nature distinction, entailing the principle that whatever is predicated of the divine nature is predicated of the three persons equally and understood to be one;

2. Clear expression that the eternal generation of the Son occurs within the unitary and incomprehensible divine being;

3. Clear expression of the doctrine that the persons work inseparably.[123]

THE WORD *MONOGENĒS* IN THE GREEK-SPEAKING FATHERS

We noted above that Eunomius and Basil both call the Son *monogenēs* and speak of him as *the Monogenēs,* as do the other two Cappadocians. They agree that the word means "unique" or "only," but they differ profoundly on what makes the Son unique. For the Cappadocians and

---

[123]Ayres, *Nicaea,* p. 236.

the other Greek-speaking fathers we have discussed, Justin, Origen, Alexander and Athanasius, Christ is called *monogenēs* to highlight his uniqueness as the only begotten Son, one in being/nature with the Father. They do not take it as a synonym for *gennaō* ("to beget"), and they do not quote the Johannine texts where this word is found to support the doctrine of the eternal begetting of the Son. For them, the Son is *monogenēs*, unique, primarily because he alone is begotten of the Father and thus one in being with him. In other words, in the Greek-speaking fathers the word *monogenēs* is given specific theological content. It alludes to what singles out the Son of God from everything else in creation. He is begotten, not created, one in being with the Father. In short, he is "the only begotten Son" (of the Father). This explains why modern scholars, competent in the Greek language and well aware of the lexical meaning of this word, support the theological translation of the word *monogenēs* as "only begotten."[124]

When Justin calls the Son *monogenēs* he is obviously stressing that Jesus is God's unique or only Son.[125] In Origen, when the Son is called "his [God's] only-begotten" (Latin, *unigenitus*), the Greek original is almost certainly *monogenēs*. This is suggested because Origen consistently uses this title as a lofty name for the Son.[126] It is the same in the writings of Bishop Alexander. He uses the word to speak of the Son's uniqueness; he never equates the terms *gennaō* and

---

[124]So Letham, *Holy Trinity*, p. 384. On this page in Letham see also n. 12, where he lists other scholars who have reached this same conclusion. Near the completion of this book I wrote to Dr. Mark DelCogliano by email to ask him to comment on his translation of *monogenēs* as "Only Begotten" in his and Andrew Radde-Gallwitz's translation of *St. Basil of Caesarea: Against Eunomius*. This is his reply. "Of course, you are right about the translation of *Monogenes* [it primarily means unique or only]. I remember when beginning the project we toyed with translating the term as 'only' or 'unique,' in line with modern biblical translations. This led to what seemed to us odd substantive usages such as, 'Only One,' but at least it was accurate, we thought. But the more we thought about it, we thought that Basil (as well as others) really understood the term in the sense of 'only offspring of the Father'—what we here in the states would call an 'only child' (see *Contra Eunomius* 2.20-21). And we thought that this understanding of the term accorded well with the traditional translation of 'Only-Begotten.' So that's why we chose that translation of *Monogenes*." Dr. Cogliano gave me permission to quote him.

[125]Justin Martyr, *Dialogue with Trypho* 105.1 (*The Ante-Nicene Fathers*, ed. A. Coxe and A. Roberts, vol. 1 [Buffalo: Christian Literature Publishing, 1885], p. 251. Hereafter *ANF* with volume number following.).

[126]Origen, *On First Principles* 2.1.2 (*ANF* 4:246).

monogenēs, and he does not appeal to Johannine texts that use the word *monogenēs* to support his doctrine of the eternal generation of the Son.[127] It is exactly the same in Athanasius's writings. He uses *gennaō* to speak of the eternal begetting of the Son and *monogenēs* to speak of the Son's uniqueness.[128]

In *Against Eunomius,* as noted above, Basil argues that the Son is *monogenēs* because he lacks siblings,[129] by which he means he is the *only* Son begotten of the divine Father. Later in *On the Spirit,* speaking of the unparalleled dignity of the Son, he extolls "the majesty of the *monogenēs,* and of the equality of his glory with the Father."[130] And then a little later in this work he lists the Son's noble and distinctive names, which set him apart as unique, among which he mentions *monogenēs.*[131] In one of his letters, in saying why the Son is rightly worshiped as God, he speaks of him as the *Monogenēs,* who uniquely was in the bosom of the Father before he became man, quoting John 1:18.[132] Likewise, Gregory of Nyssa frequently uses *monogenēs* to speak of Jesus as the only or unique Son, because he alone is eternally begotten of the Father and thus one in being with him. In *Against Eunomius,* he devotes a whole chapter to the uniqueness of Christ, in which he frequently uses this word as title for Christ.[133]

Arius and the later so-called Arians, including Eunomius, also speak of the Son as *monogenēs,* and they too indicate that they understand the word to indicate the uniqueness of the Son. However, for them the Son is unique solely because he alone was created directly by God; all other begotten or created beings were made through the Son as by an instrument.[134] The contrasting understandings of the Son's uniqueness are

---

[127]Athanasius's theology reflects closely that of Bishop Alexander. He too explicitly uses *monogenēs* to speak of the unique Son. See T. E. Pollard, *Johannine Christology and the Early Church* (Cambridge: Cambridge University Press, 1970), pp. 158-59.

[128]See particularly Athanasius, *Discourses Against the Arians* 4.24 (*NPNF* 4:443). See also Athanasius, *Defence of the Nicene Definition* 1.6 (p. 154), 1.7 (pp. 154-57), 1.9 (p. 156), 3.11 (p. 157).

[129]Basil, *Against Eunomius* 2.21 (p. 161).

[130]Basil, *On the Spirit* 6.15 (*NPNF* 8:9).

[131]Basil, *On the Spirit* 8.17 (*NPNF* 8:11).

[132]Basil, *Letters* 234.3 (*NPNF* 8:274).

[133]Gregory of Nyssa, *Against Eunomius* 2.8 (*NPNF* 5:112-13).

[134]For more on this see O. Skarsaune, "A Neglected Detail in the Creed of Nicea (325)," *Vigiliae Christianae* 41 (1987): 40-41.

thus clear. For all the Arians the Son is *monogenēs* because he is uniquely created directly by God; for all the Nicene fathers the Son is *monogenēs* because the Son is uniquely and eternally begotten, not created, and as such is of the same divine being and power as the Father.

Wayne Grudem argues that the doctrine of the eternal generation of the Son lacks biblical warrant because the Greek-speaking church fathers grounded this doctrine on appeals to Johannine texts using the word *monogenēs* of the Son, believing the word meant "begotten." He cites a clause from the Nicene Creed of 381 as proof of this assertion. He says that in this creed "'begotten of the Father before all worlds' and 'begotten not made' use the verb *gennao* (beget) to explain *monogenes*."[135] This, as we have seen, is not the case. True, most of the many creeds of the fourth century use both terms in close proximity, but none of them take *monogenēs* as a synonym of *gennaō*. In speaking of the Son's uniqueness they use *monogenēs*, and in speaking of the eternal generation of the Son they use *gennaō*.

In an early creed, originating from Alexandria and usually attributed to Athanasius, we find an example of *monogenēs* and *gennaō* in proximity expressing two separate affirmations about the Son: namely, that he is (1) the unique and only Word or Son, and (2) he is eternally begotten of the Father: "We believe in . . . one only [*monogenēs*] Word, Wisdom, Son, begotten [*gennaō*] of the Father without beginning eternally."[136]

In the creed of the Council of Nicaea (325), the word *monogenēs* modifies the phrase "begotten of the Father" and means "only" or "unique." The clause can be translated either as

> We believe . . . in one Lord Jesus Christ, the Son of God, begotten [*gennaō*] of the Father, the only [*monogenēs*] [Son] of the being [*ousia*] of the Father.[137]

[135]Wayne Grudem, "Appendix 6," in *Systematic Theology: An Introduction to Biblical Doctrine*, rev. ed. (Grand Rapids: Zondervan, 2000), p. 1233.

[136]Athanasius, *Statement of Faith* (*NPNF* 4:84).

[137]The translation is difficult because the added anti-Arian words "that is from the being of the Father" (*toutestin ek tes ousias tous patros*), break the flow of the clause. There are several good discussions of this problem. See Pollard, *Johannine Christology*, pp. 166-88; Skarsaune, "A Neglected Detail," pp. 35-37; J. N. D. Kelly, *Early Christian Creeds* (London: Longman, 1972), pp. 215-16.

Or as,

> We believe . . . in one Lord Jesus Christ, the Son of God, uniquely [*mono-genes*] begotten [*gennaō*] of the Father, of the being [*ousia*] of the Father.[138]

In the first translation the Son is confessed as begotten and unique, in the second as the uniquely begotten Son. But whichever translation is preferred, the terms *monogenēs* and *gennaō* in this creed are not synonyms.

Contra Grudem, the Nicene Creed of 381 makes two complementary assertions. The Son is the unique, or only, Son, and he is the eternally begotten Son. The Creed reads,

> We believe in one Lord, Jesus Christ, the only Son of God [*monogenēs*], eternally begotten [*gennaō*] of the Father . . . begotten [*gennaō*] not made.

There are other fourth-century creeds,[139] but none of them make *gennaō* and *monogenēs* synonyms, and thus none of them equate these two words, even if it is clear that one informs the other. The Son is *monogenēs* because he alone is eternally begotten of the Father and as such is one in being with him.

THE CREED OF 381

Before concluding this chapter, I return to where we ended with the Cappadocians. Their efforts won the day. At the Council of Constantinople in 381 a new form of the Creed of Nicaea was ratified. This is the so-called Nicene Creed, which is used in Western and Eastern churches today. It is technically designated "the Nicene-Constantinopolitan Creed" and was again ratified at the Council of Chalcedon in 451. In this creed the Son is communally confessed in these words.

> We believe in one Lord, Jesus Christ, the only [*monogenēs*] Son of God, eternally begotten of the Father, God from God, Light from Light, true God from true God, begotten not made, of one being [*homoousion*] with the Father. Through him all things were made. For us and our salvation

---

[138]In advocating this translation Pollard argues that *monogenēs* in this sentence should be taken "adverbially."

[139]See Kelly, *Early Christian Creeds*, pp. 296-332; Hanson, *Search*, pp. 812-20, 215-16; Skarsaune, "A Neglected Detail," pp. 35-42.

he came down from heaven, by the power of the Spirit he was incarnate of the Virgin Mary, and became man.

The intent of the clause "God from [*ek*] God, Light from Light, true God from true God" demands comment. So often these words have been thought to indicate that the compilers of the creed are here teaching that the Son is "derived from" the Father and is thus contingent and subordinate God.[140] To speak of the Son as "from" the Father certainly has generative sense and is appropriate given the names Father and Son and the belief that the Son is eternally begotten of the Father. However, these words were in fact included in the creed to explicitly refute the Arian assertion that the Son's begetting was a creation in time "from nothing" and thus that he is other than God the Father in being and power. This clause seeks to exclude the thought that the Son's "fromness" or eternal generation implies any diminution in divine being or power. J. N. D. Kelly, speaking of the identical words in the 325 Creed of Nicaea says, "God from God, light from light, true God from true God" is "a deliberately formulated counter-blast to the principal tenet of Arianism, that the Son had been created out of nothing and had no community of being with the Father."[141] Michel René Barnes calls this clause in the 325 and 381 creeds "the X from X" argument.[142] "True God from true God" defines what it means to be the eternally begotten of the Father. He is God in the same sense as God the Father, yet he is the Son.

Commenting on the affirmation and inclusion of the term *homoousios* ("one in being") in this creed, Letham says it thus follows that "there is only one essence or being, which the three persons share completely. Furthermore, each person is God in himself. There is nothing in the creed (C [of Constantinople]) to suggest that the Son or the

---

[140]For example, Wayne Grudem, *Evangelical Feminism and Biblical Truth* (Sisters, Ore.: Multnomah, 2004), pp. 415-22; S. Kovach and P. Schemm, "A Defense of the Doctrine of the Eternal Subordination of the Son," *Journal of the Evangelical Theological Society* 42, no. 3 (1999): 465; Charles Hodge, *Systematic Theology* (London: James Clarke, 1960), 1:462-71. For a trenchant critique of this mistaken idea see T. F. Torrance, *The Trinitarian Faith* (Edinburgh: T & T Clark, 1988), pp. 110-45; and Letham, *Holy Trinity*, pp. 134, 178, 383-89.
[141]Kelly, *Early Christian Creeds*, p. 235.
[142]Barnes, *Power of God*, p. 119.

Spirit derives his deity from the Father. If this idea was present in Origen or others, by the time of the Council of Constantinople it had been corrected."[143]

In confessing the words of this creed, Christians in every corner of the earth, from the late fourth century until today, are saying we believe what the great theologians of the fourth century concluded captures the whole scope of Scripture about the Son of God. He is fully God without any caveats, and yet for our salvation "he came down" from heaven and became man. This means that those who make this confession are affirming two things: first, this is what we believe about the Son, and second, these words prescribe the right way to read and understand the "double account" of the Son in Scripture, one as God in all might, majesty and power, and one as God in the form of a servant.

---

[143]Letham, *Holy Trinity*, p. 177.

6

The Eternal Generation of the Son

Augustine and Aquinas

◆ ◆ ◆

Augustine and Aquinas are almost universally recognized as two of the most significant contributors to the development of the doctrine of the Trinity and as the primary representatives of the so-called Western doctrine of the Trinity. For these two reasons it is important that we explore what they taught on the eternal generation of the Son. We should not make too much of the contrast between "Western" and "Eastern" models of the Trinity, a contrast widely questioned today,[1] although it must be admitted that Augustine often expresses himself in ways not found in Athanasius or the Cappadocians. However, this is also true if one compares the "Eastern" Athanasius with the "Eastern" Cappadocians. They too can differ on important issues. It is more accurate to say that Augustine introduced or highlighted elements in the Nicene doctrine of the Trinity that would be developed in the Middle Ages and reach fruition in the work of Aquinas. Aquinas is heavily dependent on Augustine, but his analytical and philosophical approach to the Trinity makes his work distinctive.[2] Augustine stands theologically nearer to the Nicene fathers than he does to Aquinas, yet he and

---

[1]See more on this in my *Jesus and the Father: Modern Evangelicals Reinvent the Doctrine of the Trinity* (Grand Rapids: Zondervan, 2006), pp. 75-77. Lewis Ayres, *Nicaea and Its Legacy: An Approach to Fourth-Century Trinitarian Theology* (Oxford: Oxford University Press, 2004), p. 365, says Augustine's *De Trinitate* gives "one of the clearest examples of fundamentally pro-Nicene Trinitarianism." I agree. For the same point see his later book *Augustine and the Trinity* (Cambridge: Cambridge University Press, 2010), especially chap. 1.

[2]As I will show later in this chapter.

Aquinas have much in common. Indeed, on the issue addressed in this book they are of one mind. For both of them the doctrine of the eternal generation of the Son is foundational to the catholic doctrine of the Trinity. They agree it is this doctrine that explains and safeguards the unity in substance and attributes of the Father and the Son and at the same time eternally distinguishes them as two divine "persons."

AUGUSTINE

One of the common criticisms made of Augustine is that in his writings Neo-Platonic philosophy influences his theology more than the Bible. This thesis has little merit. It seems rather that the Bible triumphed over the Neo-Platonic in Augustine, and in particular in his doctrine of the Trinity.[3]

Early in book one of *The Trinity*, Augustine gives a superb summary of the Bible's teaching on the Trinity as "catholic commentators" have understood it.[4] They teach, he says,

> according to the scriptures Father and Son and Holy Spirit in the inseparable equality of the one substance present a divine unity, and therefore there are not three gods but one God; although indeed the Father has begotten the Son, and therefore he who is Father is not Son, and the Son is begotten of the Father, and therefore he who is the Son is not the Father; and the Holy Spirit is neither the Father nor the Son, but only the Spirit of the Father and the Son, himself co-equal to the Father and the Son, and belonging to the threefold unity.[5]

In this brief outline of the doctrine of the Trinity, Augustine grounds divine unity and equality *and* divine threeness—the two primary truths basic to the orthodox doctrine of the Trinity—solely on the basis that the Father eternally begets, the Son is begotten and the Spirit proceeds from the Father and the Son. For Augustine, therefore, as with Athanasius and the Cappadocian fathers, the eternal begetting of the Son and procession of the Spirit stand right at the heart of the Nicene doc-

---

[3]See on this Ayres, *Nicaea*, pp. 366-83.
[4]All references to *De Trinitate* will be from the English translation by Edmund Hill, *The Trinity: Introduction, Translation, Notes* (New York: New City Press, 1991).
[5]Augustine, *The Trinity* 1.2.7 (p. 69).

trine of the Trinity. These two doctrines form the linchpin that holds divine unity and threeness together; they affirm that Father, Son and Spirit share the one divine substance and yet are three divine "persons."

On the first page of book one of *The Trinity* Augustine warns against those who base "their arguments about God on distorted and misleading rules of interpretation."[6] A little later he expands on this comment. He first says his aim is to outline the doctrine of the Trinity based on "the testimonies of the divine scriptures, used copiously by earlier writers," that is, by catholic commentators prior to him.[7] However, before he can do this he says he must outline how Scripture is to be rightly read. This must be done because of "the sophistries and errors of the heretics," who want to major on verses such as John 14:28, "The Father is greater than I," and 1 Corinthians 15:28, according to which at the end "the Son himself will be made subject."[8] The heretics err, he argues, because they take these texts in isolation giving idiosyncratic interpretations of them. In contrast, catholic commentators read them "keeping in view the whole range of scripture."[9] For him, making the whole of Scripture the context for understanding particular passages is the first rule of catholic exegesis.[10] In the scriptures, he says, God's Son is depicted in two ways: "in the form of God in which he is, and equal to the Father," and in "the form of a servant which he took and is less than the Father."[11] Given this rule many seeming "contradictions"[12] and the "multifarious diversity"[13] in the biblical passages on the Son can be rightly understood. All texts speaking of Christ as equal in divinity, majesty and authority with the Father refer to the Son "in the form of God," and all texts speaking of Christ's human limitations, subordination and obedience refer to him in "the form of a

---

[6]Augustine, *The Trinity* 1.1.1 (p. 65).

[7]Augustine, *The Trinity* 1.3.14 (p. 74).

[8]Augustine, *The Trinity* 1.3.14-21 (pp. 74-81).

[9]Augustine, *The Trinity* 1.3.14 (p. 74).

[10]On Augustine's canonical rules for rightly reading Scripture see, Keith E. Johnson, "Augustine's Trinitarian Reading of John 5: A Model for the Theological Interpretation of Scripture," *Journal of the Evangelical Theological Society* 52, no. 4 (2009): 799-810, and his footnotes.

[11]Augustine, *The Trinity* 1.4.22 (p. 82). See also 1.3.14-15 (p. 74-75), 2.1.2 (p. 98).

[12]Augustine, *The Trinity* 1.4.22 (p. 82).

[13]Augustine, *The Trinity* 2, prologue, 1 (p. 97).

servant," as the incarnate Son. Augustine finds this hermeneutical rule spelled out in Philippians 2:4-11.[14]

Following this rule, Augustine explains John 14:28 ("The Father is greater than I") as referring to the incarnate Son "in the form of a servant" and 1 Corinthians 15:28 ("then the Son himself will be subjected") as alluding to the time when the Son "brings believers to a direct contemplation of God the Father," which will not deprive him of anything, since the Father and the Son are forever one.[15] Another example of how his catholic canonical rule gives what he considers to be the right interpretation of Scripture is his handling of the Arian proof text Proverbs 8:22: "In the form of God, it says *Before the Hills he begot me* (Prv 8:25), that is, before all the immensities of creation, and also, *Before the daystar I begot you* (Ps 110:3), that is before all time and all things of time. But in the form of a servant it says, *The Lord created me in the beginning of his ways* (Prv 8:22)."[16]

However, Augustine recognized that this one "canonical rule" is not adequate on its own. There are also texts "the heretics" misquote to prove that the Son is "less than the Father," such as those that speak of the Son as "begotten of the Father," "from" the Father and "sent" by the Father.[17] Such texts, he argues, are explained by a second rule, which excludes the idea that because the Son is begotten, from and sent by the Father there is "any dearth of equality."[18] This "rule" prescribes that these texts be understood to "mark him [the Son] neither as less nor equal, but only intimate that he is *from* [Latin, *de*] the Father."[19]

Augustine develops this second rule for reading Scripture rightly because his Arian opponents[20] argued that the human language of "begetting," coming "from" and "sending" imply the subordination of the

---

[14]Augustine, *The Trinity* 1.3.14-21 (pp. 74-81).

[15]Augustine, *The Trinity* 1.3.15-16 (pp. 75-76). I have briefly summed up Augustine's conclusions on 1 Cor 15:28. See a fuller discussion in my *Jesus and the Father*, p. 192.

[16]Augustine, *The Trinity* 1.4.24 (p. 83).

[17]Augustine, *The Trinity* 2.2.1-6 (pp. 98-101)

[18]Augustine, *The Trinity* 2.1.3 (p. 99).

[19]Augustine, *The Trinity* 2.1.2 (p. 98).

[20]Ayres, *Augustine*, pp. 171-73, argues these were *homoian* Arians, but in *The Trinity* 15.5.38 (p. 425) Augustine himself names the neo-Arian Eunomius as his debating opponent.

Son.[21] For them "fromness" indicates diminution in being and power. Augustine concedes that the metaphors of "begetting" and "sending" stand together because both depict the Son as "from" the Father, but assuming the above-mentioned rule, he will not allow that they subordinate the Son in any way. For him "fromness" does not imply subordination. What these metaphors speak of, he argues, is the "intimacy" of the Father and the Son and their indelible differentiation—one begets, the other is begotten, one sends, the other is sent. He writes that one is not greater or less because "one is the Father and the other the Son; one is the begetter, the other begotten; the first is the one from whom the sent one is; the other is the one who is from the sender."[22] Then he adds a little later, "Just as the Father, then, begot and the Son was begotten. So the Father sent and the Son was sent. But just as the begetter and the begotten are one, so are the sender and the sent, because the Father and the Son are one."[23]

Augustine certainly grounds divine self-differentiation in differing divine relations of origin, and in doing so he is intent on absolutely excluding the idea that the eternal begetting of the Son results in a divine person less than the Father in being and attributes. He writes,

> So the Word of God, the only begotten Son of the Father, like the Father and equal to him in all things, God from God, light from light, wisdom from wisdom, being from being, is exactly and absolutely what the Father is, and yet is not the Father because this one is Son, that one Father. . . . Hence it is as though uttering himself that the Father begot the Word equal to himself in all things. He would not have uttered himself completely and perfectly if anything less or more were in his Word than in himself.[24]

Augustine makes it quite clear that he endorses and argues for the Nicene doctrine of the Trinity in general, and the eternal begetting

---

[21]See Augustine, *The Trinity* 2.2.7 (p. 101), where Augustine gives the "axiom" the Arians espouse: "The one who sends is greater than the one who is sent." This argument must have been well known because Augustine returns to it many times and gives much space to it. See *The Trinity* 2.1-3 (pp. 99-108), 4.5 (pp. 171-77), 15.5.5 (p. 397).

[22]Augustine, *The Trinity* 4.5.27 (p. 172).

[23]Augustine, *The Trinity* 4.5.29 (p. 174).

[24]Augustine, *The Trinity* 15.4.23 (p. 415). See also 4.5.27 (p. 172) and 7.2.4 (p. 222).

of the Son in particular, because it is received catholic teaching. He thus comes to the Scriptures not to construct the doctrine afresh but to find more in Scripture that will support what is believed and explain more adequately those texts that have been quoted by the "heretics." Augustine speaks of the Son as the "only begotten" (*unigenitus*), but he does not appeal to the Johannine texts that use the word *monogenēs* (Jn 1:14, 18; 3:16, 18) for proof that the Son is eternally begotten of the Father. Nevertheless, he finds much in Scripture in support of the doctrine of the eternal generation of the Son. He quotes the well-established texts Psalm 2:7,[25] 45:1,[26] Proverbs 8:25[27] and Wisdom 7:24-27.[28] In discussing this last text Augustine equates the Son with God's Word and Wisdom,[29] making the point that God's Wisdom streams forth like "light flowing from light . . . the light of eternal light. And therefore it is co-eternal with the light from which it comes forth."[30]

However, Augustine gives pride of place to John 5:26 in his appeal to the Bible in support of the doctrine of the eternal generation of the Son: "For just as the Father has life in himself, so he has granted the Son also to have life in himself." He cites and discusses this text many times in *The Trinity*[31] and in his *Tractates on the Gospel of John*.[32] Commenting on this text in *The Trinity*, he says, "It was not someone already existing and yet not having life, whom he gave to have life in himself, since by the very fact that he is, he is life. So this is the meaning of *he gave the Son to have life in himself*—that he begot the Son to be unchangeable life, that is to say eternal life.[33]

---

[25]Augustine, *The Trinity* 4.5.27 (p. 173).

[26]Augustine, *The Trinity* 1.4.24 (p. 120).

[27]Augustine, *The Trinity* 1.4.24 (p. 83).

[28]Augustine, *The Trinity* 2.3.14 (p. 107), 4.5.27 (p. 173). It is to be noted that Augustine considered the book of Wisdom in the so-called Apocrypha part of Scripture following the Latin Vulgate.

[29]Augustine, *The Trinity* 2.3.14 (p. 107), 4.5.27 (pp. 172-73).

[30]Augustine, *The Trinity* 4.5.27 (p. 172).

[31]Augustine, *The Trinity* 1.4.26 (p. 85), 1.4.29 (p. 87), 2.1.3 (p. 99), 7.2.4 (p. 222), 15.6.47 (p. 432).

[32]*Augustine's Tractates on the Gospel of John, 11-27*, trans., J. W. Rettig, Fathers of the Church 79 (Washington, D.C.: Catholic University of America Press, 1988).

[33]Augustine, *The Trinity* 1.4.26 (p. 85). Cf. 2.1.4 (p. 100), 15.6.47 (p. 432).

In what follows Augustine points out that John says that the Son possesses divine life ("life in himself"), which raises the question, how then did the Son receive life from the Father? Keith Johnson finds Augustine answering this question most clearly in tract nineteen of *Tractates on the Gospel of John*. Augustine's answer, he says, is "both simple and profound"[34]: "The Father 'begat' the Son. The Father is life, not 'by being born'; the Son is life by being born. The Father [is] from no Father; the Son, from God the Father."[35]

Augustine then says that the words "has been given" should be understood to mean much the same as "has been begotten."[36] Thus Augustine argues that although the Father and the Son both possess "life in themselves," they possess it in different ways. The Father has life in himself, not from the Son; the Son has life in himself, but from the Father, in that he is begotten of the Father. They are one in divine life, differentiated in that one begets divine life and one has begotten divine life. This is another instance of the "X from X" argument. The eternal begetting of the Son envisages divine life from divine life.

To understand Augustine rightly, we must appreciate that for him God's unity is grounded primarily in the one substance or essence that the divine three share equally and each express fully. This one divine substance or essence is something immaterial, spiritual and simple. The essence is not prior to or other than the persons. It is not the origin of anything. In his letter to "Consentius his most beloved brother"[37] he first denies that the one "substance" "is a sort of fourth person."[38] Then he says, it is "what is common to all as the divinity of all and in all." "The Father, Son and Spirit are the Trinity."[39] The Father eternally generates the Son, but this does not mean the divine substance is divided or that the Son is not a divine person in his own right. The divine substance or essence cannot be divided because it is spiritual and

---

[34]Johnson, "Augustine's Trinitarian Reading," p. 803.

[35]Augustine, *Tractates on the Gospel of John* 19.13 (p. 152).

[36]Augustine, *Tractates on the Gospel of John* 19.13 (p. 152).

[37]*Saint Augustine: Letters Volume II (Letters 83-130)*, trans. Sister Wilfrid Parsons, Fathers of the Church (Washington, D.C.: Catholic University of America Press, 1953), pp. 300-317. See on this also Ayres, *Nicaea*, pp. 375-76.

[38]*Saint Augustine: Letters*, p. 306.

[39]Ibid., p. 310.

simple.[40] The eternal generation of the Son is not to be understood "materially." It is like "light from light."[41] All that the Father is, therefore, the Son also is. To those "people who find it difficult to accept the equality of Father and Son and Holy Spirit,"[42] Augustine replies that if Christ is "*the power of God and the Wisdom of God* (1 Cor. 1:24)," so too is the Father and so "this makes them even more of one and the same being."[43] They are "together one being, one greatness and one truth and one wisdom."[44] This means for Augustine that there can be no division or separation in the one divine substance/being or between the attributes of the Father, Son or Spirit. Robert Letham says that in Augustine, "All elements of subordination are pruned away."[45]

One of Augustine's very important theological contributions to trinitarian theology, building on the insights of Hilary and Ambrose,[46] is that the Bible envisages both an eternal *and* a temporal "from the Father." The Son is eternally "from" the Father in his eternal generation and temporally "from" the Father in that he is sent on mission into the world to save. A number of Johannine texts (e.g., Jn 1:1-14; 8:14, 23, 42; 13:3; 16:28) that speak of Jesus as being with the Father and then coming into the world suggest this distinction.[47] For example, in John 7:29 Jesus says, "I am from [*para*] him, and he sent [*apostellō*] me." These words seem to imply two moves. It thus follows that for Augustine the temporal missions of the Son and the Spirit reflect the prior eternal generation of the Son and procession of the Spirit within the Godhead. For Augustine, therefore, what takes place in eternity within the life of God constitutes the persons, not what takes place in history. The economy simply reveals what is eternally true. Toward the end of his long discussion of the missions in book four he says, "As being born means for the Son being *from* the Father, so being sent means for the

---

[40]Augustine, *The Trinity*, 6.2.9 (p. 211), 1.1.1 (p. 65).

[41]Augustine, *The Trinity* 15.4.23 (p. 415), 4.5.27 (p. 172).

[42]Augustine, *The Trinity* 6.1.1 (p. 205).

[43]Augustine, *The Trinity* 7.1.2 (p. 218).

[44]Augustine, *The Trinity* 7.1.3 (p. 221).

[45]Robert Letham, *The Holy Trinity in Scripture, History, Theology, and Worship* (Phillipsburg, N.J.: Presbyterian and Reformed, 2004), p. 199.

[46]Ayres, *Augustine*, pp. 187-88.

[47]B. de Margerie, *The Christian Trinity in History* (Petersham, Mass.: St. Bede's, 1981), p. 153.

Son being known to be *from* the Father. And as being the gift of God means for the Holy Spirit proceeding *from* the Father, so being sent means for the Holy Spirit his being known to proceed *from* the Father."[48]

Although Augustine never uses the medieval terms *ad intra* and *ad extra* he believed that the eternal generation of the Son and the eternal procession of the Spirit take place eternally, entirely within the life of God—nothing external to God was produced. In contrast, the missions of the Son and the Spirit are temporal and external acts in history. Lewis Ayres in his 2010 book, *Augustine and the Trinity*, finds Augustine implying this in books five to seven of *The Trinity*, where he explains "subsistent relations" in God, and in book nine, where he introduces the triadic psychological analogies, and in his later writings.[49] Ayres, in his earlier book *Nicaea and Its Legacy*, concludes that all the pro-Nicene theologians, and he includes Augustine among them, believed that "the eternal generation of the Son occurs within the unitary and incomprehensible divine being."[50]

In books five to seven of *The Trinity*, Augustine addresses the basic philosophical issues raised by his Arian opponents. Their rationalistic argument was that the title "Unbegotten" defines the Father's substance/being and "begotten" defines the substance/being of the Son, therefore the Father and the Son are different substances, different in *ousia*. In reply, Augustine argues that the language of begetting and being begotten does not imply a difference in "substance" or "accidents" between the Father and the Son, but to a difference in "relations." He insists that "substance-wise" the Father, the Son and the Spirit are one and equal.[51] However, "relations-wise" the divine three are indelibly differentiated: one is unbegotten, one begotten and one bestowed. He points out that the term "begotten can only be used with reference to another,"[52] as is the case with the other two terms. Thus to call the Father "unbegotten, is to show that he is not Son,"[53] and to call the Son

---

[48]Augustine, *The Trinity* 4.5.29 (p. 174). Italics added.
[49]Ayres, *Augustine*, pp. 199-229, 231-50.
[50]Ayres, *Nicaea*, p. 236.
[51]Augustine, *The Trinity* 5.1.4 (p. 191).
[52]Augustine, *The Trinity* 5.1.7 (p. 192).
[53]Augustine, *The Trinity* 5.1.8 (p. 193).

"begotten" is to say he is not the Father, and to say the Spirit is "bestowed" or "proceeds" is to say the Spirit is not the Father or the Son. He further writes, "Therefore, although being Father is different from being Son, there is no difference in substance, because they are not called these things substance-wise but relationship-wise; and yet this relationship is not a modification, because it is not changeable."[54]

In book seven, as a conclusion to his argument that the divine three are differentiated "relationwise,"[55] and in no other way, he says,

> The Father is not God taken singularly, but only with and taken together with the godhead he has begotten; and so the Son will be the godhead of the Father just as he is the wisdom and power of the Father, and just as he is the Word and the image of the Father. . . . This means that apart from being Father, the Father is nothing but what the Son is for him. It is clear of course, that he is only called Father because he has a Son, since he is called Father not in reference to himself but with reference to the Son. But now we are forced to say in addition that it is only because he has begotten his own being or "is-ness" that he is what he is with reference to himself [that is, the Father].[56]

This is a very profound passage. The Father and the Son are the one Godhead sharing the one substance and attributes, each fully God, and thus the only thing that distinguishes them is that one is Father because he begets a Son and one is Son because he is begotten. When we come to Calvin we will find him following Augustine on this matter. Ayres, in his usual concise and sharp way, sums up what Augustine is saying in these words. For Augustine, "none of the persons is dependent on the other for anything that is essential to God."[57]

Before leaving Augustine I must say something about his so-called psychological analogies of the Trinity in general and of the Son's begetting in particular, both of which are found in books eight to

---

[54]Augustine, *The Trinity* 5.1.6 (p. 192).
[55]This is how Hill translates the Latin term *relatio* in the quote following from *The Trinity*. I think a better rendering of the Latin would be "relation-wise," meaning, as Augustine says, in "reference to another." The Latin word does not refer to congenial relationships but to how two or more people stand in relation or "in reference" to one another.
[56]Augustine, *The Trinity* 7.1.1 (p. 218), but see also 7.1.2 (pp. 218-19).
[57]Ayres, *Nicaea*, 381.

fifteen. Augustine clearly recognizes that a fundamental question, possibly the most fundamental question, is how can the Son be begotten and sent but not subordinated to the Father?[58] In books one to seven he gives biblical and rational reasons why despite his eternal begetting and temporal sending by the Father "he [the Son] is equal to him [the Father] in all things."[59] In chapters eight to fifteen, building on the biblical revelation that humanity is made in the image and likeness of God (Gen 1:27-28), Augustine seeks, by appeal to the inner life of the human person, to penetrate more deeply into the mystery of how God can be one and yet three persons and in particular how the Son and Spirit can be said to be begotten and to proceed "from" him yet be fully equal with him. Having introduced his argument in books eight, nine and ten, in book eleven Augustine explores more than twenty triadic psychological analogies and in the end concludes that the triad of self-memory (Latin, *memoria sui*), understanding and will are the most evocative.[60]

Following John the Evangelist, Augustine identifies Jesus, the Son of God, as the Word (*Logos*), and this Word he equates with the divine self-memory, or self-knowledge, which he argues is to be objectified because the more perfect the knowledge the greater the identity between the knower and the known. In God, it follows, the identity of knower (the Father) and the known (the Son/*Logos*) must be complete, or in terms of orthodoxy, *homoousios*. All that is "left" is the distinction/relationship between the knowing subject (God the Father) and the spoken Word (God the Son). Thus on this basis Augustine explains how the biblical teaching that the Son is generated yet not eternally subordinate is reasonable and explicable, even if in the end it remains a mystery.

To sum up: for Augustine the doctrine of eternal generation guarantees what is absolutely fundamental and foundational to the Nicene faith, the full divinity of the Father and the Son and thus their co-equality and their differentiation as Father and Son. Because the Father

---

[58]Hill, *The Trinity*, 265-67. See also N. Omerod, *The Trinity: Retrieving the Western Tradition* (Milwaukee: Marquette University Press, 2005), chap. 4; and Ayres, *Augustine*, 275-315.

[59]Augustine, *The Trinity* 15.4.23 (p. 415).

[60]So Hill, *The Trinity*.

eternally begets the Son, the Father and the Son are one in substance/ being; the Son is all that the Father is except for being Father. And because the Father begets the Son and the Son is begotten, the Father is not the Son and the Son is not the Father.

As I read Augustine's *The Trinity* I find my intellect constantly stretched beyond its limit and yet feel I want to sing the doxology. Here I meet with the God I find in the Bible, one God in three persons, equal and undivided in might, majesty and power. And in his profound exposition of the doctrine of the Trinity, beginning with Scripture read through the lens provided by the Nicene Creed, and the church fathers who have preceded him, the doctrine of the eternal generation of the Son is the linchpin. Once again we see that the Son is all that the Father is apart from being the Father.

THE ATHANASIAN CREED

In the so-called Athanasian Creed (probably dating from the late fifth century), Augustine's teaching on the Trinity is identified with "the catholic faith" and made necessary for salvation. In this creed the unity of the divine three is stressed, as is their "coequality." This creed is authoritative and binding for Roman Catholics, Lutherans, Anglicans and for most of the continental Reformed churches.

> The Godhead of the Father, of the Son, and the Holy Spirit is all one: the glory equal, the majesty co-eternal.
>
> Such as the Father is, such is the Son, such is the Holy Spirit.
>
> The Father is almighty, the Son is almighty, the Holy Spirit is almighty. And yet there are not three Almighties: but one Almighty.
>
> The Father is Lord, the Son is Lord: and the Holy Spirit is Lord. And yet there are not three Lords, but one Lord.
>
> In this Trinity none is before or after, none is greater or less than another. But the whole three persons are co-eternal and co-equal.[61]

---

[61] I follow the text given in *A Prayer Book for Australia*, The Anglican Church of Australia, 1995. This translation of the Athanasian Creed is from the English Language Liturgical Consultation, the ecumenical body that issues common texts. When needed I updated the archaic English.

On divine differentiation this creed makes two affirmations. First, the persons are three in number: "There is one person of the Father, another of the Son and another of the Holy Spirit." And second, the divine three are distinguished and differentiated solely in reference to origination.

The Father is made of none: neither created nor begotten.

The Son is of the Father alone: not made, nor created, but begotten.

The Holy Spirit is of the Father and the Son: neither made, nor created, nor begotten, but proceeding.

The second half of this creed, the christological section, again mentions the eternal begetting of the Son, this time to stress that he is "perfect God." The word "perfect" (*telos*) here does not speak of moral purity but of completeness or wholeness, lacking in nothing. He is "God, of the substance of the Father, begotten before the worlds." This wording reflects the wording of the Creed of Nicaea (325), in which the Son is said to be begotten "of the being of the Father."

This creed, which Western Christians have for many centuries taken as the definitive statement on the doctrine of the Trinity, speaks unambiguously and emphatically. It affirms that the catholic faith involves belief in one God in three persons who are "coequal" in might, majesty and power; differentiated in identity as Father, Son and Spirit, and relationally because the Father is unbegotten, the Son begotten and the Spirit proceeding.

THOMAS AQUINAS

Thomas Aquinas (1225-1275) may not stand in the doctrinal tradition that most evangelicals honor, but he is one of the truly great theologians in the history of the church. Thus what he says on the eternal begetting of the Son deserves, if not demands, comment, and he says much on this matter. One reason evangelicals find Aquinas difficult is that his writings are very analytical and philosophical. He sets out his work in the form of questions, which he then breaks down into parts, to answer one at a time. However, for theologians who want clear answers to complex questions, this approach can be very enlightening and helpful. He wrote extensively on the Trinity, giving the most attention to this doctrine first in his *Summa Contra Gentiles*[62] (henceforth *SCG*) and then in his *Summa Theologiae*[63] (henceforth *ST*).

The great strength of Aquinas's work on the Trinity is also its great weakness. Aquinas takes theological conceptualization of the Trinity to new heights, which opens new vistas, but at times what he concludes often seems to take us beyond anything clearly revealed or even implied in Scripture. So analytical is Aquinas's formulation of the Trinity, in fact, that it is often summed up in these terms: one God, two processions, three persons, four relations[64] and five notions.[65] Karl Rahner[66] and Catherine LaCugna,[67] each in their own way, criticize Aquinas for focusing mainly on God as he is apart from history and thus abstracting the doctrine of the Trinity. Gilles Emery, in contrast, in his two large and important books, *Trinity in Aquinas,* [68] and *The Trinitarian Theology of St. Thomas Aquinas,*[69] argues that he is one of the most important trinitarian theologians in the history of the church and defends him against his critics.

One of the distinctive features of Aquinas's exposition of the Trinity is that he speaks of two divine "processions," the eternal begetting of the Son and the "spiration" of the Spirit.[70] Procession, Aquinas says, nor-

---

[62]The text I will be using is *Summa Contra Gentiles*, trans. Charles J. O'Neil (Garden City, N.Y.: Doubleday, 1957), vol. 4. Hereafter *SCG*.

[63]The text I will be using is *Summa Theologiae, Latin Text and English Translation*, trans. Hierbert McCabe (London: Blackfriars, 1963), vols. 6 and 7. Hereafter *ST*.

[64]The four real relations are (1) Paternity (the relation of the Father to the Son); (2) Sonship (the relation of the Son to the Father); (3) "active spiration" (the relation of the Father and the Son to the Spirit); and (4) "passive spiration" (relation of the Spirit to the Father and the Son). Of these four relations only three constitute persons: paternity, sonship and active spiration.

[65]So E. J. Fortman, *The Triune God* (Grand Rapids: Baker, 1982), p. 205, Leonardo Boff, *Trinity and Society* (Maryknoll, N.Y.: Orbis, 1986), p. 91. A "notion" or "notional act" in Aquinas signifies what is not an essential act common to the three.

[66]Karl Rahner, *The Trinity*, trans. J. Donceel (London: Burns and Oats, 1970).

[67]Catherine LaCugna, *God for Us* (San Francisco: HarperSanFrancisco, 1991), pp. 143-65.

[68]Gilles Emery, *Trinity in Aquinas* (Naples, Fla.: Sapienta Press, 2003). This book comprises seven previously published long essays on specific aspects of Aquinas's doctrine of the Trinity.

[69]Gilles Emery, *The Trinitarian Theology of St. Thomas Aquinas* (Oxford: Oxford University Press, 2007). This book is an advanced introduction to Aquinas's doctrine of the Trinity as he gives it in his *Summa Theologiae*.

[70]On this matter see *SCG* chap. 2 (pp. 42-44); *ST* 1, q.27 (pp. 3-21).

mally means "movement outwards,"[71] and on this basis, he adds, Arius and others have concluded that the Father "caused" the Son. A "procession" is an "activity," he agrees, but the "procession" of the Son and the Spirit, each in their own way, takes place in eternity within (*ad intra*) the life of God. For this reason, in the divine processions "what comes forth interiorly by a spiritual process [is] . . . the more identified with its source."[72] Indeed, what proceeds in the eternal begetting and "spiration" "is perfectly one with its source and in no way diverse from it."[73]

Both *SCG* and *ST* begin by discussing the procession of the divine persons. This starting point immediately indicates that, like Athanasius and the Cappadocians, Aquinas clearly recognized that the eternal act of divine self-differentiation that constituted the one God as Father, Son and Spirit was the foundation on which the catholic doctrine of the Trinity was built. No other matter is more fundamental. The two treatises present similar accounts of the Trinity, but, as each has something distinctive to contribute, I will discuss them separately.[74] After a short introduction, Thomas's first words on the Trinity in *SCG* are these: "Let us take the beginning of our study [of the Trinity] from the secret of the *divine generation*, and first set down what one must hold about it according to the testimonies *of sacred scripture*."[75] And immediately following he adds, "Sacred scripture, then, hands on to us the names of 'paternity' and 'sonship' in the divinity,"[76] and he then gives a list of texts that speak of the divine Father and Son as correlatives. From the names "Father" and "Son" he concludes naturally comes the idea of a "divine generation."[77] *This point should be carefully noted. Like Athanasius, the Cappadocian fathers and Augustine, Aquinas predicates the doctrine of the eternal generation of the Son primarily on the revealed names, Father and Son, which he believes imply an eternal act of divine generation.* For biblical support of this inference he appeals to Psalm 2:7, Proverbs 8:22-25, Isaiah 66:8-9,

---

[71]*ST* 1, q.27, a.1.1 (6:3).

[72]*ST* 1, q.27, a.2.2 (6:7).

[73]*ST* 1, q.27, a.2.2 (6:7).

[74]For example, most of the appeal to Scripture for what Thomas is teaching about the Trinity is found in *SCG*.

[75]*SCG* 2.1 (p. 40). Italics added.

[76]*SCG* 2.1 (p. 40).

[77]*SCG* 2.1 (p. 41).

Hebrews 1:6 and assuming the Latin translation of *monogenēs, unigenitus* (only begotten), he also includes John 1:18, "The only-begotten Son who is in the bosom of the Father, he has declared him."[78] In designating him "Son" and speaking of him as "begotten," these Scriptures make it plain, he says, that "he is more than a creation." He is God.[79] Then he refutes errors arising from a false understanding of the eternal generation of the Son. The teaching of three "heretics" is mentioned: Photinus,[80] Sabellius and Arius. He concludes that "the catholic faith is the only one to confess *the true generation of a Son of God*."[81]

In chapter ten of *SCG* Aquinas addresses "arguments against divine generation."[82] He rejects that divine generation can be likened to or understood by reference to the generation of "creatures." Creaturely generation implies time, change and that the begotten "receives its nature from the generator."[83] The Son cannot have "received from the Father a nature numerically other than the Father," for this would result in two gods.[84] The correct answer, he says, is that through generation the Father and the Son share the one nature, yet they are distinguished by differing relations so that "one is Father, the other the Son."[85]

In chapter eleven of *SCG* Aquinas asks "how generation is to be understood in divinity." Among animate bodies, he notes, generation or emanation produces something external.[86] "But since God is indivisible nothing can be separated from him."[87] He thus argues that divine generation takes place within (*ad intra*) the eternal life of God, not externally (*ad extra*).[88] He develops this argument by making an analogy between how the human mind conceives of an idea before it becomes

---

[78] *SCG* 2.1 (p. 41).
[79] *SCG* 3.1-2 (pp. 42-43).
[80] Photinus lived in the mid-fourth century. He was a pupil of Marcellus of Ancyra, who denied the preexistence of Christ. It seems he held to a form of adoptionism. Jesus was given divine status by the Father.
[81] Emery, *Trinity*, 85. His italics.
[82] *SCG* 10.1 (p. 75).
[83] *SCG* 10.4 (p. 76).
[84] *SCG* 10.4 (p. 76).
[85] *SCG* 10.4 (p. 76).
[86] *SCG* 11.3-4 (pp. 80-81).
[87] *SCG* 11.8 (p. 82).
[88] *SCG* 11.9 (p. 83).

actual in words and how the Son was begotten. He says, "The divine intellect, of course, since it does not pass from potency to act, but is always actually existent, must necessarily have always understood itself." "Therefore, his Word necessarily always existed as God. His Word, then, is co-eternal with God (Jn 1:1)."[89] Explaining his argument more clearly in *ST*, he says, "Generation in God is like the springing forth of an intelligible idea."[90] Aquinas, like the Nicene fathers, believes that the eternal generation of the Word is prophesied in Old Testament texts that speak of the eternal generation of Wisdom.[91]

Finally, in chapters fifteen to twenty-five of *SCG*, Aquinas comes to discuss the Holy Spirit, concentrating on arguments for his divinity and his procession from the Father *and* the Son (the so-called *filioque*).

In turning to Thomas's discussion of the Trinity in the *ST* (questions twenty-seven to forty-three), I will simply take up matters relevant to this study that add to what we have seen in *SCG*. As noted above, Thomas in *ST* (as in *SCG*) *begins* by discussing the eternal generation of the Son. This for him is where any discussion of the Trinity must start. He sees that the primary issue to be corrected is the Arian teaching "that the Son comes from the Father as one of his creatures."[92] The Son's eternal procession, he agrees, is rightly called "generation" but not in the sense we use this word in relation to "men or animals."[93] The generation of the Son by the Father, his "coming forth is [rather] like that in the mind's action."[94] In this case the begotten "comes forth as subsisting in the same nature."[95] As a third *article* in question twenty-seven Thomas asks, "Is there another procession besides the generation of the Word?"[96] He answers in the affirmative on the basis that John 15:26 speaks of the Spirit proceeding from the Father. This he calls a "procession of love."[97] Emery argues

---

[89] *SCG* 11.9 (p. 83).
[90] *ST* 1, q.28, a.1.4 (6:23).
[91] *SCG* 12.1-5 (pp. 90-92).
[92] *ST* 1, q.27. a.1.3 (6:5).
[93] *ST* 1, q.27, a.2.3 (6:9).
[94] *ST* 1, q.27, a.2.3 (6:9).
[95] *ST* 1, q. 27, a.3.2 (6:11).
[96] *ST* 1, q. 27, a.3.2 (6:11).
[97] *ST* 1, q.27, a.3.3 (6:13).

that rather than depicting the Spirit as the outcome of the love of the Father and the Son, Aquinas thinks of the Spirit as the divine "love impulse."[98] The procession of the Spirit, Aquinas argues, should not be called "generation" because the Bible preserves this term for the Son; it should be called "a breathing of the Spirit,"[99] a "spiration." He then argues that there can only be two processions in God, ultimately because revelation only speaks of two.[100]

Thomas explores that which differentiates the divine three in question twenty-eight. He argues, following Augustine, that the only safe and sure way to distinguish the divine three who are one in substance is by their differing "real relations." I will not digress to discuss how Aquinas explains differing divine relations, or his questions on the meaning of "divine person," or how to understand plurality in God, issues discussed in questions twenty-nine to thirty-two. These questions take us away from our focus on the doctrine of the eternal generation of the Son.

Instead, we move to question thirty-three, where Thomas asks what it means to "name the Father 'principle' (*principium*) of the Son or of the Holy Spirit."[101] He says that it cannot mean the Father *causes* the Son, because this would indicate "that the Son had a beginning and so was created"—the key Arian error.[102] It also cannot mean that the Father is "first" because "there is no first and second in God."[103] The right answer is, he says, that when the word "principle" is used of the Father it "means simply that from which something proceeds."[104] Since "the Father is one from whom another originates, it follows that the Father is principle."[105] He then adds that in contrast to the Greek authors who use "'principle" and "cause" interchangeably in referring to divinity, the Latins do not use "cause" but only "principle."[106] The reason for this, he

---

[98]Emery, *Trinity*, 103.

[99]*ST* 1, q.27, a.4.2 (6:17).

[100]*ST* 1, q.27, a.5 (6:19-21).

[101]*ST* 1, q.33, a.1.1 (7:3).

[102]*ST* 1, q.33, a.1.2 (7:3).

[103]*ST* 1, q.33, a.1.3 (7:3).

[104]*ST* 1, q.33, a.1.3 (7:5).

[105]*ST* 1, q.33, a.1.3 (7:5).

[106]*ST* 1, q.33, a.1.3 (7:5).

says, is that since Latins "want to avoid even the chance of error we do not speak of the Son or Holy Spirit in terms suggesting subjection or inferiority."[107] And to drive home his point he adds, "The term principle has as its meaning not priority but simply origin."[108] For Aquinas, the one divine essence/substance/being is not and cannot be the source or origin of the essence of the Son and the Spirit. The divine essence does not beget or spirate. The divine essence is what is shared by the divine persons. Next Aquinas considers the name "Father." He argues that this name first of all applies to one divine person because a name "signifies that by which the person is distinct from others."[109] But then he allows that the name can also be used of the triune God, such as when we pray, "Our Father."[110] He thinks calling the Father the "Unbegotten" is problematic, but following Augustine he says it may be allowed if *"to say that the Father is unbegotten is equivalent to saying he is not the Son."*[111]

The next important section for our purposes in *ST* is question forty-two, where Thomas discusses the coequality and likeness of "the divine persons."[112] Following Augustine, he affirms that "we recognize an equality in the Father, Son and Holy Spirit in that *no one of them comes first in eternity, excels in greatness or surpasses in power.*"[113] Arius denied this by arguing that that which is begotten, in the sense of created in time, must be less than the one who begets in being and power—but Thomas will not allow this. The Son, he insists, is "eternally begotten," and shares perfectly the one divine nature and power.[114] Then follows a section in which Thomas argues explicitly that the Father, Son and Spirit are one in nature and power.[115]

In question forty-three, Thomas turns to the "mission of the divine persons." First, he takes up the Arian argument that sending implies

---

[107]*ST* 1, q.33, a.2.2 (7:7).
[108]*ST* 1, q.33, a.1.3 (7:7).
[109]*ST* 1, q.33, a.2.4 (7:9).
[110]*ST* 1, q.33, a.3.3 (7:13).
[111]*ST* 1, q.33, a.4.1 (7:19).
[112]*ST* 1, q.42 (7:185).
[113]*ST* 1, q.42, a.1.1 (7:189).
[114]*ST* 1, q.42, a.2.4 (7:195).
[115]*ST* 1, q.42, a.6 (7:205-7).

subordination, a thesis that Augustine gives much space to refuting. Like Augustine, he allows that this may be the case in some human examples, but this is never the case with God. The word "sent" simply speaks of someone "going forth from the sender."[116] And this is what it means and no more when used of the Son and the Spirit. The language of sending, he points out, again like Augustine, refers to the temporal mission of the Son for our salvation. The Son comes "from" the Father in eternity (generation) and in time is "sent" by the Father (mission), but the Father and the Son are "co-equal."[117] Nevertheless, he agrees, the language of sending, like that of begetting, eternally distinguishes the persons. The Father sends, the Son is sent, and this order cannot be reversed.[118] The logic of Thomas's reasoning should be noted. The divine persons are distinguished but not subordinated by their differentiation or, to use his term, by their "opposed relations" that constitute them as persons, grounded in their differing processions.

In drawing my exposition of Thomas's discussion of the eternal generation of the Son to a conclusion, I return to his argument that the two eternal divine "processions" take place within the life of God. While this idea goes back to Justin and is taught by the Nicene fathers, Aquinas spells it out in much detail by terminologically contrasting divine acts *ad intra* and *ad extra*. In making this distinction, Aquinas appeals to Aristotle, who differentiates between two types of actions: immanent actions, which take place in the agent (for example, to love, to feel, to know), and transitive actions, which are exterior to the agent (for example, to eat, to build, to trade). Thomas, by way of analogy, applies these distinctions to God.[119] He argues some of God's actions are internal (*ad intra*) and some external (*ad extra*). The eternal generation of the Son and the procession of the Spirit, he argues, must be understood as acts *ad intra*. They are eternal and interior acts of self-differentiation within the life of God, which produce nothing outside of God. Arianism is to be rejected because it makes the procession of

---

[116]*ST* 1, q.43, a.2 (7:211).
[117]*ST* 1, q.43, a.2 (7:211).
[118]*ST* 1, q.43, a.5 (7:221).
[119]In this paragraph, I am heavily dependent on Emery, *Trinity*, p. 132.

the Son and the Spirit transitive actions, effects produced by a cause.[120] Sabellianism is to be rejected because it depicts the generation, or better, the manifestation of God as the Son, simply as a mode of divine action in the world. It does not acknowledge that what takes place in history reflects what is true in the eternal life of God. It denies eternal self-differentiation in God.

I conclude this outline of Aquinas's discussion of the eternal generation of the Son with a quote from Gilles Emery. He says that Thomas's profound exposition of the doctrine of the Trinity, "with the use of analogies and philosophical resources is guided by a double motive: the defense of the faith against errors, and the contemplation of revealed truth. Trinitarian theology has as its goal to show that the Trinity is *reasonably thinkable* and therefore arguments against the Trinitarian faith are not compelling."[121]

Exactly the same could be said of the specific matter of Thomas's profound exposition of the doctrine of the eternal generation of the Son, which he places first in both his major writings on the Trinity to make the point that the eternal procession of the Son and the Spirit are foundational to the catholic doctrine of the Trinity. The two *ad intra* "processions" ground divine unity and divine self-differentiation in eternity, while the two *ad extra* "missions" reveal what is antecedently true and make possible our salvation.

---

[120]On this matter see further Richard A. Muller, *Post-Reformation and Reformed Dogmatics* (Grand Rapids: Baker, 2003), pp. 46-47.

[121]Emery, *Trinity*, p. 127.

7

The Reformation and Post-Reformation Tradition

◆ ◆ ◆

Most books on the doctrine of the Trinity with a historical overview concentrate on the patristic period. This is understandable and appropriate because this doctrine was worked out in bitter debate in between the second and fourth centuries, concluding with the ecumenical Council of Constantinople in 381, which produced what we call today "the Nicene Creed." Augustine and the Athanasian Creed, in this telling of the story, are like a concluding addendum. For all Christians the work of the Greek theologians codified in the Nicene Creed of 381 is "theological tradition" of great weight, and for most Western Christians, Catholic and Protestant, Augustine's writings on the Trinity and the Athanasian Creed are likewise weighty theological tradition, authoritative guides for interpreting Scripture properly. In outlining how the doctrine of the eternal generation of the Son developed and was grounded in Scripture, I too have concentrated on this early period, adding a discussion of Aquinas's contribution. However, for most Protestants there is another body of weighty theological "tradition," which they also highly respect, honor and listen to. It comes from the Reformation and post-Reformation period. This is when "our" distinctive Protestant doctrines of salvation by grace alone, the primacy and authority of Scripture, the sacraments and the ordained ministry were worked out.

In this period, one of the most disputed doctrines among the Protestants was the doctrine of the Trinity, and in particular the doctrine of the eternal generation of the Son. What the Reformers concluded on all these doctrines, including the doctrine of the Trinity, is for Protestants in general and evangelicals in particular of special interest. As far as evangelicals in particular are concerned, I suspect few of our number would want to openly dissent from what the Reformers taught on any of these fundamental doctrines. We evangelicals want to hold that what we believe about our triune God, salvation, the Bible, the sacraments and the ministry of the Word stands in continuity with the beliefs of the Reformers and the confessions they inspired. For this reason, in this study focusing on the doctrine of the eternal generation of the Son, it is important for me as an evangelical to explore what the Reformers and those who saw themselves standing directly in their steps said on this important doctrine.

In what follows we will see that Luther and Calvin and most of the better-known and better-informed Protestant theologians up to the Second World War clearly recognized, and for this reason emphatically endorsed, the importance of the doctrine of the eternal generation of the Son. Because of Calvin's importance as the theologian par excellence of the Reformation age, I give more attention to his work than anyone else.

THE REFORMERS' AGENDA

For the most part the Reformers considered the doctrine of the Trinity a settled theological matter, over which they had no major dispute with the Roman Catholic Church. They agreed that in the one divine being or substance there were three coequal persons, differentiated but not divided. However, most of them rejected the overly speculative and philosophical approach to this doctrine of the medieval scholastics. They wanted to express the historic doctrine in more biblical terms.

Nevertheless, there were differences between the Reformers over the Trinity and between them and those wanting a more radical Reformation, the Anabaptists. Many among their number rejected the Nicene doctrine of the Trinity on the basis that it was not "biblical." In due course, this opposition to Nicene orthodoxy, which became quite widespread, was called "antitrinitarianism," a catchall term to designate a range of dissenting viewpoints. The most famous antitrinitarians were Michael Servetus (1511-1553) and Faustus Socinus (1539-1604), but there were many others. Thus what we have to recognize is that the Reformers and their successors formulated their teaching on the Trinity in bitter debate with Protestants of other opinion. Richard Muller says the Reformers and early Protestant orthodox theologians developed their doctrine of the Trinity "in the context of a fairly consistent denial of the doctrine by a number of highly insistent thinkers and groups who became increasingly adept at using both Scripture and early patristic tradition against the church dogma."[1] And, "Statement and defense of the doctrine of the Trinity was, moreover, made increasingly difficult [for the Reformers] by the various antitrinitarian groups that sprang up in the sixteenth and seventeenth centuries, groups that often advocated a starkly rational Biblicism over against the tradition, particularly against the views of Nicene and Post-Nicene fathers."[2] And on the contentious matter of "the tradition," he says, "The Reformers and the Reformed orthodox developed their teaching on the doctrine of the Trinity in a conscious dialogue with the patristic and medieval tradition, in overt agreement with the councils of the early church and in the tradition of the medieval conciliar decisions as well."[3]

LUTHER

Martin Luther (1483-1546) never wrote a detailed exposition of the doctrine of the Trinity, but he often came to this matter in his extensive writings, and the general consensus is that he was basically faithful to the received "Western" expression of this doctrine.[4] In his most de-

---

[1]Richard A. Muller, *Post-Reformation Reformed Dogmatics: The Rise and Development of Reformed Orthodoxy, ca. 1520 to ca. 1725*, vol. 4, *The Triunity of God* (Grand Rapids: Baker, 2003), p. 19.

[2]Ibid., p. 20.

[3]Ibid., p. 18. See also p. 21, where he makes the point that for the Reformers Scripture was "the primary and necessary norm," and tradition "the secondary norm."

[4]Roger E. Olson and Christopher A. Hall, *The Trinity* (Grand Rapids, Eerdmans, 2002) p. 69, argue that Luther gave more emphasis to the divine persons than to their unity. On reading Luther on the Trinity I am not convinced of this. In his sermon on the Trinity, Luther seems to give equal emphasis to divine unity and threeness. For this sermon see <www.godrules.net/library/luther/129luther_h3.htm>. On Luther's doctrine of the Trinity see also Muller, *Triunity of God*, pp. 62-63, and his bibliography in p. 63 n. 7. See also C. Helmer, "God from Eternity to Eternity: Luther's Trinitarian Understanding," *Harvard Theological Review* 96, no. 2 (2003): 127-46.

tailed discussion of the Trinity, "The Three Symbols or Creeds of the Christian Faith,"[5] he begins by arguing that "the real Christian Church" honors and confesses these symbols, or creeds.[6] He then adds that, when he comes to the clause on the Son, he has "perceived and noted that in all histories of all Christendom that all those who have correctly had and kept the chief article of Jesus Christ have remained safe and secure in the right Christian faith."[7] In his ensuing discussion he has a lengthy section on the eternal generation of the Son and the eternal procession of the Spirit, both of which he endorses without any caveats. He finds biblical support for the first in Psalm 2:7 and the second in John 15:26. He then says, "Just as the Son is born of the Father and yet does not depart from the Godhead, but on the contrary remains in the same Godhead with the Father and is one God with him, so also the Holy Spirit proceeds from the Father."[8] Then he adds,

> Accordingly this birth is much different from the birth of men; and this proceeding is much different from the proceeding of men. For a human being born of another is not only a separate individual person from his father, but also a separate individual substance, and does not remain within his father's substance, nor does the father remain in the son's substance. But here the Son is born as another person and nevertheless remains within the Father's substance, and the Father within the Son's substance. They are accordingly distinct as to person, but remain in one single, undivided, and unseparated substance.[9]

"Consequently," he says, "the theologians call this birth an immanent birth, which does not depart from the Godhead."[10]

Then on the question as to why the Son, in particular, became incarnate, Luther makes the suggestion that it was "fitting" for him to do so because he was first born in eternity and then "was physically born and became a son."[11] When it comes to eternally differentiating the

---

[5] In L. Spitz, ed., *Luther's Works* (Philadelphia: Muhlenberg, 1960), 34:199-229.
[6] Ibid., p. 201.
[7] Ibid., p. 207.
[8] Ibid., p. 217.
[9] Ibid., p. 218.
[10] Ibid.
[11] Ibid.

Father and the Son, Luther holds that Hebrews 1:3, where the Son is described as "the brilliance of his [the Father's] glory and the image of his substance" "provides us with an excellent picture."[12] Then some lines later, speaking of the Son's oneness in substance with the Father, he says, "Christ cannot be a creature. For the scriptures describe no creature as being the brilliance of the divine substance or glory."[13]

In this exposition of the three ecumenical creeds, Luther, following the Nicene tradition, explicitly predicates both the oneness in substance/ being of the divine three and their eternal differentiation in the eternal *ad intra* begetting of the Son and the eternal procession of the Spirit.

CALVIN

In evangelical literature it is sometimes claimed that John Calvin (1509-1564) rejected the historic doctrine of the eternal begetting of the Son,[14] but this is not true. The Old Princeton theologian B. B. Warfield is mainly responsible for the popularity of this idea among conservative evangelicals today.[15]

---

[12]Ibid., p. 219.

[13]Ibid., p. 220.

[14]So Paul Helm, "Of God and the Holy Trinity: A Response to Dr Beckwith," *Churchman*, 115, no. 4 (2001): 352; and R. Reymond, *A New Systematic Theology of the Christian Faith* (New York: Nelson, 1998), pp. 324-31. It is by no means clear what Reymond is arguing in relation to Calvin, but on p. 330 he quite explicitly speaks of "Calvin's rejection of the ancient doctrine of the Father's eternal generation of the Son." So also K. A. Richardson, "Calvin on the Trinity," in *John Calvin and Evangelical Theology: Legacy and Prospect*, ed. Sung Wook Chung (Milton Keynes, U.K.: Paternoster, 2009), p. 34. On Calvin's respect for the doctrinal tradition he had inherited see D. F. Kelly, "The Catholicity of Calvin's Theology," in *Tributes to John Calvin: A Celebration of his Quincentenary*, ed. D. W. Hall (Phillipsburg, N.J.: Presbyterian and Reformed, 2010), pp. 189-216; and B. W. Swinburnson, "John Calvin, Eternal Generation, and Communication of Essence: A Reexamination of his Views," *Kerux: The Journal of Northwest Theological Seminary* 25, no. 1 (2010): 26-49.

[15]In his long essay, "Calvin's Doctrine of the Trinity" in *Calvin and Augustine* (Philadelphia: Presbyterian and Reformed, 1956), pp. 189-284, Warfield says that "although he [Calvin] taught that the Son was begotten of the Father, and of course begotten before all time, or as we would say from all eternity, he seems to have drawn back from the doctrine of 'eternal generation' as it was expounded by the Nicene Fathers" (pp. 247, 250). Later he adds, Calvin "admitted the facts of 'generation' and 'procession,' [but] he treated them as bare facts, and refused to make them constitutive of the doctrine of the Trinity" (p. 257). Then last, Warfield argues that Calvin rejected the texts "customarily relied upon" to establish the doctrine of the eternal generation of the Son, concluding that there is "little Biblical basis for the doctrine of 'eternal generation' except what might be inferred from the mere terms 'Father,' 'Son' and 'Spirit'" (p. 277). Warfield in arguing that Calvin rejected "the doctrine of 'eternal generation' as it was expounded by the Nicene Fathers" would seem to contradict his many affirmations

Calvin frequently speaks of the Son as eternally begotten of the Father;[16] he calls the Father "the unbegotten" and the Son "the begotten";[17] he discusses "the eternal generation" of the Son in some detail at least twice;[18] he designates the Father as "the fountainhead of divinity,"[19] saying, "The Son is said to come forth from the Father";[20] and he clearly recognizes that at the heart of the Arian error was the idea that the Son was begotten in the sense of created in time, an idea he totally rejects.[21] Calvin's firm belief in the Nicene doctrine of the eternal generation of the Son is probably seen most clearly in the 1545 expanded section of his Genevan Catechism, where he affirms this doctrine not once but twice.

First we have the question and answer,

M. Why do you call [God the Father] Father?

S. Primarily with reference to Christ, who is the eternal Wisdom, begotten of him before all time and being sent into this world was declared to be his Son.

And second,

M. Why do you call him the only Son of God, seeing that God designs to bestow this appellation upon us all?

S. That we are the sons of God we have not from nature, but from adoption and grace only, in other words, because God put us in that place (Jn. 1:1) but the lord Jesus who was begotten of the substance of the Father and is one in essence with the Father (Eph. 1:3) is by the best title called the only Son of God, because he alone is his Son by nature (Heb. 1:1).[22]

"that in his doctrine of the Trinity Calvin departed in nothing from the doctrine which had been handed down from the orthodox fathers" (p. 229, cf. pp. 240, 279-83).

[16]John Calvin, *Institutes of the Christian Religion* 1.13.7 (ed. John T. McNeill, trans. Ford Lewis Battles [London: SCM, 1960], p. 129 [all subsequent references to Calvin's *Institutes* are to this edition]), 1.13.8 (p. 131), 1.13.17 (p. 142), 1.13.23 (p. 151), 1.13.24 (p. 152), 2.14.5 (p. 488). On this matter see Robert Letham, *The Holy Trinity in Scripture, History, Theology, and Worship* (Phillipsburg, N.J.: Presbyterian and Reformed, 2004), pp. 261-67, who also emphatically argues that Calvin endorsed the doctrine of the eternal generation of the Son.

[17]Calvin, *Institutes* 1.13.25 (p. 153).

[18]Calvin, *Institutes* 2.14.5 (p. 488), 2.14.8 (p. 492).

[19]Calvin, *Institutes* 1.13.23 (p. 149), 1.13.25 (p. 153).

[20]Calvin, *Institutes* 1.13.18 (p. 143).

[21]Calvin, *Institutes* 1.13.4 (p. 125), 1.13.5 (p. 127).

[22]Quotations taken from *John Calvin Tracts and Letters*, ed. and trans. Henry Beveridge (Carlisle, U.K.: Banner of Truth Trust, 2009), 2:41 and 43. See also J. T. Dennison, *Reformed*

What is so significant in this wording is that it perfectly reflects historic orthodoxy. Agreeing with the Greek fathers, Calvin says the Son is the unique Son because he alone is eternally begotten of the Father. And following the wording of the Creed of Nicaea (325), he says that the Son is begotten "of [Greek, *ek*] the being of the Father," or that of the Athanasian Creed, he is begotten "of [Latin, *ex*] the substance of the Father."[23] For Calvin, the begetting of the Son means that he is one in essence/being with the Father. This is what makes him the unique Son of God.

Basic to Calvin's doctrine of the Trinity is that each of the divine three share the one divine being or essence and each is God in himself, God in his own right. Thus Calvin cannot allow the view that the doctrine of the eternal generation of the Son indicates the subordination of the Son. He says to suggest that the Father is "the essence giver"[24] is to "definitely cast the Son down from his rank."[25]

Calvin's discussion of the doctrine of the Trinity is characterized by his emphasis both on divine unity *and* the threefold distinction of Father, Son and Spirit. For him divine unity is axiomatic because the divine three share and are the one being or essence of God.[26] His writing is well informed by the Greek- and Latin-speaking Nicene fathers, but the way he expresses himself as he develops the doctrine of the Trinity is often fresh and distinctively worded.

What Calvin says on the eternal begetting of the Son is the specific issue that concerns us. Calvin developed his thinking on this matter primarily in defense of his own orthodoxy against his critics. Toward the end of his positive account of the doctrine of the Trinity (section nineteen) Calvin takes up the matter of how to think rightly of the Father as the begetter or "sole beginning" (*monarche*) of the Son. He says that sometimes "the ancients"

Confessions of the 16th and 17th Century in English Translation, 1523-1552 (Grand Rapids: Reformation Heritage Books, 2008), 1:425.

[23] *Ousia/being, substance, essence* and *nature* are all synonymous trinitarian terms speaking of what is common to the divine three.

[24] Calvin, *Institutes* 1.13.23 (p. 149).

[25] Calvin, *Institutes* 1.13.23 (p. 149).

[26] Calvin, *Institutes* 1.23.16 (pp. 140-41), 1.13.19 (p. 143). In more detail on Calvin's understanding of the Trinity see my *Jesus and the Father: Modern Evangelicals Reinvent the Doctrine of the Trinity* (Grand Rapids: Zondervan, 2006), pp. 160-67, 195-99, 231-36.

teach that the Father is the beginning of the Son; sometimes they declare that the Son has both divinity and essence from himself, and thus has one beginning with the Father. Augustine well and clearly expresses the cause of this diversity . . . when he speaks as follows: "Christ with respect to himself is called God; with respect to the Father, Son. Again, the Father with respect to himself is called God; with respect to the Son, Father. In so far as he is called Father with respect to the Son, he is not the Son; in so far as he is called the Son with respect to the Father, he is not the Father; in so far as he is called both Father with respect to himself, and Son with respect to himself, he is the same God." Therefore, when we speak simply of the Son without regard to the Father, we well and properly declare him to be of himself [Latin, *ex se ipso esse*]; and for this reason called the sole beginning [Latin, *principium*]. But when we mark the relation that he has with the Father, we rightly make the Father the beginning of the Son.[27]

In this long and convoluted paragraph Calvin introduces one of his key insights, appealing to Augustine[28] and later to Cyril of Alexandria.[29] What he says, we should also note, reflects the later teaching of the Fourth Lateran Council.[30] He argues that when we think of the Father and the Son independently of each other, then we should think of the Son and the Father as both God in their own right, both self-existent God, both, to use Calvin's terms, *ex se ipso esse* or *autotheos*.[31] Calvin is claiming that Christ possesses what theologians call *aseity*. This technical term derives from the Latin *aseitas*, meaning "of oneself." To speak of the Son's *aseity* is thus to speak of him as self-existent God like the Father, God not caused or dependent on another.[32] However, to safeguard scriptural statements that speak of the Son as "from" the

---

[27]Calvin, *Institutes* 1.13.19 (pp. 143-44).

[28]For support of Calvin's appeal to Augustine, reference should be made to Augustine, *The Trinity* 5.1.7. Other references in support are given in Calvin, *Institutes* 1.13.19 (p. 144 n. 42). On this matter see also T. F. Torrance, "Calvin's Doctrine of the Trinity," in *Trinitarian Perspectives: Toward Doctrinal Agreement* (Edinburgh: T & T Clark, 1994), pp. 59-67. Torrance finds this idea also in Athanasius and Gregory of Nazianzus, pp. 64 and 65.

[29]Muller, *Triunity of God*, p. 325 and 325 n. 249; and Torrance, "Calvin's Doctrine," p. 64.

[30]See Norman Tanner, ed., *The Decrees of the Ecumenical Councils*, vol. 1, *Nicaea I to Lateran V* (London: Sheed and Ward, 1972), pp. 231-32.

[31]On these terms see Muller, *Triunity of God*, pp. 80-81. On how Calvin came to use the term *autotheos* see Warfield, "Calvin's Doctrine of the Trinity," pp. 234-44, 252-73.

[32]Muller, *Trinity of God*, pp. 324-26.

Father, Calvin adds that we rightly think of the Father as the *monarche* or "sole-beginning" of *the person of the Son*. The Father does not give the Son his divine being/essence in the eternal act of divine generation, but rather in this act of self-differentiation the Father becomes other than the Son and the Son other than the Father—yet sharing together the one being or essence. The Father is thus the Father *of* the Son, just as the Son is the Son *of* the Father, and this can never change. These irreversible relational distinctions make one Father and one Son but in no way detract or diminish the full deity of the Son because the Father and the Son are one in being/essence and power.

At this point Calvin brings his positive presentation of the doctrine of the Trinity to a conclusion. He then begins in section twenty-one to give an extended refutation of heretical ideas of the Trinity current in his day.[33] He first mentions Servetus, whom he says argued that "in the beginning there was no distinction in God" and that the Son and the Spirit "came forth from God" in time.[34] In this comment Servetus sounds very much like Arius, but it seems Servetus was basically a modalist, denying eternal divine self-differentiation.[35] Then Calvin moves to "another similar monster,"[36] almost certainly Valentine Gentile of the Italian Reformed congregation in Geneva, along with his supporters.[37] Calvin depicts him as teaching that the Father "is truly and properly the sole God, in forming the Son and the Spirit, infused into them his own deity. Indeed, they do not refrain from this dreadful manner of speaking: the Father is distinguished from the Son and the Spirit by this mark, that he [the Father] is the only 'essence giver.'"[38] In reply Calvin insists that the name "Son" does distinguish the Son from the Father, "the fountainhead and beginning of deity," but it does not imply or necessitate that he is in

---

[33]P. W. Butin, *Revelation, Redemption and Response: Calvin's Trinitarian Understanding of the Divine-Human Relationship* (Oxford: Oxford University Press, 1995), pp. 26-38, explains who Calvin is arguing with. He says that the impact of Calvin's theological battles over the Trinity should never be minimized or ignored in seeking to understand Calvin's teaching on this doctrine.

[34]Calvin, *Institutes* 1.13.22 (p. 147). See also 2.10.8 (p. 492), where Calvin returns to Servetus's erroneous teaching on the Trinity.

[35]Butin, *Revelation*, pp. 33-34, finds Servetus's teaching on the Trinity complex and confusing.

[36]Calvin, *Institutes* 1.13.23 (p. 149).

[37]On these opponents see Butin, *Revelation*, pp. 35-38; and Muller, *Triunity of God*, pp. 80-81.

[38]Calvin, *Institutes* 1.13.23 (p. 149).

any way not fully God. He is, says Calvin, "the Word begotten by the Father before all ages (cf. 1 Cor. 2:7)."[39] He then adds, "If we consider no one but the Father to be God, we definitely cast the Son down from his rank. Therefore whenever mention is made of deity, we ought by no means to admit any antithesis between Son and Father, as if the name of the true God applied to the later alone."[40]

Muller says Calvin clearly saw that what Gentile was teaching about the begetting of the Son and the procession of the Spirit "amounted to a radical subordination of the second and third persons, with the result that the Father alone is truly God."[41]

For Calvin the Son is God in the same sense as the Father is God; the Father and the Son share the one divine essence, and this is true of the Spirit also.[42] Nevertheless, Calvin adds, there must be "some mark of differentiation in order that the Father may not be the Son."[43] He denies that this difference lies in the essence because this would "annihilate Christ's true divinity."[44] To those who say it does lie in the essence he puts the question, "Let them answer whether or not he [the Father] has shared [literally, communicated; Latin, *annon cum Filio eam communicaverit*] it with the Son." If the Father has not fully communicated his essence to the Son, Calvin concludes, then in the Son we have "a half God," and the essence of God has been torn apart. The truth is rather "that the essence is wholly and perfectly common [Latin, *communis*] to the Father and the Son."[45] What is significant in this paragraph is that here Calvin speaks of the eternal generation of the Son in terms of *a perfect communication of divine essence,* language that Zacharias Ursinus[46] (1534-1583) would develop and which from then on

---

[39]Calvin, *Institutes* 1.13.23 (p. 149).

[40]Calvin, *Institutes* 1.13.23 (p. 149).

[41]Muller, *Triunity of God,* p. 81.

[42]Calvin, *Institutes* 1.1.23 (p. 150).

[43]Calvin, *Institutes* 1.1.23 (p. 150).

[44]Calvin, *Institutes* 1.1.23 (p. 150).

[45]Calvin, *Institutes* 1.1.23 (p. 151). I am thankful to Swinburnson, "John Calvin, Eternal Generation," for drawing to my attention Calvin's use of the language of communication of essence.

[46]*The Commentary of Dr. Zacharius Ursinus on the Heidelberg Catechism,* trans. G. W. Willard, introduction by J. W. Nevin (1852; repr. Phillipsburg, N.J.: Presbyterian and Reformed, 1985). Ursinus gives the longest discussion I found on what is implied in speaking of the eternal begetting of the Son in terms of a communication of the divine essence. See pp. 129-37.

would often appear in Reformed theology until the late nineteenth century. Speaking of the eternal generation of the Son in terms of a "perfect communication of divine essence" is not to be taken to mean that at this point Calvin teaches that the Father in the act of begetting the Son gives the Son his divine essence. A communication is by definition "a sharing,"[47] an event that results in something held in "common," as Calvin himself points out in the above quote. In speaking of the eternal generation of the Son as a "perfect communion or sharing of the divine essence" Calvin does not assert anything theologically innovative. The Nicene doctrine of the eternal generation of the Son is predicated on the belief that while it distinguishes the Father and the Son it speaks of their oneness in being/essence (*homoousios*).

In section twenty-five Calvin begins by saying his opponents are "deceived," because "they dream of individuals, each having its own separate part of the essence" as constituting the Trinity. In contrast, he says, "We teach from the Scriptures that God is of one essence, and hence that the essence both of the Son and the Spirit is *unbegotten;* but inasmuch as the Father is first in order, and from himself begot his wisdom, . . . he is rightly deemed the beginning and fountainhead of the whole divinity. Thus God without particularization is *unbegotten;* and the Father also in respect to his person is *unbegotten.*"[48] Then he says there is no "quarternity," as if "the three persons came forth by derivation from one essence."[49] (Here he is rejecting the idea that the one essence/being, a kind of fourth entity, is the source or origin of the three persons.) For Calvin, the divine three share the one divine essence/being, which is fully present in each of them, and thus both as the one God and the three persons they are God without any caveats. Then, he says, "We confess that the Son since he is God, exists of himself [Latin, *ex se ipsa*], but not in respect to his person; indeed since he is the Son, we say he exists from the Father. Thus his essence is without beginning; while the beginning of his person is God himself."[50]

---

[47]And so we should note that Ford Lewis Battles in the translation of the *Institutes* we are following translates the Latin *communicaverit* as "shared."

[48]Calvin, *Institutes* 1.13.25 (p. 153). Italics added.

[49]Calvin, *Institutes* 1.13.25 (p. 153).

[50]Calvin, *Institutes* 1.13.25 (p. 154).

In these words, Calvin argues yet again that the Son considered on his own is self-existent God; he has no origin. However, as *the person of the Son*, he is distinguished from the Father as the Son because his origin lies in "God himself." This is very subtle theology yet significant nonetheless. What Calvin is seeking to do is take over from the tradition the idea that the Son is fully God and exclude any hint that his divinity is given to him by the Father. His identity as the person of the Son is given by the Father, not his divinity or divine being. He and the Father are one in divinity, one in essence/being, differentiated because one is the Father, who begets, the other the Son, who is begotten. T. F. Torrance brings this whole matter into sharp focus when he says, "Calvin will have nothing to do with the idea of derived Deity as if one Deity should borrow his deity from another. That heresy shatters on the biblical identification of the incarnate Son of God with Yahweh."[51]

In completing his argument, Calvin dismisses the claim that "the subordination of the incarnate Word to the Father" is evidence that the Son is less in essence/being and power than the Father.[52] Calvin allows that, as the "Mediator," the Son willingly subordinates himself to the Father, yet Calvin says, "His majesty is not on this account diminished. For even though he emptied himself (Phil. 2:7), he lost not his glory with the Father, which was hidden to the world." Calvin is adamant: the Son is true God and never ceases to be so, yet he freely chose subordination in becoming incarnate for our salvation.

Calvin holds that the triune God existed before he created the world and, with it, time.[53] Because for him the Son is fully God, the Son must have been "begotten of God *before* time (cf. Ecclus. 24:14, Vg.)."[54] To allow that the Son was created or begotten in time would make him a creature. Calvin is convinced; the Scriptures do not allow this. The Son is not a creature: "By his eternity, his true essence and his

---

[51] Torrance, "Calvin's Doctrine," p. 61.
[52] Calvin, *Institutes* 1.13.26 (p. 154).
[53] Paul Helm, *Calvin: A Guide for the Perplexed* (Edinburgh: T & T Clark, 2008), p. 37, says Calvin is an "eternalist; that is, he holds that God exists beyond or outside of time."
[54] Calvin, *Institutes* 1.13.7 (p. 129).

divinity is proved."[55] However, Calvin thinks, "It is foolish to imagine a continuous act of begetting, since it is clear that the three persons have subsisted in God from eternity."[56] In these words Calvin is not denying the eternal generation of the Son but "the view that the eternal generation of the Son is a sort of continuing communication of essence."[57] Later Reformed theologians, as we are about to see, have generally not followed Calvin on this matter.

What Calvin is opposing from sections twenty-one to twenty-nine of chapter thirteen of the *Institutes* is "derivative subordinationism"— the idea seen in one form in Origen—which holds that the Son in his *begetting* contingently derives his "essence" (being) from the Father and is thus less than the Father. For Calvin all three persons of the Trinity are God in an absolute sense for all eternity. Derivative subordinationism for him is a very dangerous heresy. He gives more space to opposing this error than any other matter.[58] Gerald Bray says that in insisting that the Son is *autotheos* Calvin completely excluded "any hint of causality latent in the terms 'generation' and 'procession.'"[59]

Finally, we return to the charge that Calvin rejected the doctrine of the eternal generation of the Son, or in Paul Helm's case, so "pared down" this doctrine that it has little content.[60] Calvin certainly never rejected this doctrine, as we have shown, and in arguing that the Son is *autotheos*, or possesses *aseity*, in opposition to those who saw the Father as "the sole essence giver," he is not a pioneer, nor is he paring down the doctrine of the eternal generation of the Son.[61] Athanasius certainly held that the Son is eternally begotten of the Father and is thus "true

---

[55]Calvin, *Institutes* 1.13.8 (p. 131).

[56]Calvin, *Institutes* 1.13.29 (p. 159).

[57]D. F. Kelly, "The True and Triune God: Calvin's Doctrine of the Trinity," in *A Theological Guide to Calvin's Institutes*, ed. D. W. Hall and P. A. Lillback (Phillipsburg, N.J.: Presbyterian and Reformed, 2008), pp. 65-90 (89).

[58]Calvin, *Institutes* 1.13.21-26 (pp. 145-56).

[59]Gerald Bray, *The Doctrine of God* (London: Inter-Varsity Press, 1993), p. 204.

[60]Paul Helm, *John Calvin's Ideas* (Oxford: Oxford University Press, 2004), p. 56. Helm also makes the quite startling claim, ibid., p. 41, that "a doctrine of the Trinity, then, that mentions neither 'Trinity,' nor 'person,' nor 'substance,' nor the begetting of the Son nor the procession of the Spirit, is what Calvin in principle favours." This may be what Helm favors, but Calvin himself seems to believe exactly the opposite. See *Institutes* 1.13.2-3 (pp. 122-25).

[61]Muller, *Triunity of God*, p. 81, says that in this argument Calvin is only affirming "the traditional doctrine of the Trinity . . . against any essential subordination of the persons."

God from true God," God without any caveats.[62] Calvin is heavily dependent on Augustine for what he says on these matters, and what he teaches reflects the teaching of the Fourth Lateran Council (1215), as noted earlier. This means that what Calvin says on the eternal begetting of the Son and his aseity is grounded in the tradition. Letham says, "Calvin both preserves and develops the inheritance he receives."[63] Muller writes,

> The question underlying the assignment of *aseitas* to the Father and the Son was the question of precisely what is generated in the generation or begetting of the Son. In the traditional Western model, as argued by Peter Lombard and ratified in the Fourth Lateran council, the divine essence neither generates nor is generated; rather the person of the Father generates the person of the Son—with the result that the Son, considered as to his sonship, is generated, but considered as to his essence is not. . . . The Son, therefore, has all of the attributes of the divine essence, including *aseity*.[64]

And again,

> Calvin consistently agreed with traditional orthodoxy that the person of the Son subsists in relation to the Father by generation, but he also insists that, considered according to his full divinity, the Son shares the divine attribute of self-existence, or *aseitas*. After all, the essence is undivided in the three persons, so that each of the persons contains in and of himself the full essence of the Godhead.[65]

Calvin's insistence that the doctrine of the eternal generation of the Son spoke not of the Father deifying the Son and thus of his subordination but rather of the full equality of the divine three in being and power and of their eternal divine self-differentiation became a characteristic of Reformed orthodoxy, maintained by Beza[66] and by most

---

[62]See our earlier discussion on Athanasius and note, for example, Athanasius's assertion that "the whole being of the Son is proper to the Father's essence." *Discourses Against the Arians* 3.23.3 (*NPNF* 4:395). See also in support Torrance, "Calvin's Doctrine," p. 63 and 63 n. 103.
[63]Letham, *Holy Trinity*, p. 268.
[64]Muller, *Triunity of God*, p. 88.
[65]Ibid., p. 324.
[66]Ibid., p. 81.

Reformed theologians in the seventeenth century.[67] They agreed that the Son is fully God *a se ipso*—he is *autotheos*.

POST-REFORMATION THEOLOGIANS

In what follows, I will not attempt to survey what all the more important post-Reformation Protestant theologians between the seventeenth and twentieth centuries say on the eternal generation of the Son. My aim is more modest. First, I want simply to demonstrate that orthodox Protestant theologians from the time of the Reformation have recognized this doctrine as being of very high importance, and thus many of them discuss it at length. Second, I want to make my readers aware that in this period denials of the doctrine of the eternal generation of the Son became common. This means that when taken with the sixteenth-century attacks on this doctrine we have a doctrine that has been scrutinized and defended possibly as much as any doctrine.

FRANCIS TURRETIN

I take as my first representative theologian the Swiss-Italian Reformed theologian Francis Turretin (1623-1687), who is of particular importance to American Southern Presbyterians. In the early days of the old Princeton seminary Turretin's three-volume *Institutes of Elenctic Theology*, in Latin, was a set text.[68] In his extended discussion of the doctrine of the Trinity[69] he expounds, defends and endorses the historic doctrine of the eternal generation of the Son. After warning of the limits of the human mind to explain divine generation, he begins by asserting that "All generation indicates a communication of essence on the part of the begetter to the begotten (by which the begotten becomes like the begetter and partakes of the same nature with him), so that this wonderful generation [of the Son] is rightly expressed as a communication of essence from the Father (by which the Son possesses indivisibly the same essence with him and is made perfect like him)."[70]

---

[67]Ibid., p. 324.
[68]Francis Turretin, *Institutes of Elenctic Theology*, trans. G. M. Ciger, 3 vols. (Phillipsburg, N.J.: Presbyterian and Reformed, 1992).
[69]Ibid., 1:292-302.
[70]Ibid., 1:292-93.

This generation of the Son, he goes on to say, is not to be understood to replicate human generation. It is a divine act "without time," "without place" and "without any passion or change." It occurs "not in time, but from eternity." It is "unceasing."[71]

The Son's eternal generation, Turretin argues, "may be proved" by appeal to Psalm 2:7, Acts 4:25 and 13:33, Hebrews 1:5, Proverbs 8:22-31, Micah 5:2, Colossians 1:5, and Hebrews 1:3, texts he expounds in some detail.[72] Significantly, when he comes to speak of Christ as the *monogenēs* Son, he argues that the Son is given this name because he alone is said to have been "in the beginning with God; yea also to be God by whom all things were created."[73] He insists that Christ is not given the name "Son" as an honor or by grace but because he is eternally begotten of the Father "in the most perfect manner," thereby sharing completely in the one divine essence.[74]

Then he returns to the eternal aspect of the Son's begetting. Again he describes it as a timeless act *within* the life of God without beginning or end, likening it to "the rays emanating simultaneously with the sun, only in a more eminent, inexplicable manner."[75] The Father begat the Son, he says, by a "necessary and voluntary" act, not by will. "Necessarily because he begat by nature, as he is God by nature, but voluntarily, because not by coaction [*coacte*], but freely . . . of spontaneity."[76] In the Son's generation the Father generates "a person."[77] Turretin then gives this explanation: "That which is most perfect does not generate a thing differing from itself essentially, but a person differing from itself personally. For the essence of the Father is the essence of the Son and of the Holy Spirit. . . . However, to confess that the divine three have the one essence, is not to deny personal identity. Each has their own mode of subsisting."[78]

Turretin's explanation of the eternal generation of the Son in terms of a "communication" of divine essence goes back to Calvin, but the

---

[71]Ibid., 1:293.
[72]Ibid., 1:294-99.
[73]Ibid., 1:298.
[74]Ibid.
[75]Ibid., 1:301.
[76]Ibid.
[77]Ibid.
[78]Ibid.

prominence of this idea in his work may be traced back to Zacharias Ursinus's earlier exposition of the Heidelberg Catechism. What this language underlines is that the eternal begetting speaks of the Father and the Son sharing in "common" the one divine essence or being.

JOHN OWEN

John Owen (1616-1683) is widely recognized as the greatest of the seventeenth-century Puritan theologians. He was informed on the history of the doctrine of the Trinity, and trinitarian thinking pervades his writings. This is clearly seen in his large studies on communion with God, the doctrine of the Holy Spirit and on the glory of Christ.[79] Against the English Socinians, who denied the eternal generation of the Son, and the Arminians, who argued that the eternal generation of the Son indicates his subordination, he wrote *Vindiciae evangelicae; or, the Mystery of the Gospel Vindicated and Socinianism Examined* (1655)[80] and *A Brief Declaration and Vindication of the Doctrine of the Trinity: as also of the Person and Satisfaction of Christ* (1699).[81] In these two works, one of Owen's primary concerns is to establish by appeal to Scripture the preexistence and eternity of the Son.[82] He directs most of his arguments to John Biddle, a Socinian who is often called "the father of English Unitarianism." However, the Arminian leader Episcopus and the Arminian-leaning Hugo Grotius are often named and addressed because they subordinated the Son to the Father on the premise that the begetting of the Son implied his diminution in divine being and power.

The Socinians denied Christ's pre-existence, arguing that all the texts that speak of his begetting refer to his human begetting in the incarnation. For them, Jesus grew "to be God by degrees," ultimately

---

[79]On Owen's writings see *The Works of John Owen*, ed. William Gould, 17 vols. (1850-1853; repr., London: Banner of Truth, 1972).

[80]Ibid., vol. 12.

[81]Ibid., vol. 2.

[82]So in *A Brief Declaration*, vol. 2, we note that he has just under two pages each under the following headings: "There is one God," and "The Father is God" and twenty-two pages under the heading "Jesus Christ is God, the eternal Son," pp. 282-404. In *Vindiciae Evangelicae*, vol. 12, p. 170, he says the Socinians' aim is to "despoil our blessed Lord Jesus of his eternal deity."

being "adopted Son of God" by the Father.[83] In answer to their teaching Owen concentrates on biblical exegesis. He argues that Jesus is the unique Son of God by eternal generation. He is the *monogenēs* Son (Jn 1:18), and only of him does Paul say he is God's "own" Son (Rom 8:32), his "proper" Son, his "natural" Son.[84] This honor he bears because he is "begotten of the essence of his Father."[85] And then he says, "Nothing can give such an equality but a *communication* of essence."[86] This communication of divine essence, Scripture teaches, takes place in eternity. He quotes in support Psalm 2:7, "This day I have begotten you," interpreting it in the light of the words of Proverbs 8:25, "Before the Hills were I brought you forth"; John 5:26, "The Father has given to the Son to have life in himself," taking this to mean that in eternity the Father communicated divine life to the Son; John 1:1, "In the beginning was the Word"; and John 17:5, "Glorify me" with "the glory I had in your presence before the world existed."[87]

Much of Owen's criticism of the Socinian "biblical" arguments is what we would call today hermeneutical. He argues that they quote texts in isolation, giving them a meaning that cannot be reconciled with the whole of Scripture. Thus he criticizes them for quoting only four verses that could possibly teach the eternal generation of the Son (Ps 2:7; 110:3; Prov 7:23; Mic 5:2),[88] explaining them away unsatisfactorily and ignoring much else in Scripture that speaks of Christ's eternity and of his generation in eternity. He says to them, "Let the gentlemen take their own way and method, we shall meet them at the first stile, or rather brazen wall, which they endeavour to climb over."[89]

However, the Socinian attack on the doctrine of the eternal generation of the Son was not only "biblical," it was also rationalistic. Thus they argued that

---

[83]John Owen, *Vindiciae*, p. 181.
[84]Ibid., p. 185.
[85]Ibid., p. 186.
[86]Ibid.
[87]Ibid., p. 189.
[88]Ibid., p. 236.
[89]Ibid.

this generation out of the Father's essence involves contradiction. For if Christ had been generated out of the essence of his Father, he must have taken either a part of it, or the whole. He could not have taken part of it, because the divine essence is indivisible. Neither could he have taken the whole; for in this case the Father would have ceased to be Father, and would have become the Son; and again since the divine essence is numerically one, and therefore incommunicable, this could not have happened.[90]

For Owen such reasoning was "the fruit of measuring spiritual things by carnal, infinite by finite, God by ourselves, the object of faith by corrupted rules of corrupted reason."[91] It indicated that the Socinians had set human reason over Scripture, failing to recognize the limitations of human logic and the corruption of the human mind by sin. For Owen, "What is impossible in finite, limited essences, may be possible and convenient to that which is infinite and unlimited, as that whereof we speak."[92] If Scripture spoke of eternal sonship and eternal generation, he adds, then reason should bow to Scripture.

Owen is adamant that the Son is "true God from true God." He writes, "The Scriptures never say, that the Father is the only true God. . . . We grant to the Father to be the only true God; and so we say is the Son also."[93] Again, following the tradition, he grounds the threefold divine distinctions in differing origination; it "lieth in this that the Father begetteth the Son, and the Son is begotten of the Father, and the Holy Spirit proceedeth from both."[94] What I find refreshingly distinctive in Owen's writings on the Trinity is his preoccupation with the eternity of the Son. For him if the Son is preexistent and eternal, and he finds much scriptural support for this, then this can only be explained by an eternal begetting, and an eternal begetting speaks of oneness in divine essence.

JOHN GILL

I take John Gill (1697-1771) as an example of an eighteenth-century English theologian with a concern to uphold the doctrine of the eternal

---

[90]*Racovian Catechism*, iv.1, quoted in part by Owen, *Vindiciae*, p. 237.
[91]Owen, *Vindiciae*, p. 237.
[92]Ibid.
[93]Owen, *A Brief Declaration*, p. 410.
[94]Ibid., p. 405. See also p. 406.

generation of the Son. Gill was an erudite, self-taught Baptist linguist and theologian, the only individual ever to have written a commentary on every verse of the Bible. In his *Body of Divinity*,[95] published just before his death, we see the fruits of his lifelong study of the Scriptures in their original languages and the breadth of his lifetime of reading of the Fathers and the Reformers. He devotes twenty pages of this work to an exposition of the doctrine of the eternal generation of the Son.[96] He argues that the doctrine arises because Scripture clearly speaks of one God in three persons, and this must be explained. For him the doctrine of the eternal generation of the Son is primarily grounded in the biblical revelation of God as Father and Son. These names suggest a generative act and, because this generation is divine, an eternal act. In making the case for the eternal generation of the Son primarily on this basis, Gill reflects the thinking of Athanasius, the Cappadocian fathers, Augustine and Aquinas. Much to my surprise, I found him speaking of the names "father" and "son" as "correlates," which "mutually put or suppose each other"[97]—terminology that is common in contemporary books on the Trinity. Repeatedly, he speaks of the importance of the doctrine of the eternal generation of the Son. "It is easy to observe," he says, "that the distinctions of persons in the deity, depends on the generation of the Son; take away that, which would destroy the relation between the second and first persons, and the distinctions drop."[98] To abandon speaking of the generation of the Son, he adds, "is dangerous, and generally leads into one error or another."[99] What must be avoided at all cost, he insists, is both thinking of the generation of the Son as a creative act that produces a creature and of thinking of it in "carnal and corporal" terms.[100] Like Aquinas, he says divine generation is to be likened to the coming forth of an idea in the mind.[101] It is an act that takes place in God; it is not an act that produces something external to God.

---

[95]John Gill, *Body of Divinity* (Grand Rapids: Sovereign Grace, 1971).
[96]Ibid., pp. 140-60.
[97]Ibid., p. 147.
[98]Ibid., p. 142, cf. p. 144.
[99]Ibid., p. 143.
[100]Ibid., p. 145.
[101]Ibid.

He explicitly rejects the thesis that to speak of the generation of the Son indicates his dependence, subordination and submission. He writes,

> As to the subordination and subjection and inequality, which it is supposed the Sonship of Christ by generation implies; it may be answered, that Christ in his office-capacity, in which he is the Mediator, is a servant, and as he is a man, and appeared in the form of one . . . is subordinate and subject to the Father; but not as he is the Son of God: and whatever inequality sonship may imply among men, it implies no such thing in the divine nature, among the divine persons; who in it subsist in perfect equality with one another.[102]

A better outline of the doctrine of the eternal generation of the Son in twenty pages would be hard to find. What strikes me most forcibly is that Gill does not seek to evaluate or ground this doctrine merely by appeal to a handful of proof texts, although he does reference Psalm 2:7 several times. He predicates this doctrine preeminently on the revelation that the names of the first and second persons of the Trinity are given in Scripture as Father and Son, arguing that these names imply an eternal generative act. He then seeks to show the huge importance of this doctrine for a right understanding of the triune God.

SAMUEL MILLER

Moving to America in the early nineteenth century we take as our first defender of the doctrine of the eternal generation of the Son Samuel Miller (1769-1850) of Princeton Theological Seminary. To explain his contribution, we must set his writings in the context of the debate between New England theologians and Southern Presbyterian theologians. In 1819 William Ellery Channing, the eloquent minister of the Federal Street Church in Boston, preached a sermon setting out the beliefs of "Unitarian Christianity." One of several replies to Channing's sermon came from Professor Moses Stuart (1780-1852) of Andover Theological Seminary, founded some five years before Princeton, in 1807. His reply, in the form of five "letters" to

---

[102]Ibid., p. 148.

Channing,[103] begins with a letter on how to rightly interpret Scripture, in which he asserts his own high view of Scripture. In the following "letters," the doctrines of the Trinity and Christology come onto center stage. One of his major concerns is to refute Channing's argument that the orthodox doctrine of the Trinity implies tritheism. However, in giving his understanding of the orthodox doctrine of the Trinity, he dismisses the doctrine of the eternal generation of the Son on the basis that it makes no sense. To be begotten or generated, he believes, speaks of a beginning in time and of derivation and dependency. To speak of the Son of God in these terms, he says, "is out of the question," if he is truly God.[104] Another reply to Channing came from Samuel Miller of Princeton, when he was invited to preach at the First Presbyterian Church in Baltimore in 1820. He declared that a "fatal decline of orthodoxy" occurred when creeds were called into question, and he charged Channing and his fellow Unitarians with promulgating "soul destroying errors."[105] When Moses Stuart read what Miller had written on these matters subsequent to his sermon,[106] he published his *Letters on the Eternal Generation of the Son of God, Addressed to the Rev. Samuel Miller D.D.*, 1822.[107] Stuart was unambiguously opposed to Unitarianism, but he could not endorse the doctrine of the eternal generation of the Son, as we have noted. In this book he multiplies and develops his objections. The doctrine of the eternal generation of the Son is to be rejected because it is "not taught in scripture,"[108] it reflects Platonic ideas,[109] it makes no sense,[110] and it makes the Son "derived and dependent" God and thus subordinate

---

[103]Moses Stuart, *Letters to the Rev. Wm. E. Channing, Containing Remarks on his Sermon, Recently Preached and Published in Baltimore*, 3rd ed. (Baltimore: Flagg and Gould, 1819).

[104]Ibid., p. 42.

[105]D. B. Calhoun, *Princeton Seminary: Faith and Learning, 1812-1868* (Edinburgh: Banner of Truth, 1994), 1:294, tells this story well.

[106]There were more publications than I have mentioned. For a chronological listing see D. Wells, ed., *Reformed Theology in America: A History of Its Modern Development* (Grand Rapids: Baker, 1997), p. 57 n. 12.

[107]Moses Stuart, *Letters on the Eternal Generation of the Son of God, Addressed to the Rev. Samuel Miller D.D.* (Andover: Flagg and Gould, 1822).

[108]Ibid., p. 90; see also pp. 13-17, 95.

[109]Ibid., pp. 70-74.

[110]Ibid., pp. 78-85.

God.[111] In making his case Professor Stuart strongly asserts his belief in the sufficiency and authority of Scripture.[112] In contrast, he is critical of the ante-Nicene fathers and the Nicene Creed, both of which he argues were heavily influenced by Platonic ideas.[113]

In his rejoinder, *Letters on the Eternal Sonship of Christ, Addressed to the Rev. Stuart, of Andover,*[114] Miller gives an extensive (295 pages), biblically based and historically informed defense of the doctrine of the eternal generation of the Son. He begins by saying that for orthodoxy the doctrine of the eternal generation of the Son is "highly important."[115] To deny this doctrine is to give way to "the enemies of truth."[116] Fundamental to his reply is his argument that the *Logos* and the Son are to be identified together and that both are eternal. For him there can be no Father without Son. In reply to Stuart's argument that the doctrine of the eternal generation of the Son implies the Son's derivation and dependency and thus his subordination, Miller says, "I do *not* admit into my views of the subject, any ideas of *creation,* on the part of the Father, or *derivation, inferiority,* or *subordination,* on the part of the Son. The idea of a *derived* or *inferior* God is quite abhorrent to my feelings, and as alien to my creed, as it can be of yours."[117] Early in his case he sums up his position succinctly and profoundly in these words.

> The First Person was for eternity Father, and the second Person was for eternity Son: not by creation, or adoption, or incarnation, or office but by *nature;* the true, proper, co-equal, co-essential, co-eternal Son of the Father, because for eternity possessing the same nature, and the same plenitude of Divine perfection with himself.
>
> The terms b*egotten* and *generation,* are intended by the Spirit of God to refer to the same relation which the names Father and Son express. If so, and if the Father was eternal Father, and the Son eternal Son; then the latter, in the sense meant to be conveyed by the term begotten, was

---

[111]Ibid., pp. 87, 90-92, 155.
[112]Ibid., pp. 13-14, 94.
[113]Ibid., pp. 12, 65-77, 159-60.
[114]Samuel Miller, *Letters on the Eternal Sonship of Christ, Addressed to the Rev. Stuart, of Andover* (Philadelphia: W. W. Woodward, 1823).
[115]Ibid., p. 13.
[116]Ibid., p. 18.
[117]Ibid., p. 31.

eternally begotten. In one word, the generation of the Son was eternal. This language I believe, is to be understood in Divine and ineffable sense; in a sense above earthly sense.[118]

Having read this summary of his position, we are not surprised that when he comes to the biblical case for the eternal generation of the Son, he says, "My first argument in favour is the eternal Sonship of Christ is drawn from the correlate names, *Father* and *Son*."[119] The fact that the Bible depicts God as eternally Father, eternally Son and eternally Holy Spirit, he argues, leads to the necessary conclusion that the one God is eternally triune—"self-differentiated," to use my expression. The eternal begetting of the Son and procession of the Spirit explain how this is so by speaking of differing divine "relations" in a way that safeguards and affirms oneness in divine nature/being. Some twenty pages later Miller comes "to consider some of those detached passages of Scripture, which I am constrained to regard as teaching the doctrine of the eternal sonship of Christ" and thus his eternal generation.[120] He begins with a careful exposition of Proverbs 8:22-31 and then proceeds to expound the other texts that are generally quoted in support of the doctrine of the eternal generation of the Son, adding others and in each case making telling observations. Rather than finding little or no support in Scripture to warrant this doctrine, he finds the doctrine well-grounded in Scripture.

In letter four he considers biblical counterevidence and finds it wanting. In letters five and six he gives a comprehensive outline of the teaching on the eternal sonship and generation of the Son in the Fathers, exhibiting wide-reading and attention to detail. In contrast to Professor Stuart, he thinks the Fathers have much to teach the church, and their theological reasoning and understanding of the Bible is to be commended and followed. In letter seven he considers rational and philosophical objections to the doctrines of the eternal generation of the Son and procession of the Spirit and finds them wanting. He sums up and concludes his case in letter eight.

---

[118]Ibid., p. 38.
[119]Ibid., p. 47.
[120]Ibid., p. 76.

Samuel Miller's defense of the parallel doctrines of eternal sonship and generation of the Son is dated in language and in other ways, yet it is still compelling. It represents confessional Reformed and evangelical theological work at its best. I only wish I had found this largely ignored and forgotten book at the beginning of my research, not at the end. It is a must-read for those who would seek to understand the doctrine of the eternal generation of the Son.

WILLIAM G. T. SHEDD

Another nineteenth-century American defense of the doctrine of the eternal generation of the Son is given by William Shedd (1820-1894), the Presbyterian professor of systematic theology at Union Theological Seminary, New York, from 1874-1890. In his chapter on the Trinity, in the first volume of his *Dogmatic Theology*,[121] he first discusses God in unity before discussing the divine three. He begins his discussion of the three persons by grounding their differentiation in the internal life of God. He designates the eternal begetting of the Son and procession of the Spirit "constitutional" acts, understood as *"opera ad intra* [works within the life of God] because they are not emanent or transitive acts that go out of and beyond the divine essence, and produce external results—such as the creation of a new substance from nothing, like that of the finite universe."[122] They are not "creative acts. They originate nothing external to God, and other than God."[123] And they are not temporal acts but "eternal and unceasing."[124] And they are necessary yet free acts. It is of "the nature and constitution of the Godhead that from all eternity the Father should generate the Son,"[125] and the Father and the Son "spirate" the Holy Spirit.[126] These works *ad intra* are, he finds, taught in Scripture, and he gives the texts commonly quoted which he

---

[121]William G. T. Shedd, *Dogmatic Theology*, vols. 1 to 3 (Edinburgh: T & T Clark, 1888-1894). See 1:285-300. His discussion on the eternal begetting of the Son is not finished at p. 300. In subsequent pages discussing the Father and the Son this topic comes up many times.
[122]Ibid., p. 285.
[123]Ibid., p. 287.
[124]Ibid., p. 288.
[125]Ibid., p. 289.
[126]Ibid., p. 290.

thinks prove what he has argued.[127] The generation of the Son and procession of the Spirit, he says, is to be understood as "communication of the divine essence"[128]: "The term communication must be taken etymologically. By generation the Father makes the eternal essence common (*koinonia*) to himself and the Son."[129] This means, he says, "The results of these two eternal, constitutional, and necessary activities of generation and spiration in the divine essence are two distinct *emanations* of the essence. There is no creation of a new essence, but the modification of an existing one."[130] The church fathers gave this explanation: "The Son is from the Father, not as an effect from a cause; not as an inferior from a superior; not as a created finite substance from an uncreated infinite substance; but as intelligence is from intellect, the river from a spring, the ray from the sun."[131]

He also makes the point that the divine essence "can subsist *indivisibly* and *totally* in more persons than one."[132] And, "The great mystery of the Trinity is, that one and the very same substance, can subsist as an undivided whole in three persons simultaneously."[133] This simultaneous sharing in the one divine nature, he says, led "the Nicene trinitarians to speak of the *perichōrēsis* (mutual indwelling) of the divine three."[134]

Some of Shedd's language could be disputed, but overall his is an informed and well-argued exposition of the historically developed doctrine of the eternal generation of the Son and procession of the Spirit, which shows he recognized the great importance of these two doctrines.

BAVINCK AND BERKHOF

Two early twentieth-century, well-reasoned and weighty defenses of the doctrine of the eternal generation of the Son are found in Herman Bavinck's *Reformed Dogmatics*, specifically volume two, published in

---

[127]Ibid., pp. 291-92.
[128]Ibid., p. 293.
[129]Ibid.
[130]Ibid., p. 294.
[131]Ibid.
[132]Ibid., p. 296.
[133]Ibid., p. 297.
[134]Ibid., p. 299.

Dutch between 1906 and 1911,[135] and Louis Berkhof's *Systematic Theology*, first published in 1939.[136]

Bavinck begins by stressing that the language of eternal begetting or generation is "analogical" human language, and when we use it of God "we must be careful to remove all associations with imperfection and sensuality from it."[137] And unlike human generation, divine generation takes place within the eternal life of God. It arises out of divine "fecundity," the generative and fruitful nature of God.[138] It is a "spiritual" generation, giving rise "to distinction" in the divine being but not separation or division[139]: "The most striking analogy of divine generation is thought and speech, and Scripture itself suggests this when it calls the Son '*Logos*' (Speech, Word, Reason). Just as the human mind objectivizes itself in speech, so God expresses his entire being in the *Logos*."[140]

The doctrine of the eternal generation of the Son "implies that the Father begets the Son out of the being of the Father."[141] As a consequence the Son is as fully God as God the Father. He then quotes the words of the Nicene Creed that teach just this truth: "God of God, Light of Light, very God of very God."[142] This truth, he says, is to be contrasted with the Arian view that the Son was generated by the will of the Father in time by an act of creation.[143] Finally, Bavinck makes the point that the generation, or begetting, of the Son is "an eternal unchanging act of God, at once always complete and eternally ongoing."[144]

Berkhof has a short yet excellent explanation and defense of the doctrine of the eternal generation of the Son. It stands apart because of its conceptual clarity and accuracy. He begins by saying, first, that "the personal property of the Son is that he is eternally begotten of the

---

[135]The four volumes are now in English. See Herman Bavinck, *Reformed Dogmatics*, trans. J. Vriend (Grand Rapids: Baker Academic, 2006).

[136]Louis Berkhof, *Systematic Theology* (London: Banner of Truth, 1958). Berkhof lived in America. He was the president of Calvin Theological Seminary for many years.

[137]Ibid., p. 308.

[138]Ibid.

[139]Ibid., p. 309.

[140]Ibid.

[141]Ibid.

[142]Ibid.

[143]Ibid.

[144]Ibid., p. 310.

Father."[145] In other words, what distinguishes the Son from the Father and the Spirit is that he alone is eternally begotten of the Father. Second, "the doctrine of the generation of the Son is suggested by the biblical representation of the first and second person of the Trinity as standing in the relation of Father and Son to each other."[146] In other words, the biblical names Father and Son imply a generative act called "begetting." He then lists several "particulars" demanded for a correct understanding of this doctrine.

1. The eternal generation of the Son "*is a necessary act of God*," because God is naturally generative. It is not by "optional will" or "contingent."[147]

2. "*It is an eternal act of the Father*," in the sense that "it is a timeless act, the act of the eternal present."[148]

3. "*It is the generation of the personal subsistence rather than the divine essence of the Son.*" The Father does not "generate the essence of the Son." To make this assertion, he says, "is the equivalent to saying He generated his own essence, for the essence of both the Father and the Son is the same. It is better to say that the Father generates the personal subsistence of the Son, but thereby also communicates to Him the divine essence in its entirety."[149]

4. "*It is a generation that must be conceived of as spiritual and divine.*" Rather than indicating a necessary "division and separation in the divine Being . . . it excludes all "division or change. It brings *distinctio* and *distributio* but not *diversitas* and *divisio* in divine Being."[150]

KARL BARTH

Finally, we come to Karl Barth (1886-1968), who is generally acknowledged to be one of the most important theologians of the twentieth century. Barth definitely stands within the Reformed tradition, and in

---

[145]Ibid., p. 95.
[146]Ibid.
[147]Ibid.
[148]Ibid.
[149]Ibid.
[150]Ibid., p. 94.

recent years evangelicals have been more open to learning from him than they were in the past. In the first volume of his famous fourteen-volume *Church Dogmatics,* published in German in 1936, he begins by speaking of God as the self-revealing God. Because he wrote this work on the Trinity more than seventy years ago, I do not include him in my discussion of some contemporary mainline theologians' views on the doctrine of the eternal generation of the Son in chapter ten.

For Barth, Christ is God without any caveats. He writes, "If Jesus were only a creature he could not reveal God, for the creature certainly cannot take God's place and work in his place. If he reveals God, then irrespective of his creaturehood he himself has to be God."[151] Immediately following his discussion of God the Revealer, Barth begins his exposition of the doctrine of the Trinity. In his section "The eternal Son," we find an extended discussion on the doctrine of the eternal generation of the Son in the context of an exposition of the Nicene Creed. On the second clause of the creed, beginning with the words, "We believe in one Lord, Jesus Christ," Barth comments on the first words immediately following, "the only [*monogenēs*] Son." This specific affirmation about the Son he says emphasizes "the oneness, which means the exclusiveness and uniqueness of the revelation and reconciliation enacted in Jesus Christ. To believe in him as the Son of God is to know no other Son of God alongside him."[152] And, he adds, by confessing him as *monogenēs* we are "confessing the oneness and uniqueness of the revelation that took place in Jesus Christ."[153] To confess the unique Son as eternally begotten of the Father is to confess the belief that Jesus Christ "did not come into being in time as such, that he did not come into being in an event within the created world."[154] The *pro pantōn aiōnōn,* translated either as "before all time" or "eternally," Barth says, should not be understood as a "temporal definition."[155]

---

[151]*Church Dogmatics* I/1, ed. Geoffrey W. Bromiley and T. F. Torrance, 2nd ed. (Edinburgh: T & T Clark, 1975), p. 406. I have taken the liberty in this quote and the others following of using lowercase for the first consonant in divine pronouns given in the translation as capitals.
[152]Ibid., p. 424.
[153]Ibid., p. 425.
[154]Ibid., p. 426.
[155]Ibid., p. 427.

It speaks, rather, both of what is "antecedently" true before the incarnation and of what "takes place today, that it took place yesterday, and that it will take place tomorrow."[156] This clause thus asserts that the incarnate one is "the eternal Son of the eternal Father."[157]

Next he notes that the creed speaks of the eternally begotten Son as "God from God, Light from Light, true God from true God, begotten not made." In this phrase Barth sees both identity and differentiation, "unity and distinction." He writes, "We have to distinguish light and light and God and God . . . [and] to understand this as a distinction in God himself. We have not to understand it as though there were God on the one side and a creature on the other, but in such a way that the one God is found equally on both sides."[158] The words, "True God from [*ek*] true God," Barth says, speak of

> very God grounded in and proceeding from very God—that is Jesus Christ. That is God only in this mode of being. The distinction of mode of being in which Jesus Christ exists, then, in relation to another mode of being, a relation which the *ek* shows to be a grounding in or proceeding from. Conversely the unity of the two modes of being as *modes* of being of an absolutely identical *being* is denoted by the repletion of the noun *Theos* along with the emphatic repetition of the adjective *alethinos* ["true"].[159]

In speaking of what the Western tradition has called the divine "persons," Barth uses the German word *Seinsweise*, translated "mode of being." The term reflects the Cappadocian *tropos hyparxeos*, which they use of the divine three. Barth, in speaking of "three modes of being," is not seeking to change the historic doctrine of the Trinity but to express better what orthodoxy has meant by the term "person" when used of Father, Son and Spirit.[160] What he wants to exclude is the thought that the divine "persons" are three separated individuals, as is the case when we speak of human beings. Barth will not allow that the "threeness" in God in any way undermines the unity of God. To say the one God is

---

[156]Ibid.
[157]Ibid.
[158]Ibid.
[159]Ibid., p. 429.
[160]Kevin N. Giles, "Barth and Subordinationism," *Scottish Journal of Theology* 64, no. 3 (2011): 327-46.

triune does not imply "threefold deity either in the sense of a plurality of Gods, or in the sense of the existence of a plurality of individuals or parts within the one Godhead."[161] Rather, "The name of Father, Son and Spirit means that God is the one God in threefold repetition, and in such a way that the repetition itself is grounded in his Godhead."[162]

The last words, "begotten, not made," in the clause beginning "God from God," Barth believes, are "the most decisive." The "not made," he says, "Tell us that in his mode of being in God Jesus Christ is certainly from God, yet he is not from God in the way that creatures from the highest angel to the smallest particle of sun-dust are from God, namely, by creation, i.e., in such a way that he had his existence, as an existence distinct from God, through the will and word of God."[163]

And the word "begotten," he says,

> denotes the real becoming of Jesus Christ, his eternal becoming appropriate to him as God, his relation of origin and dependence as God in his distinctive mode of being. And it uses a figure of speech from the creaturely realm to do this.[164]
>
> It denotes the bringing forth of God from God, whereas creating denotes only the bringing forth of the creature by God.[165]

However, Barth is quite emphatic that the word "begetting" is a metaphor. He says, "Obviously the natural character of the metaphor of begetting makes it clear at the outset that in all that is said about Father and Son in description of two modes of being in God we have a frail and contestable figure of speech. We denote God in this way but we do not grasp him."[166]

Barth then explores at some length what the very human and metaphorical words "begetting," "Father," "Son" and "Word"[167] might say about God. Since God cannot be defined by human terms, he argues, we must accept that the true meaning of these words is found in their

---

[161]Ibid., p. 350.
[162]Ibid.
[163]Ibid., p. 430.
[164]Ibid.
[165]Ibid., p. 433.
[166]Ibid., p. 431.
[167]Ibid., pp. 431-37.

"original and proper meaning" in God's own life. Their meaning in human speech only dimly and imperfectly reflects that reality.[168] In the end he concludes that what the "figure" of begetting speaks of is

> [the] distinction and unity in God which is inescapably presented to us in revelation itself . . . when it understands Jesus Christ, the Word of God, as the eternal Word. The Word of God in which he gives himself to be known by us is none other than that in which he knows himself.[169]
>
> As the Word which God thinks or speaks eternally by himself and whose content can thus be no other than God himself, Jesus Christ as God's second mode of being is God himself.[170]

In these words Barth makes it clear what he has implied all along, namely, that the language of eternal begetting speaks of what takes place in God *ad intra*. It is not a creative act *ad extra* that produces a Son other than God the Father but rather an act of eternal self-differentiation in the very life of God which replicates God. In this divine act *ad intra* the Son is eternally differentiated in his mode of being as the Son from the Father in his mode of being as the Father, yet they are not separated or divided; they remain the one God. The Son is fully God in all might, majesty and power, one with the Father and the Spirit.[171]

There is nothing to suggest in the subsequent volumes of the *Church Dogmatics* that Barth came to question in any way the doctrine of the eternal generation of the Son. However, in recent years a lively scholarly debate has emerged as to whether or not to follow his innovative reformulation of the doctrine of election in volume 2.2. Barth came to think that divine threefold self-differentiation, spoken of in terms of the eternal generation of the Son and the eternal procession of the Spirit, is a consequence of God's determination being "God for us" or is logically prior to and constitutive of God's being.[172] Bruce McCormack initiated the debate by arguing that in logical sequence Barth implies that God first decided to be God for us and then as a result triune. In reply Paul

---

[168]Ibid., p. 432.

[169]Ibid., p. 435.

[170]Ibid., p. 436.

[171]"Karl Barth and Subordinationism," pp. 327-46.

[172]On this debate see M. T. Dempsey, *Trinity and Election in Contemporary Theology* (Grand Rapids: Eerdmans, 2011).

Molnar argues that Barth never allows that God's freedom to be God is qualified in any way and his decision to be God-for-us is entirely all of grace. If this is the case then for Barth God exists eternally as Father, Son and Holy Spirit, and would so have existed even if he had never decided to create and save (i.e., "to be God for us").[173] I am persuaded that Molnar is right in his reading of Barth but I do not think I need say more on this debate for the purposes of this book.

CONCLUSION

We have seen in Reformation and post-Reformation theology an ongoing and emphatic defense of the creedal doctrine of the eternal generation of the Son, well grounded in Scripture, often in the face of denials or misrepresentations of it. For those evangelicals who would call themselves "Reformed," this is a "tradition" that cannot be ignored or perfunctorily dismissed.

---

[173]This assertion reflects Molnar's primary thesis that for Barth the ontological Trinity speaks of God as he is for all eternity and the economic Trinity of his revelation of himself in history in the work of creation and salvation.

8

Does the Eternal Generation of the Son Imply or Necessitate the Eternal Subordination of the Son?

◆ ◆ ◆

The Nicene fathers, as we have seen, believed that the doctrine of the eternal generation of the Son secured two essential elements in the Nicene faith: (1) the unity of being and power of the Father and the Son and (2) their eternal self-differentiation. Surprisingly evangelicals in recent years have called both these beliefs into question. Some argue that the doctrine of the eternal generation of the Son actually implies or necessitates the eternal subordination of the Son and thus should be abandoned. Others argue that there are better ways to eternally differentiate the divine persons than the idea that the Father is eternally unbegotten God and the Son eternally begotten God and for this reason the doctrine should be abandoned. In this chapter we will examine the first charge: the eternal generation of the Son implies or necessitates the eternal subordination of the Son. In the next chapter we will examine the claim by some evangelicals that either the differing works of the three divine persons is what primarily and eternally differentiates them or that differing authority of the three divine persons is what primarily and eternally differentiates them.

ETERNAL GENERATION IMPLIES OR NECESSITATES THE SON'S ETERNAL SUBORDINATION

Many evangelicals today believe that the doctrine of the eternal generation of the Son implies or necessitates the eternal subordination of the Son, but there agreement ends. Some evangelicals endorse the doctrine because they think it supports their belief that the Son is eternally subordinated to the Father; some reject it for exactly the same reason. However, within these two alternatives there are two variants. I will therefore need to outline four evangelical views that in one way or another presuppose that the eternal begetting of the Son implies or necessitates his eternal subordination and submission to the Father. The people representing these differing positions were all introduced in chapter one when discussing evangelical calls to abandon the doctrine of the eternal generation of the Son.

THE FOUR VIEWS

1. The doctrine of the eternal generation of the Son should be *endorsed* because it teaches the ontological subordination of the Son, something evangelicals should believe.

I have already mentioned that my interest in the doctrine of the Trinity, and in particular the doctrine of the eternal generation of the Son, goes back to my reading in late 1989 of John Dahms's article "The Generation of the Son" in the *Journal of the Evangelical Theological Society*.[1] In this essay he says he is writing in support of the words "eternally begotten by the Father" in creedal definitions of the faith because they provide "an *ontological* basis for the subordination of the Son of [*sic*] the Father."[2] This doctrine, he says, speaks of the "*derivation* of the Son from the Father"[3] and thus his dependency on him and subordination to him, thereby providing "an *ontological basis* for the *dissimilarity* of the Father and the Son."[4] Throughout the essay, Dahms makes it plain that he thinks the ontological subordination of the Son is what orthodox Christians should believe. It is what the Bible and the creeds teach.[5]

---

[1] John Dahms, "The Generation of the Son," *Journal of the Evangelical Theological Society* 32, no. 4 (1989): 493-501. See also Dahms, "The Subordination of the Son," *Journal of the Evangelical Theological Society* 37, no. 3 (1994): 351-64.
[2] Ibid., p. 497.
[3] Ibid., p. 499.
[4] Ibid., p. 497. Italics added.
[5] His very last paragraph, ibid., p. 501, says this explicitly.

2. The doctrine of the eternal generation of the Son should be *rejected* because it teaches the Arian error of the ontological subordination of the Son.

This position is most starkly stated by Walter Martin in his widely read book *The Kingdom of the Cults*.[6] In discussing the theology of Jehovah's Witnesses he argues at length that orthodox Christians should give up the doctrine of the eternal generation of the Son because it has "fed the Arian heresy through the centuries and today continues to feed the Christology of Jehovah's Witnesses."[7] It is a mistake to think of Jesus as the eternal Son who is generated in eternity because this "definitely suggests [his] inferiority and derivation."[8] Jesus is the eternal Word, not the eternal Son.

Similarly, Mark Driscoll and Gerry Breshears argue that the doctrine of the eternal generation of the Son should be abandoned because the term "begotten unavoidably implies a beginning of the one begotten. That would certainly lend support to the Arian heresy that the Son is a created being and not the Creator God."[9]

3. The doctrine of the eternal generation of the Son should be *accepted* because it reflects the belief that the Son is eternally subordinated in role and authority, but not ontologically, a belief all evangelicals should hold. (역할 권위 . not 존재론)

The belief that the eternal generation of the Son implies or necessitates the eternal subordination and submission of the Son to the Father is now well entrenched in the evangelical community. However, most evangelicals of this persuasion want to avoid speaking of the *ontological* subordination of the Son, as Dahms did, even if what they say might appear to imply it. Most of those who opt for this third position assume that the eternal begetting, or generation, of the Son speaks of his derivation from the Father and thus his subordination. One example of this assumption is seen in Geoffrey W. Bromiley's article on eternal gener-

[6]Walter Martin, *The Kingdom of the Cults* (Grand Rapids: Zondervan, 1965), pp. 101-3.
[7]Ibid., p. 102.
[8]Ibid., pp. 103-4.
[9]Mark Driscoll and Gerry Breshears, *Doctrine: What Christians Should Believe* (Wheaton, Ill.: Crossway, 2010), p. 28.

ation in the *Evangelical Dictionary of Theology*[10] and another in the essay on Calvin's doctrine of the Trinity by the Australian Anglican evangelical theologian Robert Doyle.[11] A third example, given in more detail, is found in Stephen Kovach and Peter Schemm's essay in the *Journal of the Evangelical Theological Society*, ten years after Dahms wrote his.[12] They argue that "the idea that the Son is begotten and the Father unbegotten means that the Father is primary and Sonship secondary." And, "The eternal begottenness of the Son" indicates "the eternal subordination" of the Son, something taught in the creeds.[13] They find proof of this in the words of the Nicene Creed, which speak of the Son as "God from God, Light from Light, true God from true God," which they think speaks of his derivation from the Father and thus "the dependence of the Son on the Father."[14] We should carefully note that Kovach and Schemm argue for the *eternal subordination of the Son in function and authority*, the most common evangelical way of speaking of the Son's subordination, arguing that eternal subordination in "role," meaning authority, has no ontological implications.[15] We will say more on this distinctive conservative evangelical doctrine of the Trinity in the next chapter. Again we find that those arguing for this position claim their views are historic orthodoxy.

4. The doctrine of the eternal generation of the Son should be *rejected* because it implies or necessitates the Son's eternal subordination to the Father.

Millard Erickson, a much-respected conservative evangelical theologian, argues that the doctrine of the eternal generation of the Son should be abandoned because it implies or necessitates the eternal sub-

---

[10]Geoffrey W. Bromiley, "Eternal Generation," in *Evangelical Dictionary of Theology*, ed. Walter E. Elwell (Grand Rapids: Baker, 1984), p. 368.

[11]Robert Doyle, "Strategies and Consequences in Calvin's Teaching on the Trinity," in *Engaging with Calvin: Aspects of the Reformers Legacy*, ed. M. D. Thompson (Nottingham, U.K.: Apollos, 2009), pp. 99-101. He expresses this as his view, not that of Calvin.

[12]Stephen Kovach and Peter Schemm, "A Defense of the Doctrine of the Eternal Subordination of the Son," *Journal of the Evangelical Theological Society* 42, no. 3 (1999): 461-76. See also Wayne Grudem, *Evangelical Feminism and Biblical Truth* (Sisters, Ore.: Multnomah, 2004), pp. 415-24.

[13]Kovach and Schemm, "A Defense," p. 465.

[14]Ibid.

[15]We will discuss and document their ideas in the next chapter.

ordination of the Son. He writes, the generation of the Son, "thought of as an eternal occurrence, involves the subordination of the Son to the Father. . . . [And], to speak of one of the persons as unoriginate and the others as eternally begotten or proceeding from the Father is to introduce an element of causation or origination that must ultimately involve some type of subordination among them."[16] Erickson, expressing historic orthodoxy, endorses "the complete equality of the three [divine persons]"[17] and contends that arguments for the *eternal functional* subordination of the Son imply that he is "inferior" and subordinate to the Father within the immanent Trinity.[18]

Paul Helm and William Lane Craig, two well-informed and well-respected evangelical philosophers, are of much the same opinion. Helm argues for the rejection of the doctrine of the eternal begetting of the Son because the word "begotten" "must carry the implication that the Father caused the Son to be, thus an asymmetry between the being and agency of the Father (who begets) and the being and agency of the Son (who is begotten) is implied, and in some undeniable sense the Son is subordinate to the Father."[19]

William Lane Craig is starker in his wording: "This doctrine of the generation of the *Logos* from the Father cannot, despite assurances to the contrary, but diminish the status of the Son because He becomes in effect contingent upon the Father. Even if this eternal procession takes place necessarily and apart from the Father's will, the Son is less than the Father because the Father alone exists *a se*, whereas the Son exists through another (*ab alio*)." And, "To be dependent upon the *Unoriginate* for one's existence is to lack a ground of being in oneself alone, which is surely less great than being able to exist on one's own. Such derivative being is . . . the same way in which created things exist. De-

---

[16]Millard Erickson, *God in Three Persons: A Contemporary Interpretation of the Trinity* (Grand Rapids: Baker, 1995), p. 309. See also his *Who's Tampering with the Trinity? An Assessment of the Subordination Debate* (Grand Rapids: Kregel, 2009), pp. 179-84.

[17]Erickson, *God in Three Persons*, p. 331.

[18]Ibid., p. 309.

[19]Paul Helm, "Of God, and the Holy Trinity: A Response to Dr Beckwith," *Churchman* 115, no. 4 (2001): 350. Helm is much more careful in his wording in *John Calvin's Ideas* (Oxford: Oxford University Press, 2004), pp. 41-45. In this later work (p. 56) he speaks of Calvin so "paring down" the doctrine that it is left with little content.

spite protestations to the contrary, Nicene orthodoxy does not seem to have completely exorcised the spirit of subordinationism introduced into Christology by the Greek Apologists."[20]

I noted earlier in this book that the most commonly voiced reason evangelicals give for abandoning the doctrine of the eternal generation of the Son is that it has no biblical warrant. What we now discover is that the belief that the eternal generation of the Son implies or necessitates the *eternal subordination* of the Son is also a very weighty additional reason why some evangelicals want to abandon this doctrine and paradoxically why others want to uphold it.

RESPONSES TO EVANGELICAL ARGUMENTS THAT GENERATION IMPLIES SUBORDINATION

For someone versed in historical theology, this widespread evangelical belief that the doctrine of the eternal generation of the Son implies or necessitates "the eternal subordination and submission of the Son" is quite mind-boggling. It indicates that those making this case have a minimum of knowledge of the historical development of the doctrine of the Trinity and do not understand what this doctrine teaches and safeguards. The arguments outlined above by contemporary evangelicals neatly fit into two categories: the perverse and the philosophical.

The perverse. In the dictionary I keep by my desk, the primary meanings of the word *perverse* are "persistent in error, different from what is reasonable, against the weight of evidence."[21] I use the word in these senses, not in any other. I dare to call the conclusions of John Dahms, Walter Martin, and Mark Driscoll and Gerry Breshears "perverse" because, as theological teachers, it is their responsibility to be informed and not to teach something contrary to well-established facts. It is hard to believe that any theologian could claim that the doctrine of the eternal generation of the Son, endorsed by the Nicene and

---

[20]William Lane Craig, "A Formulation and Defense of the Doctrine of the Trinity" (2003), <www.lastseminary.com/trinity/CraigWilliamLTrinity.pdf>, p. 15. See also J. P. Moreland and William Lane Craig, "Christian Doctrines (1): The Trinity," in *Philosophical Foundations for a Christian Worldview* (Downers Grove, Ill.: InterVarsity Press, 2003), p. 594. I put the key Arian term "Unoriginate" in italics.

[21]*The Concise Oxford Dictionary of Current English* (Oxford: Clarendon Press, 1964).

Athanasian Creeds and most of the Reformation and Post-Reformation confessions, actually teaches the ontological subordinationism and the Arian error. I know of no informed theologian who believes that the ontological subordination of the Son is historic orthodoxy, as Dahms argues. There is nothing to support his opinion. Walter Martin for his part argues that this doctrine should be abandoned because it has "fed the Arian heresy through the centuries," while Driscoll and Breshears say the word "begotten unavoidably implies a beginning of the one begotten. That would certainly lend support to the Arian heresy that the Son is a created being and not the Creator God."[22] Dahms, Martin, and Driscoll and Breshears all exhibit a profound ignorance of what the Arian debate was all about. It was the Arians who taught the eternal subordination and submission of the Son on the basis of their understanding of his begetting, and it was the Nicene fathers who argued against the eternal subordination of the Son on the basis of their understanding of divine begetting. The Arian understanding of the Son's begetting was that he was contingently created in time by the will of the Father and is thus dependent and subordinated God. The Nicene fathers' understanding was that the Son is eternally begotten not by will and is thus of the same divine being as the Father. He is not subordinated to the Father but is his equal in being, power and rank, yet other than the Father as the Son. J. N. D. Kelly eloquently sums up scholarly opinion. "The principal aim of those who manufactured the creed [of Nicaea] was to call a halt, once and for all, to the Arian heresy."[23] And he adds, in speaking of the Son as "begotten of the being of the Father," and anathematizing all the Arian slogans, the Nicene bishops placed "Arian theology . . . under a total ban."[24]

The more common evangelical opinion that the doctrine of the eternal generation of the Son implies or necessitates the eternal subordination of the Son *in role and authority,* not his ontological subordination, has nothing to commend it. This verbal distinction makes little or no difference. A *necessary* and *eternal* subordination of the Son in role

---

[22]Driscoll and Breshears, *Doctrine,* p. 28.
[23]J. N. D. Kelly, *Early Christian Creeds* (London: Longmans, 1960), p. 231.
[24]Ibid., p. 239.

and authority in the immanent Trinity implies the ontological subordination of the Son.[25] If the Son is *necessarily and eternally* subordinated, his subordination defines his *being* as the Son. His subordination is, then, what indelibly distinguishes him from the Father. What is more, arguing for the eternal subordination of the Son in authority reflects one of the basic elements of historic Arianism. Everyone knows that the Arians subordinated the Son in *being*, but few realize that they also subordinated him in authority. In chapter four, in explaining Arian teaching, I substantiated this assertion. In all forms of fourth-century Arianism the Son is eternally set under the Father in authority and is bound to obey him. For the Arians subordination in being implied subordination in authority, and vice versa. All the Nicene fathers believed just the opposite. For them, if the divine three are one in being, then they are one in power and authority, and vice versa. Being and authority cannot be divided in divine life. Triune divine sovereignty is unitary.

Wayne Grudem's argument that the Nicene and the Athanasian Creeds, along with the Anglican Thirty-Nine Articles and the Westminster Confession of Faith, actually teach the eternal subordination in authority of the Son is profoundly perverse.[26] The Athanasian Creed speaks of the "coequality" of the divine three, explicitly excluding any hierarchical ordering in being or authority, and the Anglican Thirty-Nine Articles and the Westminster Confession teach that the divine three are one in being and power. Kovach and Schemm build on Grudem's work, arguing that when the Nicene Creed speaks of the Son as "God from God, light from light, true God from true God," it is speaking of the Son's "derivation" from the Father and his "dependence" on the

---

[25]So Erickson, *Who's Tampering*, pp. 169-94. See also Kevin Giles, *Jesus and the Father: Modern Evangelicals Reinvent the Doctrine of the Trinity* (Grand Rapids: Zondervan, 2006), p. 46; T. McCall and K. Yandell, "On Trinitarian Subordinationism," *Philosophia Christi* 11, no. 2 (2009): 339-58; Thomas McCall, "'Eternal Functional Subordination': Considering a Recent Evangelical Proposal," in *Which Trinity? Whose Monotheism?* (Grand Rapids: Eerdmans, 2010), pp. 175-88; Keith E. Johnson, "Trinitarian Agency and the Eternal Subordination of the Son: An Augustinian Perspective," *Themelios* 36:1 (2011): 7-25.

[26]Grudem, *Evangelical Feminism*, pp. 415-17. In this book Grudem appeals to the doctrine of the begetting of the Son as proof of his eternal subordination to the Father. In his *Systematic Theology: An Introduction to Biblical Doctrine*, rev. ed. (Grand Rapids: Zondervan, 2000), pp. 1233-34, he argues for the abandonment of this doctrine. These two positions are hard to reconcile to say the least.

Father and thus his subordination to the Father. This again is indicative of a complete ignorance of the fourth-century debates over the Trinity and the content of Nicene orthodoxy. As we have demonstrated earlier, for the Nicene fathers, the words "God from God, light from light, true God from true God" indicate their belief that the Son is as much God as the Father, with whom he is *homoousios* ("one in being").[27] These words were included in the creed *not* to indicate the subordination of the Son but the exact opposite. Claims that the Nicene Creed (let alone the Athanasian Creed) allows or implies the eternal subordination of the Son do not bear critical scrutiny. The primary goal of the Nicene fathers was to *exclude* the idea that in the eternal life of God the divine three are hierarchically ordered in being or power.

Robert Letham, in his refutation of those who argue that "the eternal generation of the Son either implies or entails a subordinate status for the Son," is of the same opinion.[28] He rejects that speaking of the eternal generation of the Son reflects Neo-Platonic ideas that would make him a lesser "emanation from the Father"[29] and that the Son's eternal generation can be likened to human generation in time, suggesting a subordinate.[30] Rather, he argues, the Nicene fathers believed this doctrine spoke of the Son's oneness in being/nature and omnipotence with the Father yet identified him as other than the Father. He quotes with approval from the *Expositio fidei,* a work attributed to Athanasius, which he says reflects the language of the Creed of Nicaea (325). "The Son is 'true God of true God . . . omnipotent from omnipotent . . . whole from whole.'"[31] And then he says that the "creedal statements connected with eternal generation underline the *homoousios* of the Father and the Son."[32] In other words, Letham is arguing that in these ways the creeds exclude the idea that the Son is eternally subordinated in being or power.

---

[27]See, e.g., Kelly, *Early Christian Creeds,* pp. 236-39.
[28]Robert Letham, *The Holy Trinity: In Scripture, History, Theology, and Worship* (Phillipsburg, N.J.: Presbyterian and Reformed, 2004), p. 384.
[29]Ibid., p. 388.
[30]Ibid.
[31]Ibid.
[32]Ibid., p. 389.

David Cunningham, a well-informed trinitarian theologian, is even more emphatic. He says the Council of Nicaea intentionally excluded all expressions of subordinationism known at that time.

> In order to rule out Arianism and other forms of subordinationism, the Nicene Council rejected a whole variety of attempts to place the three in hierarchical order—logical, causal, temporal or otherwise. The Council's clarity on this point is especially visible in the Nicene anathemas, which claim that there was no time when the Word was not. And to make it clear that the begetting of the Son need not imply temporal order, the Creed states that this begetting takes place eternally. Nor is there any logical hierarchy among the Three; they all imply one another and are dependent on one another, so that no one of them can be understood in a position of primacy over the others.[33]

These "perverse" evangelical interpretations of the doctrine of the eternal generation of the Son not only disclose a profound ignorance of doctrinal history but also a profound misunderstanding of what theology is and how all theological language works. They assume that the meaning of words used of God must be derived from their use in everyday speech, referring to created realities, particularly words related to human birth. For the Nicene fathers, as we have shown, giving meaning to words used of God in this way only leads to error and heresy. To do so is to depict God in human terms, which is idolatry. Words used theologically are not to be given content or definition on the basis of human experience but are to be adapted to the proper object of reference—namely, God. No word can be used of God in exactly (univocally) the same way as it is used of creation since God is not a creature. This means specifically that the Son's begetting cannot be understood in terms of human begetting, nor can the divine names Father and Son be understood in terms of human fathers and sons.

The philosophical. We must take the philosophical arguments of Erickson, Helm and Craig—that the doctrine of the eternal generation of the Son should be rejected because it implies or necessitates his eternal

---

[33]David Cunningham, *These Three Are One: The Practice of Trinitarian Theology* (London: Blackwell, 1998), p. 112.

subordination—more seriously because they are based on a rational argument. But as we will show they too exhibit a profound and perverse ignorance of what the orthodox doctrine of the eternal generation actually teaches and safeguards. They make the case that the orthodox doctrine of the eternal generation of the Son subordinates him to the Father by depicting him as "caused" by the Father, begotten "contingently" by the Father and "dependent for his being" on the Father. Craig says that speaking of the Son in this way implies that the Son is unlike the Father because he lacks *aseity*. (This technical term derives from the Latin *aseitas*, meaning "of oneself." To speak of the Father's or the Son's *aseity* is thus to speak of them as self-existent God. Craig argues that if the Son is said to be begotten of the Father, then he lacks *aseity*.)

This rationalistic approach to doing trinitarian theology reminds us of Eunomius, the neo-Arian whom the Cappadocian fathers opposed. In this case it presupposes a logical syllogism with the major premise, the Father causes the Son; the minor premise, what is caused is less than and subordinate to what causes him; and the conclusion, the Son is thus less than and subordinate to the Father.

Origen, Arius and Eunomius certainly taught that the Father "caused" the Son by an act of will and that the Son was begotten contingently, dependent for his existence on the Father, lacking in aseity and thus subordinated God. He was God in second degree. This understanding of the Son of God is exactly what the Nicene fathers opposed. What Athanasius argued against *more than anything else* was the consistent Arian argument that the Father's begetting of the Son is to be understood as a creative act of the divine will that produced a Son different in being from the Father and subordinate to the Father. For Athanasius the doctrine of the eternal generation of the Son speaks of the eternal begetting of the Son in the inner life of God by necessity, not will, that resulted in "God from God," a "true offspring," "one in being" (*homoousios*) with the Father.

Possibly the most important contribution the Cappadocian fathers made to the developing orthodox understanding of the doctrine of the eternal generation of the Son was their exclusion of the Neo-Platonist premise that what is caused is less than its originating cause, a premise

Origen, Arius and Eunomius all presupposed. Basil and the two Gregories saw clearly that speaking of the Son as eternally begotten of the Father implied derivation and cause, but they would not allow that this language resulted in any subordination whatsoever. They argued that what is caused is not necessarily separated or subordinate to its cause, giving the illustration of a fire and its light and the sun and its rays. The fire and the sun are the cause of the light, but they are not other than the cause or secondary to the cause. Their depiction of the Father as the "cause" (*aitia*) and "origin" (*archē*) of the Son has its critics, as we have noted, but what cannot be denied is that the Cappadocian fathers insisted on the unity in being and power of the three divine persons. The Father may be conceived of as the *archē* of the Son and the Spirit, but for them this implied no subordination whatsoever. For them, the divine three share the one divine being and power, they are bound together in the most intimate communion, they interpenetrate one another, and they work inseparably and have one will. Thus they cannot be ranked hierarchically.

Before leaving the Cappadocian fathers it is important to comment on their theological method. They would not allow that logic or rational arguments are ways of *knowing God,* which for them is what *theo-logy* is all about, or that human analogies or the meaning of words as they apply to creation can tell us anything about God. For them the path to knowing God is prayerful reflection on the Scriptures read holistically and christologically.

The Creed of Nicaea of 325 and the Nicene Creed of 381 were compiled specifically to exclude the Arian belief that the Son was created by the Father in time and was thus subordinate God. Immediately following the assertion that the Son is "eternally begotten of the Father" the creed explains what this means by saying he is "God from God, light from light, true God from true God, begotten not made, of one being with the Father." If one wanted to exclude subordinationism in any form, one could not devise better wording. The Son is "from the Father," and "begotten of the Father," yet he is God in exactly the same way and sense as God the Father. Thus his begetting is like "light from light," which results in "God from God," a Son "one in being with the Father."

Augustine is likewise adamant that the eternal generation of the Son in no way diminishes the Son. Each divine person is the fullness of the Godhead, and together they are the one God.[34] The Son is begotten and sent by the Father, yet he is "equal" with the Father, one in substance and attributes. For Augustine the one divine essence is not the origin of anything; it is what unites the divine persons. Reflecting Augustine's construal of the Trinity, the Athanasian Creed speaks of the Father as "not begotten" and of the Son as not "created but begotten," yet it excludes any subordination in the Godhead whatsoever. This creed says that the three divine persons are all "Lord" and "Almighty": "none is before or after, greater or less"; they are "coequal."

Thomas Aquinas, in the thirteenth century, spoke explicitly of the Son's begetting and the Spirit's "spiration" as divine acts *ad intra,* to be contrasted with divine acts *ad extra.* This distinction absolutely ruled out any thought that the Son and the Spirit are contingently produced by the Father, or that they derive their divine *being* from the Father, or that they are other to the Father in being and power.

Calvin made his own important contribution in answer to those who argue that the Son's begetting implies or necessitates the idea that he is contingent God, God in second degree. Building on Augustine's argument that the Father is the Father only in relation to the Son and the Son vice versa, he argued "that the Son since he is God, exists of himself, but not in respect to his person; indeed since he is the Son, we say he exists from the Father. Thus his essence is without beginning; while the beginning of his person is God himself."[35] In other words he is arguing that when we think of the Father and the Son independently of each other, then we should think of the Father and the Son as both true God in their own right, both self-existent God, both, to use Calvin's Latin term, *ex se ipso esse,* and his Greek term, *autotheos.*[36]

---

[34]Lewis Ayres, *Augustine and the Trinity* (Cambridge: Cambridge University Press, 2010), pp. 208-11.

[35]John Calvin, *Institutes of the Christian Religion* 1.13.25 (ed. John T. McNeill, trans. Ford Lewis Battles [London: SCM Press, 1960], p. 154).

[36]On these terms see Richard Muller, *Post-Reformation Reformed Dogmatics: The Rise and Development of Reformed Orthodoxy, ca. 1520 to ca. 1725,* vol. 4, *The Triunity of God* (Grand Rapids: Baker Academic, 2003), p. 19.

What Calvin is claiming for the Son in these words is his *aseity*. Like the Father and the Spirit, the Son is self-existent God, God not dependent on another.[37]

Erickson, Craig and Helm all seem to assume that to speak of the Son as "begotten of the Father" indicates that he is created or produced by the Father and that human begetting explains divine begetting. The Nicene fathers with one voice oppose the idea that the begetting of the Son should in any way be paralleled with human begetting, except that like produces like in nature. They emphatically oppose the Arian idea that begetting implies a creative and contingent act and thus the Son's subordination. Thus historic orthodoxy, the catholic faith, on the basis of the doctrine of the eternal generation of the Son and eternal procession of the Spirit, affirm that the Father, the Son and the Holy Spirit eternally share the one divine being and power and cannot be separated or divided, only distinguished and differentiated as persons. Rather than the received doctrine of the eternal generation implying or necessitating the eternal subordination of the Son, it excludes this very idea while at the same time affirming eternal divine self-differentiation.[38]

T. F. Torrance says that for historic orthodoxy, "No distinction between underived deity and derived deity is tenable; there can be no thought of one person being ontologically or divinely prior to another or subsequent to another. Hence while the Father in virtue of his Fatherhood is first in order, the Father, the Son and the Spirit eternally coexist as three fully co-equal Persons in perichoretic togetherness and in-each-otherness."[39]

TO SUM UP

I sum up my reply to my fellow evangelicals who argue that the doctrine of the eternal generation of the Son speaks of him as "derived" God, "dependent" God, "contingent" God, and thus subordinate and submissive God in a number of points.

---

[37]See ibid., pp. 324-26.
[38]Letham, *Holy Trinity*, p. 389, comes to virtually the same conclusion.
[39]T. F. Torrance, *The Christian Doctrine of God: One Being, Three Persons* (Edinburgh: T & T Clark, 1996), p. 180.

- The eternal begetting of the Son does not involve a change in God. God is eternally triune; he does not become a Trinity in time. There never was a time when the Son (or the Spirit) was not.

- The eternal begetting of the Son cannot be likened to human generation, except on one matter: like produces like, and thus fathers and their offspring are of the same nature. Divine begetting is "immaterial," "spiritual," like the unceasing light coming from the sun, or "light from light," or the utterance of the divine Word.

- The eternal begetting of the Son is not to be understood in terms of temporal, contingent causation or as human begetting in the created order. The eternal generation of the Son and procession of the Spirit are necessary divine acts *ad intra*. Nothing is produced outside of God.

- The Son, on the basis of his eternal begetting, is to be confessed as "true God from true God, one in being [*homoousios*] with the Father."

- The eternal begetting of the Son eternally and indelibly differentiates the Father and the Son as "unbegotten God" and "begotten God." It does not differentiate or separate them in being or power, or as underived deity (the Father) and derived deity (the Son and the Spirit), or as contingent and noncontingent God. The Father, the Son and the Spirit all possess *aseity*. They are each "true God," each self-existent God.

9

Are There Better Ways to Ground the Father-Son Distinction than the Eternal Begetting of the Son?

◆ ◆ ◆

This chapter explores two alternatives to the eternal generation of the Son and procession of the Spirit as the ground of divine self-differentiation, both of which are put forward by contemporary conservative evangelicals. One is that the differing *works* of the divine three seen in the economy eternally and primarily differentiate them; the other is that the differing *authority* of the divine three seen in the economy eternally and primarily differentiates them. These two positions are united in their belief that how the triune God is revealed in history (that is, in the economy) reveals what is true of God in eternity (that is, in the immanent Trinity). That is, if we see in the economy the divine three doing different works, then they must be differentiated on this basis in eternity; or, if we see the Son subordinate, submissive and obedient in the incarnation, then he must be differentiated from the Father on this basis in eternity.

In answer to these counterproposals to the historic way of eternally differentiating the divine three, I will argue in what follows that nothing that takes place in history determines God's life in eternity—God is free. God's actions in the world should be understood strictly in terms of what God reveals in his Word. God's revelation of himself in historical acts in the economy is certainly to be trusted—God is not other than he reveals himself—but what we conclude about God in eternity from his acts in the economy should not be based on human experience, ideas and agendas but on what God reveals in Scripture.

DIFFERING THE DIVINE THREE PRIMARILY ON THE BASIS OF DIFFERING ECONOMIC ACTIVITIES

The evangelical theologians John Feinberg[1] and, in less detail, Millard Erickson[2] reject the doctrines of the eternal begetting of the Son and the eternal procession of the Spirit as the basis for eternal divine self-differentiation because, first, they think these doctrines lack biblical warrant and, second, they eternally subordinate the Son to the Father, *which they oppose.* Instead, they argue that the divine three should be differentiated primarily on the basis of their differing works/operations/roles seen in the economy. Having rejected differing origination, or relations of origin, as the basis for eternally differentiating the divine three, Feinberg asks, "How can we distinguish the three persons? Here we must focus on predicates that are true of each alone in their economic *roles.* For example, the Son alone became incarnate, and he alone was baptized. The Father alone spoke words praising Jesus at Christ's baptism, and the Holy Spirit alone descended as a dove in that event. We could multiply other unique predicates that would distinguish the three, but the point is already served."[3] In this quote Feinberg uses the modern word *role* in the dictionary sense to speak of divine actions, the distinctive works of the Father, Son and Spirit. This is perfectly acceptable but we will see shortly that many evangelicals use this same word in a non-dictionary sense to speak of person-defining differing authority.

Erickson's solution is very similar. The Son is to be distinguished from the Father because he is the one who became incarnate, and the

---

[1]John Feinberg, *No One Like Him: The Doctrine of God* (Wheaton, Ill.: Crossway, 2001), pp. 488-98. I found on the Web a reference to an unpublished lecture given at the Evangelical Theological Society annual meeting, November 2008, by Brandon Jones, titled "The Unbegotten Son? A Defense of the Eternal Generation of the Son Against the Arguments of Evangelicals like John S. Feinberg." I emailed Jones, and he kindly sent me an electronic copy. I found his work of high standard and helpful.

[2]Millard Erickson, *God in Three Persons: A Contemporary Interpretation of the Trinity* (Grand Rapids: Baker, 1995), pp. 309-10; Erickson, *Who's Tampering with the Trinity? An Assessment of the Subordination Debate* (Grand Rapids: Kregel, 2009), pp. 179-84.

[3]Feinberg, *No One Like Him*, p. 498. Italics added.

Spirit is to be distinguished from the Father and the Son because of the specific works he does in the world.[4]

There are two important reasons why predicating eternal divine self-differentiation on the differing works of the three divine persons in the economy is to be rejected. Both counter arguments appeal to what Scripture teaches and both reflect what the church fathers recognized long ago. First, the thesis that the differing works of the divine persons in the economy eternally differentiates them is to be rejected because what God does in the world does not establish in any sure way what is true in eternity. God may appear in the world as three persons who do different things but this in itself does not tell us God is eternally triune and it could suggest the three divine persons are not in fact one God. We believe that God is one yet three persons not because of God's actions in the world but because Scripture says God is one and three persons. God's actions in the world are not self-explanatory. We need Scripture to tell us what they mean and imply. In the second century the Monarchian Modalists argued that the differing operations or works of the one God in the world spoke only of what is revealed in the economy. Ultimately we have one undifferentiated God who simply appears in history in three differing modes or roles. For them the revelation of three divine persons and their differing works in the world spoke only of what was seen in the economy. God in fact is a monad. Modalism was rejected by the early church fathers because they reasoned that if the Bible reveals God as both one and three persons and God is unchanging then he must be triune for all eternity. God is certainly revealed in the economy as three persons but it is Scripture that tells us the one God is eternally the Father, the Son and the Holy Spirit. It is the same with divine unity. God's actions in the world would if anything lead us to believe that there are eternally three separated divine persons, the Father, the Son and the Spirit. God's work in the world does not infer divine unity. We believe that God is one even though we have a revelation of three divine persons in history because the Bible says: God is one.

---

[4]Erickson, *God in Three Persons*, pp. 309-10.

Second, we should reject any attempt to base eternal divine self-differentiation on the differing works of the three divine persons in the economy because the Bible does not differentiate the divine persons on this basis. The Bible teaches clearly that no divine work is the work of any one person of the Trinity. Their works unite them not distinguish them.[5] Jesus said quite emphatically, "whatever the Father does the Son does likewise" (Jn 5:19). On this biblical basis from the time of Athanasius, Ayres says, the doctrine of "inseparable operations" has been one of the three fundamental axioms of the Nicene understanding of the Trinity.[6] This doctrine recognizes that the Bible often associates specific divine actions with one divine person, such as creation with the Father, redemption with the Son, and sanctification and empowerment with the Spirit. What it highlights is that the Bible always speaks of the divine three working together jointly and harmoniously—operating inseparably.

Augustine enunciated the doctrine of inseparable operations most forcefully. He gave the principle, "Just as the Father, Son and Holy Spirit are inseparable, so do they work inseparably."[7] This principle he supplements and explains by what later Latin theologians would call "the doctrine of appropriation," an idea first seen in the Cappadocians, especially Gregory of Nyssa.[8] Because the divine "persons" share and are one "substance," he argues, whatever can be said of one can be said of all three. Thus no act of God in the economy is the work of the Father, Son or Spirit alone. Augustine recognized that in Scripture

---

[5]In the Bible no divine act or operation is ever depicted as the work of one divine person in isolation from the other two. The three persons baptize as one (Mt 28:19), bless as one (2 Cor 13:13) and minister through believers as one (1 Cor 12:4-6). Creation is a work of God involving the Father, Son and Spirit (Gen 1:1; Jn 1:2-3; Col 1:16; Heb 1:10). So too is election (Mt 11:27; Jn 3:3-9; 6:70; 13:18; Acts 1:2; Rom 8:29; Eph 1:4; 1 Pet 1:2). And so too is salvation (Jn 3:1-6; Rom 8:1-30; 2 Cor 2:6; Eph 1:3-14). When it comes to divine rule both the Father and the Son are named "Lord," the supreme ruler, and it would seem also the Holy Spirit (2 Cor 3:17). In the book of Revelation the Father and the Son rule from the one throne (Rev 5:13; 7:10). Last, it is to be noted that judgment is ascribed to both the Father and the Son (Ps 7:8; 9:7-8; Rom 2:16; Rev 16:7; Mt 25:31-32; Jn 5:27; Acts 10:42; Phil 2:10).

[6]L. Ayres, *Nicaea and Its Legacy: An Approach to Fourth-Century Trinitarian Theology* (Oxford: Oxford University Press, 2004), pp. 236, 280-81.

[7]Augustine, *The Trinity* 1.7 (p. 70), 2.9 (p. 103). The translation used is by Edmund Hill, *The Trinity: Introduction, Translation, Notes* (New York: New City Press, 1991).

[8]Ayres, *Nicaea*, pp. 296-300.

certain actions are ascribed to the Father or the Son or the Spirit, and so he said we rightly appropriated them to one or another of the divine three. Thus creation is ascribed to the Father because he is the originator of all, the incarnation to the Word because revelation comes through the Word, and love to the Holy Spirit because he is the gift of love between the Father and the Son.[9] Ayres says the doctrine of "appropriation is for pro-Nicene [theologians] an important habit of Christian speech because it is central to Scripture's own speech about the divine persons."[10] The differing works/operations of the divine three in the economy are neither a biblical nor a theologically safe basis on which to ground eternal divine self-differentiation.

Once it is recognized that there is absolutely nothing to commend in the argument that eternal divine self-differentiation is to be predicated on the differing works of the divine three persons in the economy, the strength and depth of the explanation and ground for divine self-differentiation given by historic orthodoxy can be seen. This teaches that divine self-differentiation takes place within the life of God apart from history through the eternal begetting of the Son and the eternal generation of the Spirit. The historic missions of the Son and the Spirit reveal what is true in eternity: they do not constitute or make God three persons. Bruce Marshall says that the older Scholastic Roman Catholic and Protestant theologians were absolutely correct in arguing that God would be eternally triune even if he had not created or come to redeem.[11] Given this premise, he says, we need a "conceptual means for apprehending the distinctions among the divine persons, and their unity as God, other than the means we use to apprehend the totality of their activity in creation and redemption."[12] He writes,

> The traditional disjunction between the eternal processions of the divine persons and their temporal missions serves just this conceptual and logical purpose. The distinctions among the persons of the Trinity

---

[9]This is discussed mainly in books 6 and 7 but see also 2.9 and 2.18.
[10]Ayres, *Nicaea*, p. 297. See his excellent discussion of this whole matter on pp. 296-300.
[11]Bruce Marshall, "The Unity of the Triune God: Reviving an Ancient Question," *The Thomist* 74 (2010): 14-15.
[12]Ibid., p. 19.

are fully secured by the two divine processions, that is, by the non-contingent coming forth of the Son from the Father and the Holy Spirit from the Father and the Son.[13]

Thus,

Working in terms of procession and mission gives us conceptual tools for explaining quite clearly how the distinctions among the divine persons do not arise from the economy of salvation, but are presupposed to it. . . . Mission includes procession, but procession does not include mission; procession is necessary for mission, but mission is not necessary for procession.[14]

Marshall eloquently captures what Christians have historically believed and found theologically compelling. Divine self-differentiation takes place within the life of God in eternity; what takes place in history simply reveals what is true in eternity. In other words, the economic Trinity reveals the immanent Trinity—understood as the threefoldness of God. God is triune for all eternity; events in the world neither make him triune nor explain how he is eternally triune. God is certainly revealed in the economy as Father, Son and Spirit, three distinct persons, but it is the Bible that tells us these three persons coexist for all eternity and that these three divine persons are in fact one God. Thus what the doctrines of the eternal generation of the Son and procession of the Spirit do, and do well, is explain how the one God is eternally three persons and how the divine three persons are the one God.

DIFFERING THE DIVINE THREE PRIMARILY OR EXCLUSIVELY ON THE BASIS OF DIFFERING AUTHORITY

Far more common among contemporary conservative evangelical theologians is the view that the divine "persons" are primarily if not exclusively eternally differentiated on the basis of differing authority. In the previous chapter I pointed out that there is today a profound and widespread division among conservative evangelicals over whether or not the Son is *eternally* subordinated in authority to the Father. The thesis

---

[13]Ibid.
[14]Ibid., p. 20.

of the Son's eternal differentiation from the Father on the basis of differing authority has emerged directly out of this debate, which is in
turn directly connected to the debate about the subordination of
women. Virtually every evangelical who argues theologically for the
Son's eternal subordination in authority[15] is committed to the permanent subordination of women.[16] It is believed that just as the Father
is "head over" the Son, husbands are "head over" their wives in the
home and men "head over" women in the church.[17]

Both my book *Jesus and the Father: Modern Evangelicals Reinvent the
Doctrine of the Trinity* and Millard Erickson's book *Who's Tampering
with the Trinity? An Assessment of the Subordination Debate* explain and
fully document this divisive intramural evangelical doctrinal dispute.
The most influential exposition of the subordination case is found in
Wayne Grudem's *Systematic Theology: An Introduction to Biblical Doctrine*, first published in 1995.[18] He devotes a full chapter in this book
arguing for the eternal subordination of the Son in authority and then
a second chapter to arguing for the permanent subordination of women
in authority. For Grudem, the relationship between human fathers and
sons explains and defines the relationship between the divine Father
and Son. Just as "the Father has authority over the Son in the Trinity,

---

[15]To find a quote in an evangelical egalitarian biblical scholar's writings where on exegetical
grounds he or she concludes that one or more texts may speak of the subordination of the Son
is not counterevidence. No one denies some texts speak of the Son subordinating himself to
the Father, for example, Philippians 2:6-8. In this case these verses allude to his voluntary
subordination in the incarnation for our salvation. The theological question is, should this
subordination seen in the incarnation be read back into the life of God in eternity? This is not
an exegetical question but a theological question answered by a holistic reading of Scripture.

[16]Someone of this conviction could reply, "But we only argue for the subordination of wives to
husbands and women to male church leaders not the subordination of women to men," but this
is not the full story. This position is grounded on the premise that women are subordinated to
men in *creation* before the fall. If this is the case, then the subordination demanded must apply
to all men and women in the whole of creation, not just the home and the church. True, today
only the subordination of women in the home and in church is mentioned, but the position is
predicated on a putative "creation order" that subordinates all women, all the daughters of Eve,
to all men, the sons of Adam.

[17]On this see Kevin N. Giles, *The Trinity and Subordinationism: The Doctrine of God and the
Contemporary Gender Debate* (Downers Grove, Ill.: InterVarsity Press, 2002); and Giles, *Better
Together: Equality in Christ* (Melbourne: Acorn, 2010).

[18]Wayne Grudem, *Systematic Theology: An Introduction to Biblical Doctrine* (Grand Rapids:
Zondervan, 1995).

so the husband has authority over the wife in marriage."[19]

The influence of Grudem's *Systematic Theology* on evangelicals, charismatics and Pentecostals is pervasive. It is the most widely used theology text in Bible colleges and evangelical and Pentecostal seminaries around the world. More than 300,000 copies are in print in the American edition alone. He is emphatic both that the *eternal subordination of the Son in authority* stands right at the heart of the orthodox doctrine of the Trinity and that this teaching in no way implies the ontological subordination of the Son, the Arian heresy.[20] He repeatedly claims that the best of theologians from the past and the creeds teach precisely what he teaches. For Grudem, the Father has "the role of commanding, directing, and sending," and the Son has the role of "obeying, going as the Father sends, and revealing God to us."[21]

In this quote just given, Grudem speaks of the differing "roles" of the Father and the Son, by which he means their differing authority. The word *role* is foundational in the literature arguing for the permanent subordination of women predicated on the eternal subordination of the Son. If we are going to understand what is being said, we must recognize the special meaning given to this word by Grudem and those who follow him. In this literature the word *role* does not refer to characteristic behavior that can change, or to the works or operations of

---

[19]Ibid., p. 257.

[20]To prove that this so-called role subordination does not imply subordination in *being* or inferiority in person at either the human or divine level, Grudem and those who follow him use carefully chosen illustrations. They cite the examples of the ship's captain and the crewman, the officer and the private, and the manager and the worker. In each of these cases the point is valid. These illustrations of differing "roles" do not suggest ontological subordination or personal inferiority because the roles can change and the higher position invariably has some basis in competence, training, age, etc. However, these carefully chosen and selective illustrations in fact do not parallel what Grudem and other evangelicals today are arguing. The exact parallels to their distinctive usage of the terms *function* and *role* are to be found in classic aristocracy, race-based slavery and in apartheid, where one's so-called role or function is ascribed by birth and can never change. In this usage the one who rules is understood to be of a superior class and the one who obeys of an inferior class. In these cases, "difference in role" speaks of a *necessary, essential and unchangeable* difference, predicated on the premise that some are born to rule and some obey. The rulers and the ruled are not social equals and never can be. So what Grudem and his followers are actually arguing is that women are only equal in a spiritual sense, not in any substantive way. They *are* the subordinated sex, and this can never change. When the word *role* is used in trinitarian discourse in this sense it thus necessarily involves the ontological subordination of the Son.

[21]Ibid., p. 250.

the divine persons (as Feinberg does), but to the supposed *differing au-thority* given to men and women and the divine Father and Son. Men and the divine Father have the "role" or "function" of leading ("headship"); women and the divine Son have the "role" of obeying. These so-called roles can never change; they are person-defining. The choice of the word *role* is deliberate because it sounds acceptable to the modern ear and because it obfuscates what is really being said, namely, that men permanently have authority over women and the Father eter-nally has authority over the Son. This means that whenever we see the expression "different roles" in this literature we are to take it, at all times, to mean "different authority" that is unchanging and thus person-defining.

WHAT "COMPLEMENTARIAN" EVANGELICALS ARE TEACHING

Grudem, following the seminal work by George Knight, *New Testament Teaching on the Role Relationship of Men and Women*,[22] argues that men and women and the divine Father and the Son are primarily, if not exclu-sively, *eternally* distinguished by their differing authority, spoken of in terms of "differing roles." Evangelicals who follow in the steps of Knight and Grudem euphemistically call themselves "complementarians."

Grudem specifically rejects the doctrine of the eternal generation of the Son, saying it would be best if the words "'begotten of the Father' (signifying the 'eternal generation of the Son') were not retained in any modern theological formulations,"[23] because this teaching is not war-ranted by Scripture and it does not ground the eternal distinctions be-tween the Father, Son and Spirit in any "meaningful" way.[24] His alter-native is that "authority and submission between the Father and the Son . . . and the Holy Spirit, *is the fundamental difference* between the

---

[22]George Knight, *New Testament Teaching on the Role Relationship of Men and Women* (Grand Rapids: Baker, 1977). Knight "invented" the so-called complementarian position, which grounds the subordination of women in the eternal life of God, using the language of "role differentiation" to speak of both women's and the Son's unchanging and unchangeable subor-dination. See Kevin N. Giles, "The Evangelical Theological Society and the Doctrine of the Trinity," *Evangelical Quarterly* 80, no. 4 (2008): 323-48.

[23]Wayne Grudem, "Appendix 6," in *Systematic Theology: An Introduction to Biblical Doctrine*, rev. ed. (Grand Rapids: Zondervan, 2000), p. 1234.

[24]Ibid.

persons of the Trinity."[25] If we did not have "subordination [in the Godhead] then there would be no inherent difference in the way the three divine persons relate to one another, and consequently we would not have three distinct persons."[26] And again, "If we did not have such differences *in authority* in the relationships among the members of the Trinity, then we would not know of any differences at all."[27] In his later book *Evangelical Feminism*, he adds, "The differences in authority among the Father, Son and Holy Spirit are the *only* interpersonal differences that the Bible indicates that exist *eternally* among the members of the Godhead."[28] For Grudem, nothing is more important than the authority structure both in the Trinity and between men and women. It is, he says, "the *most fundamental* aspect of interpersonal relationships in the entire universe."[29]

Bruce Ware in his monograph on the doctrine of the Trinity, *Father, Son, and Holy Spirit: Relationships, Roles, and Relevance,*[30] follows Knight and Grudem in grounding eternal divine threefold differentiation primarily, if not exclusively, on differing authority.[31] This is the only evangelical book that I know of that is devoted entirely to arguing for a doctrine of the Trinity in which the divine persons are primarily if not exclusively differentiated on differing authority within the Godhead for all eternity. In speaking specifically of what "distinguishes" the divine persons, Ware says that the Father's authority is "supreme among the Persons of the Trinity."[32] In contrast, the Son is distinguished because he is in "submission to the leadership, authority and headship of his Father," or as he puts it a few lines later, because he "stands in a relationship of eternal submission under the authority of his

---

[25]Wayne Grudem, *Biblical Foundations for Manhood and Womanhood* (Wheaton, Ill.: Crossway, 2002), p. 31. Italics added.

[26]Grudem, *Systematic Theology*, p. 251.

[27]Wayne Grudem, *Evangelical Feminism and Biblical Truth* (Sisters, Ore.: Multnomah, 2004), p. 433.

[28]Ibid. Italics added.

[29]Ibid, p. 429. Italics added.

[30]Bruce Ware, *Father, Son, and Holy Spirit: Relationships, Roles, and Relevance* (Wheaton, Ill.: Crossway, 2005).

[31]Ibid., pp. 21, 45-46, 55, 59, 71-72.

[32]Ibid., p. 46. See also p. 47, where he says, "The Father is supreme in the Godhead," and p. 59, where he says, "He is supreme among the persons of the Godhead."

Father."[33] He agrees that the divine persons cannot be differentiated on the basis of differing nature/being, arguing that "the inherent authority of the Father and the inherent submission of the Son" is what *eternally* differentiates them.[34] Then, when speaking of the "difference between the Son and the Spirit," he says the Spirit's "position is third—all the time third."[35] "The Son along with the Father (now) have authority over him."[36] We are thus not surprised to find him speaking of the "hierarchical structure of authority [that] exists in the eternal Godhead."[37] He is quite emphatic that the differing authority of the divine persons is eternal and person-defining. He says, "Within the Godhead, not only is authority eternally exercised [by the Father] but submission marks the relationship of the Son to the Father from eternity past to eternity future."[38] Ware characteristically speaks of the eternal "submission" of the Son, in contrast to Grudem, who characteristically speaks of the eternal "subordination" of the Son, but I can see no significance in the alternative renderings of the one Greek word, *hypotassō*. If the Son is *eternally* submissive to the Father, always bound to obey him, because this is what indelibly and eternally distinguishes him from the Father, then he *is* a subordinate. Subordination in authority defines *who he is*, his being/nature; submission describes how he functions. The latter follows from the former. His *being* prescribes his eternal submissive "role."

A number of parallels between Ware and Grudem's teaching are significant. First, like Grudem, Ware asserts that he is teaching what "the church" has always believed,[39] and in support he appeals to Athanasius[40] and Augustine[41] among others. Second, he defines the divine Father-Son relationship in terms of human father-son relationships. Third, he grounds the subordination of women in the home

---

[33]Ibid., p. 70.
[34]Ibid., p. 80.
[35]Ibid., p. 127.
[36]Ibid. See also p. 153 for a similar assertion.
[37]Ibid., p. 21.
[38]Ibid., p. 98.
[39]Ibid., p. 79.
[40]Ibid., p. 37.
[41]Ibid., p. 80.

and the church on the supposed subordination of the Son in the immanent Trinity.[42] And fourth, he dismisses the doctrine of the eternal
generation of the Son.[43]

This distinctive evangelical understanding of divine differentiation
raises two questions acutely. Is it possible to speak of the *eternal* subordination or submission of the Son without falling into both the errors of
subordinationism and tritheism? And is differing authority a sure way,
even the only way ultimately, as Grudem argues, of differing persons,
whether human or divine? These two questions merge with each other,
but I will deal with them separately, beginning with the last one.

DOES DIFFERING AUTHORITY INDELIBLY DIFFERENTIATE PERSONS HUMAN AND DIVINE?

Arguing that human beings, specifically men and women, are indelibly
and permanently differentiated on the basis of differing God-given,
person-defining authority is unconvincing. Differing authority does
not categorically differentiate human beings. In differing contexts and
at differing times someone's authority can change. For example, a man
or woman may be the managing director of a large company with many
hundreds of people under their authority and be in the reserve army on
the weekends, where they are under the authority of officers "above."
And one day the managing director may lose their position and have no
one under them. And when it comes to men and women, authority
certainly does not categorically differentiate them. In a marriage the
authority exercised can change. In many a marriage, in the early days
when the man is insecure and finding his way, he may insist on having

---

[42]Why a threefold, analogically described all-male relationship in heaven should prescribe a
twofold male-female relationship on earth completely escapes me. The argument seems to be
special pleading of the worst kind. If divine threeness is prescriptive, then threesomes on earth
would be the ideal, and if the Father-Son relationship is prescriptive then all male twosomes
on earth would be the ideal! I very much doubt if the evangelicals making this argument would
be happy with these conclusions! I believe perfect divine relations in heaven do not give us a
social agenda to be put into operation in any detail in a fallen world. I also wonder if Christ and
women stand in parallel should men address their wives as "Lord"? I am of the opinion that
the man-woman relationship and the doctrine of the Trinity should not be coupled. Those
who turn to the Trinity to establish either equality or hierarchical ordering in the man-woman
relationship too easily end up corrupting the doctrine of the Trinity. The tail wags the dog.
[43]Ware, *Father, Son, and Holy Spirit*, p. 162 n. 3.

the final decision on important matters but thirty years later may be quite happy for his wife to make all the major decisions. It is true that once men held the reins of power and this differentiated them from women. But this is no longer the case. Today there are women presidents, prime ministers, governors, judges, managing directors, bishops and generals of the Salvation Army. Women seem to be very competent at exercising authority and do so well as a general rule. I can think of nothing to support the assertion that differing authority is what essentially differentiates people. How could this possibly distinguish twins, especially as children? And how could this possibly distinguish children in a schoolroom, or ordinary soldiers in an army?

When it comes to divine persons, differing them on the basis of *eternal* differing authority not only distinguishing them, but it also separates and divides them. Divine unity is lost. The Father and the Son are not "one" (Jn 10:30; 17:11). Instead of the orthodox doctrine of three "coequal" divine persons, where "none is before or after, greater or lesser," as the Athanasian Creed says, we have a hierarchy where the Father *eternally* rules over the Son and the Father and the Son rule over the Spirit. Knight, Grudem and Ware endorse just this view of the Trinity. Rather than reflecting historic orthodoxy, as they claim, this construal of the Trinity would seem to embrace the error of "subordinationism." This heresy is defined in the scholarly literature as the hierarchical *ranking* of the divine persons in the immanent Trinity, the ascribing of differing *status* to each person *on any basis,* something that in the end implies the ontological subordination of the Son and usually the Spirit as well.[44] For Ware, Grudem and those who follow them, to

---

[44]H. E. W. Turner, "Subordinationism," *A Dictionary of Christian Theology,* ed. A. Richardson (London: SCM, 1969), p. 329, defines the error of subordinationism as a positing of "a difference of *status* among the three [divine] persons." Gerald O'Collins, *The Tripersonal God: Understanding and Interpreting the Trinity* (Mahwah, N.J.: Paulist, 1999), p. 206, says that the error of subordinationism is seen in "those who assign an inferior *status* to the Son and the Holy Spirit as being 'under' and derived from the Father." Robert Letham, *The Holy Trinity in Scripture, History, Theology, and Worship* (Phillipsburg, N.J.: Presbyterian and Reformed, 2004), p. 502, defines subordinationism as the error of "teaching that the Son and the Holy Spirit are of lesser being or *status* than the Father." In the body of his book, p. 400, he defines Arianism, a form of subordinationism, as "the heretical idea that the Son was of a lesser *rank* or *status* than the Father." He does not define it simply as ontological subordinationism. See also pp. 147, 179 n. 29, 383, 482, 484, where Letham also comments on the heresy of Arianism

assert that they reject the ontological subordination of the Son does not avoid this charge. If the Son is primarily defined by his subordination, and this is what indelibly and eternally differentiates him from the Father, then no matter what language is used the implication is that he is other than the Father in what makes him the Son, his being. In other words, he is ontologically subordinated.

Furthermore, if the divine three are to be distinguished because the Father commands and the Son obeys, as Knight, Grudem and Ware maintain, what happens to the orthodox doctrines of inseparable operations and unity of will? Surely such teaching produces a radical social model of the Trinity, where we have three divine persons, each with their own will, each doing what the one above dictates—and as a result, tritheism.

It would seem impossible to speak of the *eternal* subordination or submission of the Son without falling into both the errors of subordinationism and tritheism. This is why with one voice the church has never allowed differing authority as a basis for differentiating the divine persons. Evangelicals who speak of the eternal subordination or submission of the Son attempt two strategies to avoid the charge of subordinationism. The first and most common is to argue that the subordination or submission of the Son envisaged only speaks of his *functional* or *role* subordination, not his ontological subordination. If the so-called differing function or role of the Father and the Son referred only to the operations of the divine persons, which could change and thus would not be person-defining, as these sociological terms normally indicate, then their reply would have force. However, the so-called distinctive roles or functions of the Father and the Son, namely, the Father's ruling "role" and the Son's obeying "role," are in fact *eternal, necessary and person-defining.*[45] They eternally distinguish the Father as the Father

---

and other forms of subordinationism. The italicizing of the word "status" in the above quotes is added. I have tracked down some twenty definitions of the error of subordinationism in theological dictionaries and theological books, and not one of them endorses the Knight-Grudem-Ware thesis that this error entails solely endorsing the ontological subordination of the Son. They agree it is anything that implies or necessitates this.

[45]The force of these two terms should be noted. The word *eternal* refers to what is divine. God alone is eternal, all else is temporal. The word *necessary*, in theological and philosophical usage, refers to what could not be otherwise. It is something true in all possible worlds. If the Son of

and the Son as the Son. If this is the case, then what differentiates them is not their "role" but who they are, their very being. The Son's *eternal* subordinate "role" is dictated by who he is, his being. This is the error of ontological subordinationism.

The second strategy in attempting to avoid the charge that the eternal subordination or submission of the Son does not entail the error of subordinationism is to assert that the Son's eternal submission and obedience is *voluntary*, not *necessary*. To argue this way is to suggest that the Father-Son relationship could be otherwise. The Father could have voluntarily chosen to be subordinate to the Son. My debating opponents would not be happy with this conclusion, but what they need to acknowledge is that if the Son's submission and obedience is entirely voluntary, and he could act otherwise, then his subordination in authority does not indelibly differentiate him from the Father. Differing authority in this case is not something that intrinsically differentiates the Father and the Son.

Another problem with the voluntary argument is that if there is no reason why the Son is necessarily and eternally submissive and obedient to the Father, then his choice to be so must be arbitrary. It is generally believed nothing in God is arbitrary. God's own life is ordered.

The claim may be made that the Son's submission and obedience is voluntary but I do not see Grudem, Ware or any other evangelical who teaches this hierarchical doctrine of the Trinity arguing this. They all insist that there is something in the Son that makes it appropriate for him to be eternally submissive and obedient that is not true of the Father. This something is that he is like a human son, set under his father. He is bound to obey his father. If this is the case then his submission and obedience is person-defining and *necessary*. It is what makes him a son. His submission and obedience indelibly and eternally differentiates him from the Father. At least as far as authority is concerned the Son is not coequal with God the Father. He does not just

---

God is eternally and necessarily subordinate or submissive, then it means this status defines his person or being. It speaks not of how he functions or his "role" but of his ontology—what makes him who he *is*. He *is* the subordinate Son, and he cannot ever be otherwise; he does not simply function subordinately.

voluntarily function subordinately; he *is* subordinated and cannot be otherwise. Again we have ontological subordinationism.

I make two last points very briefly. First, *eternally* ranking the Father and the Son in status and authority and thus in being not only differentiates them; it also divides and separates them. This is the error of tritheism. Second, differing the Father and the Son in authority finds absolutely no support in the orthodox theological tradition. It reflects Arian teaching. Not one of the great theologians of the past or any of the creeds or confessions allows that the Son is *eternally* subordinate, submissive and obedient to the Father; indeed, they all strongly oppose this idea.

I thus conclude that differentiating the three divine persons on this basis of eternal differing authority is to be rejected, first, because it leads to the errors of both tritheism and subordinationism and, second, because neither the Bible nor the historic theological tradition gives any support to making differing authority the basis for eternally differentiating the three divine persons in the immanent Trinity.

CONCLUSION

The case for grounding divine self-differentiation primarily if not exclusively on the eternal generation of the Son and procession of the Spirit may stretch our human minds beyond their limits, and we may wish the Bible said more on this, as we do on so many other important theological questions, but the two alternative grounds for eternal divine self-differentiation given by evangelicals, which we have just considered, are far more difficult and have far less biblical support and theological weight than the doctrines of the eternal generation of the Son and the eternal procession of the Spirit. Each in their own way, as we have shown, is deeply flawed, raising more problems than they solve. Both in the end ground divine self-differentiation on what is revealed in the economy. The Nicene fathers rejected this approach. They insisted that divine self-differentiation must be understood to have taken place in eternity, within the life of God, and be independent of creation. What is revealed of God's triunity in history simply reflects what is true apart from history in the immanent Trinity; God is eternally triune.

10

The Eternal Generation of the Son in Contemporary Theology

◆ ◆ ◆

To complete the argument of this book, which has concentrated on the intramural divisions among conservative evangelicals over the doctrine of the eternal generation of the Son, something needs to be said more generally about how contemporary Protestant and Catholic theologians treat this doctrine. Adequately dealing with this matter would take a book in itself. In what follows my aims are again quite modest. I only want to alert my readers to what they can expect to find in the literature. In doing this I note that (1) most of the historical studies cover this doctrine well; (2) the general trend in contemporary books on the Trinity is to say very little on this doctrine; and (3) some of the better-known contemporary mainline theologians offer alternative ways to understand and ground divine self-differentiation other than in two eternal "processions" in God.

THE GOOD NEWS

In my reading of works on the Trinity I first note that most of the scholarly books on the historic development of the doctrine of the Trinity up to A.D. 450 deal with the doctrine of the eternal generation of the Son very well. This is not surprising because this was one of the most disputed issues in the Arian debates. The books by G. L. Prestige,[1] J. N. D. Kelly,[2] R. P. C.

---

[1]G. L. Prestige, *God in Patristic Thought* (London: SPCK, 1952).
[2]J. N. D. Kelly, *Early Christian Doctrines* (London: Adam and Charles Black, 1968).

Hanson,[3] John Behr[4] and most of all Lewis Ayres[5] are excellent on this doctrine. The tragedy is that so many contemporary theologians, especially evangelicals, show no evidence of a mastery of such books, let alone the historic sources on which these books build. Ayres agrees. He says that too many "modern Christian theologians" have "engaged in the legacy of Nicaea at a fairly shallow level, frequently relying on assumptions about Nicene theology that are historically indefensible."[6] We saw classic examples of this in the evangelical theologians who assert that the doctrine of the eternal generation of the Son is an Arian idea or that it implies or necessitates the eternal subordination of the Son.

In more wide-ranging historical introductions to the doctrine of the Trinity, the Roman Catholic theologian Edmund Fortman consistently sees the importance of the doctrine of the eternal generation of the Son.[7] In his coverage of the more important contributors to the doctrine of the Trinity, from the first century to the present, he gives time to outlining what most of the theologians he discusses say on the eternal generation of the Son.

Turning to those who identify themselves as either conservative evangelicals or conservative Reformed theologians who defend the doctrine of the eternal generation of the Son in more than a passing comment, I mention first of all Robert Letham. In his comprehensive and informed account of the historical and theological development of the doctrine of the Trinity, *The Holy Trinity in Scripture, History, Theology, and Worship,*[8] he almost invariably discusses how each of the theologians he is considering speaks of the eternal generation of the Son, and he has an excursus defending this doctrine.[9] Other noteworthy evangelical defenses of the doctrine of the eternal generation of

---

[3]R. P. C. Hanson, *The Search for the Christian Doctrine of God: The Arian Controversy 318-381* (Edinburgh: T & T Clarke, 1988).

[4]John Behr, *The Nicene Faith,* 2 vols. (Crestwood, N.Y.: St. Vladimir's Seminary Press, 2004-2006).

[5]Lewis Ayres, *Nicaea and Its Legacy: An Approach to Fourth-Century Theology* (Oxford: Oxford University Press, 2004).

[6]Ibid., p. 1.

[7]Edmund Fortman, *The Triune God: A Historical Study of the Doctrine of the Trinity* (Grand Rapids: Baker, 1982).

[8]Robert Letham, *The Holy Trinity in Scripture, History, Theology, and Worship* (Phillipsburg, N.J.: Presbyterian and Reformed, 2004).

[9]Ibid., pp. 383-89.

the Son are found in Donald Macleod, *The Person of Christ*,[10] Fred
Sanders, *The Deep Things of God: How the Trinity Changes Everything*,[11]
Keith E. Johnson's essays on Augustine's teaching on the eternal generation of the Son[12] and the Korean theologian Jung S. Rhee's five
studies on the eternal generation of the Son.[13]

Next, I mention David Cunningham, who in his 1998 book, *These
Three Are One: The Practice of Trinitarian Theology*, gives a full chapter
to the doctrine of the eternal generation of the Son.[14] He writes to
present the historical doctrine of the Trinity in its varying elements in
contemporary form and wording. His chapter on the eternal generation
of the Son is titled "Producing," and the issue he explores is "how God
produces God."[15]

T. F. TORRANCE

Thomas F. Torrance demands special consideration. Paul Molnar, in his
definitive study, *Thomas F. Torrance, Theologian of the Trinity*[16] says he is
"one of the most significant English-speaking theologians of the twentieth century,"[17] and as the title of this book indicates, the doctrine of the

---

[10]Donald Macleod, *The Person of Christ* (Leicester, U.K.: Inter-Varsity Press, 1998), pp. 72-
74, 131-35.

[11]Fred Sanders, *The Deep Things of God: How the Trinity Changes Everything* (Wheaton, Ill.:
Crossway, 2010), pp. 83-89, 91-92, 155-56.

[12]Keith E. Johnson, "Augustine's Trinitarian Reading of John 5: A Model for the Theological
Interpretation of Scripture," *Journal of the Evangelical Theological Society* 52, no. 4 (2009): 799-
811; Johnson, "Trinitarian Agency and the Eternal Subordination of the Son: An Augustinian Perspective," *Themelios* 36 no. 1 (2011): 7-25; Johnson, "Augustine, Eternal Generation,
and Evangelical Trinitarianism," *Trinity Journal* 32, no. 2 (2011): 141-63.

[13]See "Chapter 1. A History of the Eternal Generation of the Son and Its Significance in
Trinitarianism" <www.jsrhee.com/QA/thesis1.htm>. "Chapter 2. The Doctrine of the Eternal Generation of the Son in Opposition to the Logos Doctrine of the Early Church" <www
.rsrhee.com/QA/thesis2.htm>. "Chapter 3. The Triumph of Ontological Realism and Eternal Generation in the Nicene Creed" <www.jsrhee.com/QA/thesis3.htm>. "Chapter 4. John
Calvin and Reformed Theology on the Doctrine of the Eternal Generation of the Son"
<www.jsrhee.com/QA/thesis4.htm>. "Chapter 5. The Significance of the Eternal Genera-
tion of the Son Doctrine in the Contemporary Trinitarian Teaching." He has also written the
Theopedia Web-based article on the doctrine of the eternal generation of the Son <www
.theopedia.com/Eternal_generation_of_the_Son>.

[14]David Cunningham, *These Three Are One: The Practice of Trinitarian Theology* (Oxford: Blackwell, 1998), chap. 2.

[15]Ibid., pp. 59-88.

[16]Paul D. Molnar, *Thomas F. Torrance, Theologian of the Trinity* (Surrey, U.K.: Ashgate, 2009).

[17]Ibid., p. 1.

Trinity is foundational for all his work. In Torrance's two seminal books *The Trinitarian Faith*[18] and *The Christian Doctrine of God*,[19] he gives a fresh and contemporary enunciation of the doctrine of the Trinity in the light of biblical revelation, the best insights of the fourth-century Greek fathers and the Reformed tradition, especially as it is expressed by Karl Barth. Because he wrote on the Trinity constructively Torrance did not major on the errors of Arianism, and for this reason his writing does not say a lot on the Arian denial of *the eternal* begetting of the Son, although he is consistently opposed to Arianism and all expressions of subordinationism. Nevertheless, the doctrine of the eternal generation of the Son is for him a doctrine of huge importance. He says "the decisive" question raised by the teaching of Arius was "the nature of relation between Jesus Christ the incarnate Son and God the Father."[20] This question was answered when the bishops of Nicaea concluded that the church should confess belief in "one Lord Jesus Christ, the Son of God, begotten from the Father, only begotten, that is from the being of the Father, God from God, Light from Light, true God from true God, begotten not made of one being with the Father (*homoousios to patri*), though whom all things were made."[21] With these words, he says, the bishops

> gave expression to the actual content of the New Testament presentation of Christ in which faith in Christ perfectly coincided with faith in God. To have faith in the one Lord Jesus Christ is to have faith in one God the Father, and acknowledge him as God equally with the Father. This unique relation of Christ to the Father within the oneness of God was spelled out by the phrase "the only begotten Son of God, begotten from his Father before all ages . . . begotten not made."[22]
>
> . . . The import of these words was then gathered up in concentrated form by the emphatic, "of one being with the Father" (*homoousios to patri*), to express oneness in being between the incarnate Son and God the Father.[23]

[18]T. F. Torrance, *The Trinitarian Faith* (Edinburgh: T & T Clark, 1988).

[19]T. F. Torrance, *The Christian Doctrine of God: One Being, Three Persons* (Edinburgh: T & T Clark, 1996).

[20]Torrance, *The Trinitarian Faith*, p. 116.

[21]Ibid.

[22]Ibid., p. 117.

[23]Ibid.

Torrance is saying that at the Council of Nicaea the bishops predicated belief in Jesus Christ as "true God from true God" on the eternal begetting of the Son, which indicated that he is "one in being" (*homoousios*) with the Father. In these words, they asserted that Jesus Christ is God without any caveats, yet he is God the Son, not God the Father.

For Torrance the church took a theological "giant step forward"[24] when it agreed that the Father and the Son were *homoousios*. He writes, "The *homoousion* is the ontological and epistemological linchpin of Christian theology. It gives expression to the truth with which everything hangs together, and without which everything falls apart."[25] By including this word, the Nicene fathers decisively excluded "the damaging heresies of Arianism, subordinationism and Sabellianism. Against all tritheist and modalist conceptions of the Trinity, they insisted that God really is indivisibly and eternally in himself the one indivisible Being, three coequal Persons which he is toward us in the redemptive missions of his Son and Spirit."[26]

Although neither Athanasius nor the Cappadocian fathers use the term *perichōrēsis* to speak of the mutual indwelling of the three divine persons, Torrance rightly sees them all teaching what this word came to mean, namely, that "they coinhere in one another by virtue of their one Being for one Another and by virtue of the dynamic Communion which they constitute in their belonging to one Another."[27] For him the *perichōrēsis* of the Father and the Son is just as important as the *homoousios* of the Father and the Son. Indeed, we might say that for Torrance they are two sides of the one coin. Both speak unequivocally of the unity of the divine persons and of their *hypostatic* distinctions.[28] These terms envisage a fully personal and communal understanding of the triune God of Christian revelation. He writes, "The Being of God is the personal, living and active Being, fellowship-seeking and communion-constituting Being,"[29] and further that "the one triune Being

---

[24]Torrance, *Trinitarian Faith*, p. 144.
[25]Torrance, *Christian Doctrine of God*, p. 95.
[26]Ibid., p. 115.
[27]Ibid., p. 133.
[28]Ibid., p. 175.
[29]Ibid., p. 132.

of God is to be thought of, then, as essentially and intrinsically a mutual movement of loving self-communication between the Father and the Son and the Holy Spirit, an intensely personal Communion, an ever-living ever-loving Being, the *Being for others* which the three divine Persons have in common."[30]

Given this emphasis on divine communal unity, we are not surprised to find that Torrance is critical of Basil and his brother Gregory of Nyssa's teaching that the person of the Father is the "source" (*archē*) and "cause" (*aitia*) of the person of the Son and Spirit. This understanding of the eternal generation of the Son, he argues, divides the divine persons and implies subordinationism because it conceives of the Father as "uncaused deity" and the Son and Spirit as "caused deity."[31] In contrast for Torrance, "While in the Father/Son relation the Father is the Father of the Son, he is in no sense the deifier of the Son, for he himself in his eternal Being is not the Father without the Son, and as the Son in his eternal Being is not Son without Father. As Son of the Father he is not less than the Father, but is himself 'whole God' (*holos Theos*), whole from whole (*holos holou*)."[32] Appealing to the teaching of Athanasius,[33] Didymus the Blind, Epiphanius, Gregory of Nazianzus and Cyril of Alexandria,[34] Torrance argues that the one triune being of God is to be understood as the *monarche* of the divine persons, not the person of the Father alone.[35] In support of this view he draws attention to the wording of the 325 Creed of Nicaea, which speaks of the Son as begotten not *from the person* of the Father but "from the being of the Father."[36] This understanding of the *monarche* is predicated on the belief that the three divine persons eternally share and constitute the one being of God. If this is the case, then one of them cannot be thought

---

[30]Ibid., p. 133.

[31]Ibid., pp. 178-79. See also pp. 127, 182.

[32]Ibid., pp. 135-36.

[33]See my earlier discussion of this matter in the section on Athanasius.

[34]Ibid., pp. 157, 161, 175, 178.

[35]Torrance, *Trinitarian Faith*, pp. 241, 302-4, 321, 329; Torrance, *Christian Doctrine of God*, pp. 141, 176-79, 188-90. See further Molnar, *Thomas F. Torrance*, pp. 64-67. On this matter see also R. Del Colle, "'Person' and 'Being' in John Zizioulas' Trinitarian Theology: In Conversation with Thomas Torrance and Thomas Aquinas," *Scottish Journal of Theology* 54, no. 1 (2001): 70-86; and Molnar, *Thomas F. Torrance*, pp. 54-65.

[36]Torrance, *Christian Doctrine of God*, pp. 128, 141, 179.

of as the cause of the divine being of another.[37] In this construal of the *monarche*, the Son is *eternally begotten of the being of the Father* and the Spirit eternally proceeds "*from the Father through the Son*," but *the person* of the Father is not the *monarche* ("sole source") of the Son, or the cause of the Son, or "the deifier of the Son."[38] And, "Any notion of subordination in the Trinity is completely ruled out."[39]

To understand what Torrance is saying we need to note that he makes a clear distinction between naming God absolutely as the Father, referring to the Godhead, and naming God relatively as the Father, one divine person, in relation to the Son and the Spirit.[40] Torrance argues that these two meanings of the name Father are found in Scripture,[41] and we have seen that Augustine, Calvin and Aquinas make this distinction. He writes, "When the Father is considered relatively, that is *ad alios* in relation to the Son and the Holy Spirit, he is thought of as the Father of the Son, but when the Father is thought of absolutely, that is *in se*, as God himself (*Autotheos*) the name 'Father' is often applied to God (*Theos*) or the Godhead (*Theotes*). The name 'Father,' then, may refer to the one being of God or *ousia* of God, but it may also refer to the Person or *hypostasis* of the Father."[42] While Torrance will not allow hierarchical ordering within divine life in any way, he does emphatically endorse, in agreement with the tradition, order in divine life. For him, the term "order" (*taxis*) in trinitarian discourse speaks of the unchanging and irreversible "relations" that exist between the three divine persons. He says that there can be "no thought of one Person being ontologically or divinely prior to another or subsequent to another."[43] Nevertheless, in reference to the relation of the person of the Father to the person of the Son, there is an order "governed by the irreversible relation between the Father and the Son": the Father begets and the Son is begotten. This order also per-

---

[37]Ibid., pp. 176-80.
[38]Ibid., pp. 115, 178-79. See also T. F. Torrance, *Trinitarian Perspectives; Toward Doctrinal Agreement* (Edinburgh: T & T Clark, 1994), pp. 112, 135.
[39]Torrance, *Trinitarian Perspectives*, p. 112.
[40]Torrance, *Christian Doctrine of God*, pp. 137-41.
[41]Ibid.
[42]Ibid., p. 140
[43]Ibid., p. 180.

tains to the Father and the Son and the Spirit because the Spirit *proceeds from* "the Father in the Son."[44] In this order the persons are "distinguished by position and not status, by form and not being, by sequence and not power, for they are fully and perfectly equal."[45]

The importance of Torrance's work on the Trinity cannot be overestimated. More than anyone else he is responsible for possibly the most significant theological breakthrough in the twentieth century. For more than a thousand years the inclusion of the *filioque* clause had divided the Eastern and Western churches. In a series of meetings of the international dialogue between the World Alliance of Reformed Churches and the Orthodox Church, which began in 1977, Torrance was able to find a way of speaking of the triune being of God as the *monarche* of the three divine persons that was acceptable to both sides. This outcome was so momentous that all fourteen Orthodox patriarchs in the Pan-Orthodox Communion attended the meeting ratifying the "Joint Statement of the Official Dialogue between the Orthodox Church and the World Alliance of Reformed Churches," issued on March 13, 1991. It announced that an "agreed Statement on the Holy Trinity" had been reached.[46] They concluded that the *monarche* is the divine triune being of God, not the person of the Father.

> Since there is only one Trinity in Unity, and one Unity in Trinity, there is only one indivisible Godhead, and only one Arche (*arche*) or Monarchia (*monarchia*). As such, Gregory the Theologian reminds us, "It is a Monarchy that is not limited to one Person" (*Or.* 29.2). "The Godhead is one in Three, and the Three are One, in whom all the Godhead is, or, to be more precise, who are the Godhead" (*Or.* 39.11). "Each person is God when considered in himself; as the Father, so the Son, and as the Son, so the Holy Spirit; the Three One God when contemplated together; Each God because consubstantial; one God because of the Monarchy. I cannot think of the One without

---

[44]On Torrance's understanding of the *Filioque* see Molnar, *Thomas F. Torrance*, pp. 65-67.

[45]Torrance, *Christian Doctrine of God*, p. 176. See also Torrance, *Trinitarian Perspectives: Toward Doctrinal Agreement* (Edinburgh: T & T Clark, 1994), p. 136.

[46]The results of these discussions are found in T. F. Torrance, ed., *Theological Dialogue Between Orthodox and Reformed Churches*, 2 vols. (Edinburgh: T & T Clark, 1985-1993).

being enlightened by the splendour of the Three; nor can I distinguish them without being carried back to the One" (Gregory the Theologian, *Or.* 40.41).[47]

In this understanding of the Trinity, Torrance says, "there are no degrees of deity in the Holy Trinity, as implied in a distinction between the underived Deity of the Father and the derived Deity of the Son and the Spirit. Any notion of subordination is completely ruled out."[48]

THE BAD NEWS

My general impression from reading contemporary writings on the Trinity, especially by Protestant theologians, is that the trend today is not to see the importance of the doctrine of the eternal generation of the Son and thus to say very little about it. Other issues get far more attention, *perichōrēsis,* the economic and immanent Trinity, the social doctrine of the Trinity, the implications of a social doctrine of the Trinity, and in the case of many evangelicals, the Trinity as the ground of women's subordination. Paul Molnar's criticism of "much of contemporary theology [is that it] is interested merely in the economic Trinity."[49] The immanent Trinity, which is foundational and antecedent to what takes place in the world, too often gets eclipsed. When this is the case then the doctrine of the eternal generation of the Son also gets eclipsed.

This modern trend stands very much in contrast to the writings of Athanasius and the Cappadocians, in which the doctrine of the eternal generation of the Son is possibly the most discussed issue because for them it is the basis for their belief that the Father and the Son were one in being and power, yet two "persons." The modern trend is also in contrast with the Nicene and Athanasian Creeds, in which Jesus is twice confessed as "begotten"; with Augustine, who thought this doctrine was hugely important; with Aquinas, for whom the two eternal

---

[47]For the full text see World Alliance of Reformed Churches, "Agreed Statement on the Holy Trinity," <http://warc.ch/dt/erl1/13.html>. See also T. F. Torrance, *Trinitarian Perspectives,* pp. 110-22.

[48]Torrance, *Trinitarian Perspectives,* p. 112.

[49]Molnar, *Thomas F. Torrance,* p. 31.

"processions" are primary and foundational to the doctrine of the Trinity because they safeguard divine unity, affirm the eternal self-differentiation of the three divine persons and establish the four relations in the one God; and with the post-Reformation theological tradition, which fully recognized the great importance of this doctrine. I noted in an earlier chapter that John Gill devotes 20 pages to discussing the doctrine of the eternal generation of the Son and that Samuel Miller of Princeton Theological Seminary wrote a 295-page defense of the doctrine of the eternal generation of the Son: *Letters on the Eternal Sonship of Christ, Addressed to the Rev. Stuart, of Andover.*[50]

In so many books on the Trinity written in the last thirty years, the doctrine of the eternal generation of the Son is mentioned only in passing as an issue of contention in the Arian controversies. In some, as we have seen in evangelical works and will see in a moment in mainline contemporary works on the Trinity, it is even rejected or radically modified. Many simply do not recognize the huge importance and theological implications of this doctrine. The immanent Trinity, where divine self-differentiation takes place within the life of God in eternity, gets eclipsed by concerns about the practical significance of the Trinity in everyday Christian living. Why and how God is one and three is not considered, or if it is, it is dealt with superficially. These theologians do not recognize that internal and eternal divine self-differentiation actually is the foundation of our Christian triune doctrine of God. Without this foundation, Christian faith, hope and love are undermined and our worship is damaged.

FOUR ALTERNATIVE EXPLANATIONS OF DIVINE SELF-DIFFERENTIATION IN CONTEMPORARY MAINLINE THEOLOGY

Last, I briefly outline alternative explanations of divine self-differentiation in the writings of four modern theologians: two Roman Catholics, two Lutherans. These men do not reject the historic doctrines of the eternal generation of the Son and procession of the Spirit; rather, they argue that divine self-differentiation can be explained and better

---

[50]Samuel Miller, *Letters on the Eternal Sonship of Christ, Addressed to the Rev. Stuart, of Andover* (Philadelphia: W. W. Woodward, 1823).

grounded in other ways. I make no attempt to expound their overall teaching on the Trinity, and I do not attempt a detailed response to their alternative construals of the Trinity, which are complex and nuanced. I nevertheless do raise what I think are significant weaknesses in the alternatives given in each instance.

Robert Jenson. The American Lutheran Robert Jenson (b. 1930) is widely recognized as one of the more significant and innovative contributors to the late twentieth-century renaissance of the doctrine of the Trinity. He has written much on this doctrine. His two most important works on the Trinity are *The Triune Identity: God According to the Gospel* (1982)[51] and the first volume of his *Systematic Theology* (1997).[52] Jenson says his goal is to reformulate the historic doctrine of God by listening afresh to Scripture and by appeal to what he calls "revisionist metaphysics."[53] He begins this quest by first identifying the God revealed in the biblical narrative as the triune God of Christian faith. In this narrative, he argues, God is not a timeless metaphysical being outside of history but a God identified by events in time who is only fully who he will be at the eschaton.

His commitment to narrative theology and eschatological metaphysics leads him to criticize the way classical theology has spoken of the eternal generation of the Son and procession of the Spirit "from" the Father as internal acts of self-differentiation outside and above history. Instead, he says, we should "follow scripture in understanding eternity as faithfulness to the last future. . . . Truly, the Trinity is simply the Father and the man Jesus and their Spirit as the Spirit of the believing community. This 'economic' Trinity is *eschatologically* God 'himself,' an 'immanent' Trinity. And that assertion is no problem, for God is himself only eschatologically, since he is Spirit."[54]

This is certainly a radical departure from historic orthodoxy. He seems to be denying the preexistence of Christ, depicting him entirely

---

[51]Robert Jenson, *The Triune Identity: God According to the Gospel* (Philadelphia: Fortress, 1982).

[52]Robert Jenson, *Systematic Theology* (Oxford: Oxford University Press), vol. 1. See also his recent article, "Once More the *Logos Asarkos*," *International Journal of Systematic Theology* 13, no. 2 (2011): 13-133.

[53]Robert Jenson, "A Reply" [to Paul Molnar], *Scottish Journal of Theology* 52, no. 1 (1999): 132.

[54]Jenson, *Triune Identity*, p. 141.

as "the man Jesus" and defining the Holy Spirit as "the Spirit of the believing community." It would seem that right at the heart of Jenson's theology is his view that the human Jesus reveals God. He says, "Our divine savior is not an extra metaphysical entity. . . . He is Mary's child, the hanged man of Golgotha."[55] In contrast, in historic orthodoxy the eternally begotten Son in becoming incarnate reveals God and is God.

He continues by arguing that in the traditional understanding of the two "processions" the Son and the Spirit "derive their deity from the Father, but Father and Son do not derive deity from the Spirit."[56] This, he says, stands in tension with the New Testament, according to which the Spirit is the witness to the Son and God is defined as Spirit. He thus opts for a more dynamic picture of divine self-differentiation, where each divine person is who he is by giving and receiving.

In his later *Systematic Theology* he spells out what this more dynamic picture of eternal self-differentiation involves in these words: "The Father begets the Son and freely breathes the Spirit; the Spirit liberates the Father for the Son and the Son for the Father; the Son is begotten and liberated, and so reconciles the Father with the future his Spirit is."[57] The first ten words of this quote are orthodox and understandable, but after this what he says becomes problematic. How does the Spirit liberate "the Father for the Son and the Son for the Father," and what does that mean? And how does the Son in his begetting and liberation reconcile "the Father with the future his Spirit is"? Seeking new ways to speak of eternal divine self-differentiation is fine; even seeking to reformulate the doctrines of the eternal generation of the Son and procession of the Spirit is acceptable. However, alternatives to be taken seriously must be understandable and explicable and not conflate the persons or breach divine unity. It could be in the above quote that Jenson does both, but the language is so poetic that it is almost impossible to know what he is saying.

Much more could be said on Jenson's reformulation of the doctrine of the Trinity in general and of the doctrines of the eternal generation

---

[55]Ibid., p. 145.
[56]Ibid., p. 142.
[57]Jenson, *Systematic Theology*, 1:161.

of the Son and procession of the Spirit in particular, but to go further would demand a much fuller exposition of his work and ideas.[58] What I have made clear, I hope, in these brief comments on Jenson's writings on the Trinity is that he not only questions and seeks to reformulate the historic doctrine of the two eternal processions in God that constitute God as triune but that he also questions and wants to reformulate in a radical way the historic doctrine of the Trinity itself.

Wolfhart Pannenberg. The German Lutheran Wolfhart Pannenberg (b. 1928) is another important voice in contemporary exploratory thinking on the Trinity. Following Barth he begins his three-volume *Systematic Theology*[59] with a discussion of revelation, which he sees as the history of God's activity in the world. In his prolegomena, again like Barth, he immediately begins with an exposition of the doctrine of the Trinity, a doctrine he believes is foundational to all theology. He gives first of all a concise account of what the Bible says on the Trinity and how the church fathers developed this teaching into the doctrine of the Trinity.[60] He argues that a retrograde step was made in the High Scholastic period, when the practice became to discuss God in his unity before turning to the doctrine of the Trinity, a practice that post-Reformation dogmaticians followed.[61] To find a better way, he says, "we must begin with the way in which Father, Son and Spirit come on the scene and relate to one another in the event of revelation."[62]

Beginning with the threefold revelation of God in the economy Pannenberg questions the traditional way of differing the divine persons by differing origination. He argues that a "sharp distinction between begetting [the Son] and breathing [the Spirit] on the one side, sending and gift on the other [the divine missions], can perhaps be justified linguistically but can hardly be justified exegetically."[63] He

---

[58]On this see Stanley J. Grenz, *Rediscovering the Triune God: The Trinity in Contemporary Theology* (Minneapolis: Fortress, 2004), pp. 106-16; Paul D. Molnar, *Divine Freedom and the Doctrine of the Immanent Trinity* (Edinburgh: T & T Clark, 2002), pp. 68-81.

[59]Wolfhart Pannenberg, *Systematic Theology*, trans. Geoffrey W. Bromiley, 3 vols. (Grand Rapids: Eerdmans, 1991-1998).

[60]Ibid., 1:259-80.

[61]Ibid., 1:280-99.

[62]Ibid., 1:299.

[63]Ibid., 1:305. See also on this matter Wolfhart Pannenberg, "Divine Economy and Eternal

says that there is no reference in Scripture to an eternal breathing or proceeding of the Spirit or of an eternal begetting of the Son. However, on the last matter he adds that this observation is "not to rule out the idea of eternal generation."[64] Another problem with the historical doctrine of the Trinity, Pannenberg believes, is that it results in an unhelpful prioritizing of the Father, which undermines a fully trinitarian doctrine of God.[65]

In attempting to give a better explanation of eternal divine self-differentiation, Pannenberg introduces the idea of "mutual dependence."[66] For him, the term "person" is a correlative concept. Personhood is found in the self-giving of oneself to another whereby one's identity is established by the other. This leads him to speak of the Son's subjecting himself to the Father and the Spirit's subjecting himself to the Son and the Father. However, he then immediately goes on to speak of the dependence of the Father on the Son and Spirit. This, he says, discloses the "mutuality in their relationships."[67] The Father's dependence on the Son takes place, Pannenberg argues, "after Christ's resurrection when he is given all power and authority being made head over all things (Matt. 28:18, Lk 10:22, Jn 5:23, Phil. 2:9ff)."[68] Rather than finding 1 Corinthians 15:28 a troublesome verse that could be read to teach that on the last day the Son will be subordinated to the Father, Pannenberg finds this text vindicating his position. Commenting on this text he says,

> In the handing over of lordship from the Father to the Son, and in its handing back from the Son to the Father, we see mutuality in their relationship. . . . By handing over lordship to the Son the Father makes his kingship dependent on whether the Son glorifies him and fulfils his lordship by fulfilling his mission. The self-distinction of the Father from the Son is not just that he begets the Son, but that he

Trinity," in *The Theology of John Zizioulas: Personhood and the Church,* ed. D. H. Knight (Aldershot, U.K.: Ashgate, 2007), p. 79.

[64]Pannenberg, *Systematic Theology,* 1:306. Italics added.

[65]Ibid., 1:311-13.

[66]Ibid., 1:309-19.

[67]Ibid., 1:313.

[68]Ibid., 1:312.

hands over all things to him, so that his kingdom and his own deity are now dependent on the Son.[69]

Pannenberg finds biblical support for the dependency of the Father and the Son on the Spirit and thus their self-differentiation in the Johannine statements on the divine three glorifying each other. "As Jesus glorifies the Father and not himself, and precisely in doing this he shows himself to be the Son of the Father, so the Spirit glorifies not himself but the Son, and in him the Father."[70]

There is much in Pannenberg's distinctive doctrine of the Trinity that demands our attention and consideration even if we can see profound weaknesses in it, for example in his tendency toward tritheism.[71] Another significant problem is that for Pannenberg the historical missions of Jesus and the Spirit not only differentiate the divine persons from each other but they also constitute their deity. So, Samuel Powell says, for Pannenberg, "The Trinitarian persons are what they are because of their mutual relations in salvation history."[72] In other words "the economic Trinity may be said to be the self-actualization of the triune God in the world."[73] This means that, rather than the immanent and eternal Trinity having primacy, the economic Trinity constitutes the immanent Trinity. God, in other words, is not triune apart from history.

Thomas Weinandy. Thomas Weinandy (b. 1946) is a Roman Catholic scholar who has published widely on the Trinity. In the preface to his 1995 book, *The Father's Spirit of Sonship: Reconceiving the Trinity,* he tells his readers that his stimulus for writing this book came "as a result of being baptized in the Spirit within the Charismatic renewal" movement.[74] This experience led him to reflect on how the Spirit is eclipsed

---

[69]Ibid., 1:313.

[70]Ibid., 1:315.

[71]A problem given careful consideration by Veli-Matti Kärkkäinen, *The Trinity in Global Perspective* (Louisville: Westminster John Knox, 2007), pp. 141-43. Most studies on Pannenberg's doctrine of the Trinity raise this problem.

[72]Samuel M. Powell, *The Trinity in German Thought* (Cambridge: Cambridge University Press, 2001), p. 238.

[73]Grenz, *Rediscovering*, p. 105.

[74]Thomas Weinandy, *The Father's Spirit of Sonship: Reconceiving the Trinity* (Edinburgh: T & T Clark), p. ix.

in traditional trinitarian theology. In this, the Son and the Spirit eternally proceed from the Father, almost as if they are God in second and third place. His "revolutionary thesis," as he calls it, is this: "The Father begets the Son in or by the Holy Spirit. The Son is begotten by the Father in the Spirit and thus the Spirit simultaneously proceeds from the Father as the one in whom the Son is begotten. The Son being begotten in the Spirit simultaneously loves the Father in the same Spirit by which he himself is begotten (is loved)."[75]

This new conception of the Trinity, he says, "finds its distinctiveness in the specific and precise role ascribed to the Holy Spirit within the immanent Trinity, a role that has been obscured throughout the history of trinitarian theology."[76] In this explanation of eternal divine self-differentiation, the historic grounds of eternal begetting and procession are replaced by a dynamic interacting between the divine three. He speaks of divine self-differentiation being grounded in "action and origin."[77]

Giving greater prominence to the Holy Spirit in trinitarian theology is certainly a commendable goal. The Spirit has all too often been sidelined in traditional theology. Weinandy tells us in his first chapter that he is seeking to reformulate the doctrines of "procession" "to give trinitarian theology a more biblical foundation."[78] This again is a commendable goal. In his second chapter he outlines his trinitarian thesis given above. In chapters three and four he then seeks biblical support for his thesis in the narratives of Jesus' baptism, death, resurrection and in the Gospel of John. He finds much that speaks of the Father, Son and Spirit, but whether any of it directly supports his thesis is not at all clear. The baptism of Jesus (Mt 3:17; Mk 1:11; Lk 3:22) is one of his key texts, but that this indicates that "the sonship of Jesus is here presented as dependent upon his being the bearer of the Holy Spirit" is not convincing.[79] With most commentators, I think the bestowal of the Spirit on Jesus at his baptism speaks of the bestowal of the Spirit on the Son to empower him for his *earthly*

---

[75]Ibid., p. 17.
[76]Ibid.
[77]Ibid., pp. 53, 65.
[78]Ibid., p. 2.
[79]Ibid., p. 27.

mission. I am definitely not persuaded that what takes place in his baptism "constitutes" him as the Son[80] and the Father as the Father in the immanent Trinity[81] because this would make God's triunity dependent on historical events.

In chapter one, he says that another of his goals is to retrieve "the distinct personalities" of the divine three,[82] lost in Western trinitarian theology. However, he then proceeds to define the Spirit in "Western" impersonal terms as "the bond of love between the Father and the Son"[83] and their "common breath."[84] T. R. Thompson concludes that for Weinandy the Holy Spirit is presented as not "much more than a depersonalized handmaid of the Father and the Son."[85]

Most questions regarding Weinandy's thesis arise in connection with chapter four, in which he enunciates a "new trinitarian ontology," not least because it is impossible to comprehend what he is saying. For example, I wonder what the following words mean: "The Father is the Father because, in the one act by which he is eternally constituted as Father, the Spirit proceeds as the Love (Life and Truth) in whom the Son is begotten of the Father."[86] This quote, and many others speaking of how the three persons interact in constituting one another, seems to depict each divine person as an individual who "acts" relatively independently of the others, thereby making the other two who they are. Surely this undermines divine unity.

David Coffey. David Coffey (b. 1934) is another well-known Roman Catholic theologian who has published widely on the Trinity. In his 1999 book, *Deus Trinitas: The Doctrine of the Triune God*,[87] he argues that the traditional "Western" doctrine of the Trinity, according to which the Son is eternally generated by the Father and the

---

[80]Ibid., p. 66.

[81]Ibid., p. 29.

[82]Ibid., p. 4.

[83]Ibid., p. 30.

[84]Ibid., p. 75.

[85]See T. R. Thompson, review of *The Father's Spirit of Sonship*, *Calvin Theological Journal* 32 (1997): 195.

[86]Weinandy, *Father's Spirit*, p. 72.

[87]David Coffey, *Deus Trinitas: The Doctrine of the Triune God* (Oxford: Oxford University Press, 1999).

Spirit eternally proceeds from the Father and the Son, needs to be rethought and reformulated. His case is that the New Testament gives not one but two models of the Trinity.[88] The first one, which orthodoxy has embraced, exhibits the order, or *taxis*, Father, Son and Spirit. It may be called "the model of mission," as it is structured according to the historic missions of the Son and the Spirit. Taken back to the immanent Trinity, it becomes what he calls "the procession model" because what takes place in time (*ad extra*) reflects what takes place in eternity (*ad intra*). This model, he believes, owes the most to John's Gospel. The second model he calls "the return model." This he believes owes most to the Synoptic Gospels. In this model the order is Father, Holy Spirit, Son, or to state it more fully, Father—Holy Spirit—Son—Holy Spirit—Father. This model reflects Augustine's thought, who spoke of the Holy Spirit as the outcome of the love of the Father and the Son. Taken back to the immanent Trinity it speaks of the Father, Son and Spirit in a dynamic equilibrium, that is, "of the relations of the three divine persons among themselves."[89] Coffey holds that these two models can be seen as complementary, but he argues that "the return model" is far more theologically fruitful and insightful because it is comprehensive, "i.e. inclusive of the procession model, whereas the converse is not the case."[90]

Coffey outlines this "return model" in these words: "The Father bestows the Holy Spirit on Jesus as his love for him in a uniquely radical way in which Jesus is brought into human existence as his beloved Son. Jesus further appropriates his unique gift of the Holy Spirit and the divine Sonship which it brings about in the course of his life through his unfailing obedience and answering love of the Father, and in his death definitively returns to the Father in love returning the Holy Spirit to him."[91]

Again we have a very complex picture that for clarity and precision does not match what Coffey calls "the procession model": what I would

---

[88]For what follows see ibid., pp. 35-45.
[89]Ibid., p. 45.
[90]I sent my explanation of Dr. Coffey's position to him to read, and he added these words of explanation. I thank him for this.
[91]Ibid., p. 41.

call the historic doctrine of the eternal generation of the Son and procession of the Spirit. The problems with Coffey's book on the Trinity,
however, go much further than this,[92] particularly in regard to the doctrine of the eternal generation of the Son, our primary concern.

First, Coffey, following Rahner, embraces what has been called "a
Christology from below."[93] Jesus is a man who is uniquely filled with
the Spirit. He says, "The uniqueness of Jesus' Sonship is evident in the
utter radicality of this [the Father's] bestowal of the Holy Spirit,"[94] and
our relation to the Father "is essentially the same as for Christ, except
that it lacks the radicality present in his case."[95] Coffey denies that his
Christology is adoptionist,[96] but this error is implied throughout his
book. For example, he says, "The Father's radical bestowal of the Holy
Spirit on Jesus at the moment of his conception brings about his divine
Sonship,"[97] and there is "a progressive realization of divine Sonship in
Jesus."[98] This means that for Coffey, Jesus Christ is not the eternally
begotten Son of the Father who becomes incarnate but a man who is
adopted into the Godhead.

Second, Coffey argues that "God is first an absolute person and only
later becomes triune (three relative persons)."[99] He distinguishes "between two 'stages' of the Trinity *in fieri* (in the process of becoming)
and *in facto esse* (as already constituted)."[100] Later he adds, "Faith assigns
no priority of the unity of God over his threeness (or vice versa). It is the
prerogative of theology to do this if it so chooses."[101] This line of
thinking, no matter how qualified, calls into question that God is
triune for all eternity and that his triunity is grounded in an eternal act
of self-differentiation *ad intra*.

---

[92]See Paul Molnar, "*Deus Trinitas:* Some Dogmatic Implications of David Coffey's Biblical
    Approach to the Trinity," *Irish Theological Quarterly* 67 (2002): 35-54.
[93]See further on this my *Jesus and the Father: Modern Evangelicals Reinvent the Doctrine of the
    Trinity* (Grand Rapids: Zondervan, 2006), pp. 267-69.
[94]Coffey, *Deus Trinitas*, p. 37.
[95]Ibid., pp. 43, 48.
[96]Ibid., p. 62.
[97]Ibid., p. 152.
[98]Ibid., p. 138.
[99]Molnar, "*Deus Trinitas*," p. 39; Coffey, *Deus Trinitas*, pp. 72, 153.
[100]Coffey, *Deus Trinitas*, p. 51.
[101]Ibid., p. 73.

Third, following Augustine, Coffey speaks of the Spirit "as the objectivization of the mutual love of the Father and the Son."[102] This definition of the Spirit has been often criticized for depersonalizing the Spirit and for subordinating the Spirit. Coffey adds to this latter problem by giving precedence to the Father's love. He says, "The Father's love for the Son always has a priority over the Son's love for the Father, and the latter is always answering love."[103]

Concluding thoughts on the revisionists. In the end, I must admit, as open as I am to considering alternative ways of speaking of and preserving divine unity and self-differentiation, I find that none of these proposals tempt me to abandon the historic doctrine of the eternal generation of the Son and eternal procession of the Spirit, worked out by some of the best minds the church has known, honed over the centuries and sanctified by centuries of confession by millions upon millions of Christians. These correlated historic doctrines have a simplicity and profundity not matched by these idiosyncratic proposals I have just discussed. Each of the revisionist proposals has specific weaknesses, which I have mentioned, and each has a complexity to it that makes it hard to comprehend what the author is saying.

In particular, certainly with Jenson and Pannenberg and possibly with Weinandy and Coffey, it is of major concern that, apparently, events in history constitute the Father-Son-Spirit relationship. Rather than God's triunity being established in eternity in the begetting of the Son and procession of the Spirit *ad intra,* apart from history, God becomes triune in history. God's freedom to be God is thus compromised.

---

[102]Ibid., p. 50.
[103]Ibid., pp. 51, 63.

11

The Final Summing Up
of the Case in Defense

◆ ◆ ◆

It is now time to bring this book to a conclusion. In what precedes we have explored two questions.

1. Is the doctrine of the eternal generation of the Son warranted by Scripture?

2. Why has the church come to believe that it is so theologically important to confess that Jesus Christ, the Son of God, is eternally begotten of the Father?

The answers to these two questions we have discovered in brief are these.

1. There is good biblical warrant for the doctrine of the eternal generation of the Son.

All Christians who confess the Nicene Creed affirm belief in eternal divine self-differentiation: the one God revealed in history and Scripture is the Father, the Son and the Holy Spirit. In confessing God's triunity, we are agreeing this is what the Bible teaches. Any debate among trinitarian Christians about the doctrines of the eternal generation of the Son and the eternal procession of the Spirit, therefore, are debates *not* about eternal divine self-differentiation, God's triunity, but about whether the doctrines of the eternal generation of the Son and the eternal procession of the Spirit are the best and theologically safest way to understand eternal divine self-differentiation in the light of scriptural revelation.

The conclusion that the eternal self-differentiation of the Father and the Son should be understood in terms of a begetting or an act of generation by the Father of the Son goes back to Justin Martyr in the second century. He noted that the scriptures speak of a divine Father and Son and frequently use birth language to describe their relationship. The *Logos,* his favored name for Jesus Christ, taken from John 1:1-18, is, he observes, called "the Son of God" and said to be "begotten," "born" and called the "firstborn." This suggested to him that the correlated names Father and Son imply a generative act, a "begetting." He found support in Scripture for this conclusion in texts in his Greek translation of the Old Testament that spoke of the begetting of divine Wisdom and a royal son (Ps 2:7; Prov 8:25), which he took to speak prophetically of the begetting of the *Logos* before he was incarnate, and in other texts that he thought suggested this idea (e.g., Ps 45:1; 110:3; Is 53:8).

Later, Athanasius built on Justin's work, speaking more consistently of the Father-Son relationship and adding that if the begetting of divine Wisdom or an elect Son spoken of in the Old Testament ultimately referred to the Son who was God, then his begetting must be an eternal act. For Athanasius, and all the Nicene fathers, the Johannine designation of the Son as *monogenēs* ("unique, only") was highly significant. They did not appeal to this word to support the doctrine of the eternal generation of the Son but rather to highlight the Son's uniqueness. For them, what marked him out from all others—what was unique about him—was that he alone was eternally begotten of the Father.

The doctrine of the eternal generation of the Son was also of great significance for Augustine. For him, the most important text in support was John 5:26, which speaks of the Father, who has divine life in himself, giving life to the Son, who likewise has divine life in himself. He also makes much of the Johannine idea that the Son is "from" the Father. He argues that this "fromness" is twofold. The Son is from the Father in his eternal begetting and "from" the Father in his historic mission. This profound theological insight made crystal clear that the Father-Son distinction is not grounded in anything that takes place in history but is grounded in what takes place apart from history. What is revealed in the economy reflects what is antecedently true in eternity.

On this basis the Nicene fathers, first at the Council of Nicaea in 325 and then at the Council of Constantinople in 381, included two separate clauses that speak of the eternal begetting of the Son. About a century later, the eternal begetting of the Son was again endorsed twice in the Athanasian Creed. This repetition demonstrates the importance of this belief to the compilers of these creeds. In these creeds and the later Reformation and post–Reformation Protestant confessions belief in the eternal begetting of the Son is demanded of Christians because those who drafted them believed this doctrine faithfully and accurately reflects the teaching of Scripture.

2. The doctrine of the eternal generation, or begetting, of the Son, along with its corollary, the eternal procession of the Spirit, is of huge theological importance.

First, this doctrine is hugely important because it grounds divine self-differentiation in the inner life of God in eternity, as does the doctrine of the eternal procession of the Spirit. God is not triune because of anything that takes place in this world. God would be triune even if he had not created the world. What takes place in the world reveals what is true in eternity. In other words, this doctrine safeguards the freedom of God, the freedom of God to be God.

Second, this doctrine is hugely important because the doctrine of the eternal generation of the Son (and procession of the Spirit) affirms that the three divine persons are of the one divine *ousia*. They are all true God. To speak of the Son as "begotten of the Father" indicates that he is of the same nature or being as the Father and thus of the same power and majesty. This doctrine was developed as a counter-blast to the Arian thesis that the Son's begetting was to be understood as a creative act in time that produced a son external to God the Father and thus subordinate to him. To find evangelical theologians today arguing that the doctrine of the eternal generation of the Son speaks of his eternal subordination is thus very worrying. It indicates a profound ignorance of the historical development of the doctrine of the

Trinity and thus of the doctrine itself, the primary doctrine of the Christian faith—"our" Christian doctrine of God.

Third, this doctrine is hugely important because it indelibly and eternally differentiates the Father and the Son, as does the doctrine of the eternal procession of the Spirit in reference to the Spirit, yet it neither divides the one God nor subordinates one divine person to another. No other way of differing the three divine persons has been conceived that is as sure and safe a way to affirm divine self-differentiation.

Fourth and last, the story of the emergence and development of the doctrine of the eternal generation of the Son reminds us that *theology*, the science of the study of God, is not done by moving from the creaturely to the Creator, that is, by seeking to understand God in human terms and relationships. This error stood right at the heart of all the diverse "Arian" theologies of the fourth century, and today it stands right at the heart of the Knight-Grudem-Ware evangelical doctrine of the Trinity. In each case the Father-Son relationship is understood in terms of the human father-son relationship. For the Arians, the Son, like a human son, was born in time, subordinated to the Father in being/nature and authority, with the result that divine unity was lost. Today what would seem to be the prevailing opinion among conservative evangelicals, at least in America and Australia, my home country, is that the divine Father-Son relationship is to be understood in terms of a human father-son relationship and is analogous to a husband-wife relationship in which the man is understood to be "head-over" his wife. In both cases, what is taken to be essential to these relationships—namely, differing authority—the rule of one party over the other, is read back into the divine Father-Son relationship in eternity. This reasoning is enunciated in every "complementarian" work I have read outlining this distinctive evangelical doctrine of the Trinity. In the case of the evangelical rejection of the doctrine of the eternal begetting of the Son, the most common reason given, after that of the "no biblical warrant," is that to speak of the Son's "begetting" indicates his eternal subordination. Sadly, evangelicals who make this argument do not realize this is precisely the Arian argument rejected by the pro-Nicene fathers.

In direct opposition to this way of doing theology the great theologians of the past in establishing the doctrines of the eternal generation of the Son laid down the principle that the Creator cannot be understood in terms of the creaturely; God cannot be defined in terms of human life and relationships. Specifically they insisted that the language of begetting, when used of the Father-Son relationship, is not to be taken literally or in a creaturely sense. Scripture suggests the language of "begetting" and "generation" and it is sanctioned by the theological tradition, but like all human speech and imagery used of God, who is infinite in glory, power and majesty, it is beggarly and inadequate. Words used of God are not to be understood univocally, but rather analogically, being given content on the basis of what is revealed in Scripture read holistically and theologically, never by reference to human life on earth.

When we have such a powerful and profound doctrine that safeguards the priority and historical independence of the triune God as he is in himself, the full deity of the three divine persons and their indelible and eternal self-differentiation, and it establishes one of the most important principles in doing *theo-logy*, why, I ask, should any Christian seriously consider abandoning it?

To Conclude

We now see why the Nicene and Athanasian Creeds, the Reformation and Post-Reformation Protestant confessions and the greatest theologians across the centuries, have endorsed and defended the doctrine of the eternal generation of the Son. It is warranted by Scripture, and it unambiguously teaches that the Father and the Son are one in being and power, each true God, and yet it distinguishes them indelibly and eternally as "the Father" and "the Son." I would argue also that this doctrine should be endorsed and defended because it is the agreed doctrine of the church for almost two thousand years, and today it marks out those who confess this doctrine as members of the one catholic (universal) church.

I hope I have convinced you that there is biblical warrant for this doctrine and that it is of great theological importance. If I have, will you join with me in confessing Jesus Christ as God's unique [*monogenēs*] Son, "eternally begotten, not made, one in being [*homoousios*] with the Father," "true God *from* true God," "through whom all things were made," who "came down from heaven," and for our salvation was crucified, and now reigns in heaven with the Father and the Spirit, in the words of the Nicene Creed?

We believe in one Lord, Jesus Christ,

The only Son of God, *eternally begotten of the Father,* God from God, Light from Light,

True God from true God,

Begotten, not made,

Of one Being with the Father.

Through him all things were made.

For us and for our salvation

he came down from heaven:

By the power of the Holy Spirit

He was incarnate of the Virgin Mary, and became man.

For our sake he was crucified under Pontius Pilate;

He suffered death and was buried.

On the third day he rose again

In accordance with the scriptures

He ascended into heaven

and is seated at the right hand of the Father.

He will come again in glory to judge the living and the dead,

And his kingdom will have no end.

Author Index

Subject Index

Scripture Index